Will Pope Francis or a Successor Call a Vatican III Council?

Will Pope Francis or a Successor Call a Vatican III Council?

Some Global and Historical Perspectives on Ongoing Crises

John Raymaker and Gerald Grudzen

Hamilton Books
Lanham • Boulder • New York • Toronto • London

Published by Hamilton Books
An imprint of The Rowman & Littlefield Publishing Group, Inc.
4501 Forbes Boulevard, Suite 200, Lanham, Maryland 20706
Hamilton Books Acquisitions Department (301) 459-3366

6 Tinworth Street, London SE11 5AL, United Kingdom

Copyright © 2020 by The Rowman & Littlefield Publishing Group, Inc.

All rights reserved. No part of this book may be produced in any form or by any electronic means, including information storage and retrieval systems, without written permission from the publisher, except by a reviewer who may quote passages in a review.

British Library Cataloguing in Publication Information Available

Library of Congress Control Number Available

ISBN 978-0-7618-7225-2 (pbk)
ISBN 978-0-7618-7226-9 (electronic)

Contents

Introduction		1
Part I: Challenges Facing the Church in the Twenty-First Century		**5**
1	A Glimpse at the Church's Reconciling Role through the Centuries: How Faith Differs from and Underlies Beliefs	11
2	The Challenges of Globalization, Migration, and Religious Fundamentalism	23
3	The Challenges of Secularity, Alienation, Ideologies and Pluralism	53
Part II: Has the Church Been Out of Touch with the Modern World?		**83**
4	Conflicts between the Church's Resistance and Openness to Modernization	85
Part III: Principles and Strategies for the Church to Help Us Bridge Our Divides		**111**
5	Liberation Theology in the Light of Scripture and Justice Issues	113
6	Interfaith and Cross-cultural Implications of Globalization	125
7	Historical, Philosophical, and Ecumenical Perspectives on World Problems	155
8	Solutions Based on Small Christian Communities Striving for Social Justice: Some of the Ironies in the Fall and Rise of SCCs in Christian History	175
Appendix 1: Tyrrell's Argument that Church Authorities had Usurped the Laity's Role		195

Appendix 2: The Hindu Notion of Bliss Consciousness, *Saccidananda*. Brahma, Brahman, Mantra— and a Contemporary Ideology ... 197

Appendix 3: How the Church May Help Us from Falling Victim to the Hyperreality of Images ... 199

Appendix 4: Fathoming how Mystics, Philosophers, and Theologians Address the Unfathomable: Pioneer Christian Thinkers Rephrasing Ancient-Medieval Thought in Modern Terms ... 201

Appendix 5: How Philosophers and Historians Have Developed Notions of Lived Experience which can Buttress Integrating Bridges Based on a Global Mysticism ... 207

Appendix 6: Pope Francis' "Glocal" World View ... 211

Glossary ... 213

Selected Bibliography ... 215

Index ... 217

About the Authors ... 219

Introduction

This update of our *Steps toward Vatican III* (2008) focuses on the fact that the world, religion and Catholicism are all in various stages of crises. *Steps* outlined a method for clarifying the basis on which Church renewal can be effected and for fostering dialogue with other religions. We believe that Pope Francis has a similar agenda. The world is almost paranoid about "security." In 2003, President G. W. Bush led America into a precarious attempt to topple Saddam Hussein. In 2019, President Trump betrayed the Kurds who had helped the States recover from the Bush mistake by pulling US Forces from NE Syria. In the meantime, anti-democratic leaders such as Putin in Russia and Xi in China have undermined the democratic process in their countries as they profit from Trump's adventurism. Families today are everywhere under pressure; alienation and individualism confront us at every turn. Not only is the common good threatened, but so is the environment. Can we learn to be worthy stewards of mother earth?

The lives of mystics illustrate how to live spiritually in a rapidly changing world. Global spiritualities transcend but do not compete with the particular claims of the world religions—as shown in the lives of Mahatma Gandhi, the Dalai Lama or Bede Griffiths. Our aim is to interlink intra- and interfaith issues by asking how has the seed of faith been developed in the world religions. Vatican II taught us how to renew Christian ministries.[1] Yet, more than 50 years later, the Church must reassess its forms of ministries in the light of new, pressing needs. The synodal process Pope Francis initiated at the Amazon Synod (October, 2019), could serve as a model for a Vatican III.

Many contemporary philosophers hold that humans are confined to "immanence." They view transcendence as an unattainable illusion. We seek bridges between persons' actual lives today and a loving, transcendent God. Each one has his/her lived experience, which remains a deeply personal reality to be shared with others, but which is prone to misunderstanding if confined to limited perspectives. We hope that our references to the conflicting claims of such philosophers and theologians as Marx, Kierkegaard, Cardinal Newman, Nietzsche, Paul Tillich, Bernard Lonergan and Karl Rahner can help readers evaluate how ecclesial policies might best promote the Church's transformative roles in the world. Our recent book, *Pope Francis, Conscience of the World*, studies how the Pope has been encouraging Christians and other believers to build bridges of understanding. It notes that the heroic work of Dorothy Day (1897–1980), the co-foundress of the *Catholic Worker Movement*, would not have been possible without the mystical insights that guided her. Building upon *Conscience of the World*, the present volume insists with Pope Francis that we must overcome the Enlightenment's legacy that overturned the once impregnable Christian edifice of the Middle Ages.

Pope John XXIII became a symbol of hope for a New Pentecost. He stressed the Church's role as a true leaven for establishing God's Kingdom on earth. Vatican II was pivotal to his hope. It helped the Church remain a vital agent serving humanity's needs. But it may now be time to again assemble the world's bishops, which is now a much more diversified, international body than was the case in 1959. Pope Francis' reliance on other bishops in the synodal process suggests that a Council could better coordinate the global and local needs of the Church. Despite or perhaps because of our divides, people are still much interested in such topics as that of God's existence, the relationship between religion and science and ways in which religion can contribute to world peace. This update of *Steps toward Vatican III* approaches the issues affecting the world today in the light of the respective roles of the ecclesial hierarchy and the "Church from below." It links intra- and interfaith ecclesial issues in cross-fertilizing ways. It explores some of the intangibles affecting human life, such as the commonalities among Buddhist, Christian and Muslim mystics which point to the deepest spiritual aspects of life. It outlines paradigms in the light of which strategies can be developed so as to aid efforts to unite humanity. It proposes potential ways to solve global problems in the light of post-Vatican II theology and socio-cultural realities (chapters 1–7). Chapter 8 suggests ways the hierarchy could help develop small Christian communities (SCC's) so as to better address glaring problems in the world.

NOTES

1. https://www.ncronline.org/news/people/ncr-today/church-needs-vatican-iii. That had been "foreseen" in David Tracy, Hans Küng and Johann Metz's Toward Vatican III. (New York: Seabury, 1978). There is a need for more input from others for such an event.On Faggioli, see https://international.la-croix.com/news/what-the-synod-of-bishops-means-for-vatican-ii-and-vatican-iii/11145. Faggioli regrets that many US bishops have neutered Pope

Francis' message in the States by dismissing synodality. See Faggioli, The Church in a Change of Era: How the Franciscan Reforms are Changing the Catholic Church (e-book available at https://international.la-croix.com). In his pre-Christmas message to the Church's cardinals (Dec. 21, 2019), Pope Francis made it clear that the era of Christendom is over. In some ways "the Church is 200 years behind the times." We need courage to live the faith today. This will need a further reform of the Roman Curia. "Rigidity, which is born of the fear of change, ends up erecting fences and obstacles on the terrain of the common good, turning it into a minefield of incomprehension and of hatred. . .. Only love conquers weariness." Quoting St. John Henry Newman, he stressed that "To live is to change, and to be perfect is to have changed often." https:// /inter national.la-croix.com/news/sodano-resigns-as-dean-of-the-college-of-cardinals/ 11537?utm_source=Newsletter&utm_medium=e-mail&utm_content=23-12-2019& utm_campaign=newsletter_crx_lci&PMID=0964dbe689e61e205168552536593154.

Part I

Challenges Facing the Church in the Twenty-First Century

LEARNING FROM THE TRANSFORMATIVE EXPERIENCES OF SMALL CHRISTIAN COMMUNITIES, FROM THE DISCIPLES ON THE WAY TO EMMAUS, AND FROM THE PAST THREE POPES

Overspecialization in our modern world has led to a loss of wholeness that must be recaptured. Rituals help connect humans to one another and to nature. Ancient societies felt connected to the cosmos through many types of observances such as that of the summer and winter solstice and the rituals marking the change of seasons. Today, small Christian communities (SCC's) can be an effective means of recapturing a sense of unity among humans, with the earth and the cosmos. SCC's treat persons as persons. It is our aim to develop an "on-the-way" strategy, which may be compared to the experience of Jesus' disciples on the way to Emmaus, to Cervantes' Don Quixote, to Martin Luther King's dream, and to Pope Francis "dream of a Church close to the people."[1] All these instances point to facets of our "own-the-way" strategy aimed to make humans aware of the tensions between our dreams and our traumatic experiences. "Dream" is *Traum* in German. Trauma in both languages points to a hurt that leaves psychic damage in need of remedial action. It is a shock to the body or an emotional one that often creates lasting damage to a person's psychological development. We recapitulate such dream-trauma experiences both here and in the Glossary that point to foreign words touching on this.

- For the disciples at Emmaus and for Pope Francis a different dynamic occurs. The Emmaus disciples and Pope Francis both underwent trauma. In the case of the Emmaus disciples, their trauma is overcome when their eyes are opened at the inn. Pope Francis underwent his own traumas at the hands of the Argentina military. But he realized that for the Church to revitalize itself, it must move on, it must ever dream anew.
- For Cervantes, the road was always better than the inn. His fictional hero Don Quixote rebels against the waning of the Middle Ages through "feats" of an imaginary chivalry. (The point is that in all three cases a resolution depends on one's eyes being opened).
- Martin Luther King's "I have a dream speech" opened new doors, new opportunities for blacks in America but this came in the wake of much suffering, trauma, turmoil.

Ever keeping in mind, the potential roles of SCC's in the Church of the Future, we shall comment on some of the traumas of a Church-ever-on-its-way-to-meet-Christ in committed, if sometimes uncertain ways. The past three popes, John Paul II, Benedict XVI and Francis, have been Catholicism's "most influential" leaders since 1978. The first was a first-rate philosophical mind: his charisma was partly responsible for his successes. The second is a first-rate theologian. Pope Francis—also a charismatic figure—is in touch with many pressing issues now facing the globe and its inhabitants. All three have had to be ever "on the way." John Paul II was first oppressed by Nazism; later he had to face down Communism and then, capitalism.[2] Benedict, too, has been on the way from being a progressive theologian to a conservative one trying to counter what he views as relativism. Pope Francis transcends the issue of relativism. He asks us to live the authentic message of Jesus' Good News. In their own way, these three popes have sought to bridge the divides facing humanity. John Paul II, although very much engaged in peace and justice issues, sought to re-centralize Church authority in the Vatican. Benedict XVI's view on life has been much influenced by his Western, classicist training. Pope Francis, the first pope from South America, has warned us against populism. He is a universalist who respects diversity. Everyone is unique but is much influenced by the culture one lives in. The Church's role is to help people from many cultures serve God and neighbor. Effective theological bridges are needed to span people's cultural divides.

A CALL FOR RENEWAL AND TRANSFORMATION
BASED ON LIVED EXPERIENCE

How can people today discern and interrelate their personal standpoints with communal interests in ethical ways? How close can their leaders come to finding global approaches to deal with the multitude of our problems? Humanity has begun to realize the depth of the crises it is now facing. The environment is threatened in ways we are only beginning to grasp. The effects of global warming are now everywhere evident. The world economy did "thrive" but at the price of unsustainable inequalities and imbalances in many parts of the globe. Religions are polarized between liberal and fundamentalist wings; religion as a whole is marginalized. The Church has been in a state of recurring crises in Europe for over four centuries. The pedophilia scandals have recently diminished its credibility. Just as a great part of Europe is now de-christianized, so the USA is being threatened with a similar phenomenon. The crises in the world, in religion and in the Church are an interconnected set of problems which all point for the need of a Vatican III Council.

As cardinal and as pope, Joseph Ratzinger made mistakes in his approaches to Islam and to Amerindians. He gave short shrift to Third World concerns such as poverty. His entire career was marked by the perspective of a Western classicist theologian. The election of Pope Francis changed such parochialism. It helped highlight some bright spots in the Church. Some now see the papacy and the Church as beacons of moral authority in an unhinged, threatened world. Another bright spot is that the churches in the developing world have become harbingers of hope. The West needs to be more engaged with these churches and learn from them. These churches' lived experience of *communal sharing* point to the deeper roots of human life as traditionally taught in the Western churches.

Unlike the early Church, the Church is now a global one. Christ gave the Church the mission to go to all nations. The early Church's greatest missionary was St. Paul. Later, St. Boniface, St. Patrick, the brothers St. Cyril and Methodius helped bring the message of Christ to Europe. But it took the age of exploration and modern methods of travel to allow the Church to be established in other continents. The Church, now a global entity, faces the problems attendant upon serving a diversity of peoples. Globalization and secularism have conspired to marginalize sacred rituals that can link humans to God. Pope Francis has recently been distracted from his wanting to reach to all of humanity due to some of the Church's internal crises. The Church and its faithful might do well to set up mediating structures that might effectively communicate the Gospel message to disaffected youths and adults. Today's mass media often frame key issues such as political balkanization or economic trends in very divisive, confrontational ways rather than by providing us with a set of ethical-spiritual values that would unite humanity. In reality, the Gospel message is still a valid, even a needed means to help humanity solve its problems, but the Church must re-adapt itself to effectively preach Jesus' Good News.

The spiritual ideals of the Abrahamic faith traditions and of Buddhism offer us guidelines for remedying the conflicts now facing the human community. Mystically speaking, these ideals converge on being *enlightened* in a *dark night* of the soul of which St. John of the Cross spoke. Buddhist meditation—mindfulness is now widely practiced in the West; it is used by psychotherapists to treat conditions such as depression. There are stories of psychological damage due to such meditation. It takes experienced spiritual directors to guide aspirants in the mysteries of a dark night of the soul so as to help them transcend the subject/object dichotomy promoted by many scientists. Martin Buber spoke of the I/Thou unity found in the embrace of the soul with the divine lover and with others. Such profound experiences of unity can help one find an emotional and spiritual connection with all living beings. Drawing upon the rich spiritual traditions of the Abrahamic faith religions and of Buddhism, we explore ways humans could bridge the present divides between the secular and the sacred in the West. We do so, in part, by developing a cosmic spirituality rooted in the earth and in the writings of mystics. We seek to integrate the insights of many creative people with the ways the divine manifests itself in the world's religions—as grounded in people's own lived experiences.

In part I, we study the phenomena of globalization and secularism with the view of outlining the challenges now facing the Church. We argue that global changes are so overwhelming and the need of solutions so great that a Vatican III Council may be required to assess the situation and prepare the Church to adequately address today's complexities. Most if not all Ecumenical Councils were assembled to address major problems facing the Church. Who has the right to call such a Council was once a hotly debated question. Present Canon Law specifies that only the reigning pope can do so.

Our overall intention in this volume is to repeatedly come back to Jesus' prayer for the "coming of God's Kingdom" (Mt 6:9–15). We end each chapter with a "strategic conclusion" that asks whether Christians are indeed effectively seeking God's Kingdom.

NOTES

1. https://international.la-croix.com/news/i-dream-of-a-young-church-close-to-the-people-pope-tells-jesuits-in-thailand-japan/11437?utm_source=Newsletter&utm_medium=e-mail&utm_content=07-12-2019&utm_campaign= newsletter_crx_lci&PMID= 0964dbe689e61e205168552536593154. At Alcoholic Anonymous, recovering addicts undergo a painful total-abstinence process; it helps them realize what has traumatized them. See also https://psycnet.apa.org/record/2006-23055-003 on dream-trauma links.

2. Appointed bishop at 38, Wojtyla had a personal hand in shaping Vatican II. The first Polish Pope dealt with East-West problems as an insider; he influenced the demise of Communism. Today it is debated whether, as Pope, he retrenched Vatican II's ecumenical approach in favor of recentralization or whether, like Leo XIII, he sowed seeds that germinated for example in the election of Pope Francis. Noting the difficulties that both Leo XIII and John Paul II had

to face during their pontificates, we stress their courageous examples to help us "cross" a threshold of mutual cross-fertilization among humans.

Chapter One

A Glimpse at the Church's Reconciling Role through the Centuries

How Faith Differs from and Underlies Beliefs

The Church, born from the faith of Christ's disciples when their eyes were opened, is ever on its way. Our modern world is torn by many forms of dissension, not the least of which is that between Christian, secularist and Islamic perspectives. In 1986, Pope John Paul II invited religious leaders from around the world to pray for peace in Assisi. First, they all prayed in silence before dispersing to various parts of Assisi to pray in their own way. William Johnston, an expert on mysticism noted that their silent prayer "was a prayer of union . . . there was unity in diversity."[1] The diversity came when each group used its own Scriptures. Johnston calls for a global mediation of mysticism on the model of Hans Küng's global ethics. We seek to answer Johnston's call by trying to bridge the divides between secular and religious approaches to social ethics on the one hand, and secularist-atheists' misunderstanding of mysticism and spirituality, on the other. In terms of our twofold strategy, chapters 1–7 often refer to a global ethics, a global spirituality. Chapter 8 explores concrete ways of living with both a local and a global consciousness. Many people today identify Christian churches with dogmas about Christ and the Church he founded. Our text makes an important distinction between faith and beliefs. Faith transcends, but does not negate beliefs in particular dogmatic expressions. In a way analogous to Gabriel Marcel's distinction between Problem and Mystery, faith is an *archetypal ground* of human consciousness. Through faith one enters a realm of Mystery in one's life. In the realm of faith, love precedes^e knowledge.

God has entered history with a gift of his love. We accept this initiative from God through faith—the eye of love. It is this eye, which enables humans to become heroic in daily life or in times of difficulty. It is a "mystical eye" that penetrates below the surface of life's sordid aspects so as to react with justice. Faith is an embryonic mystical experience; it lets one transcend the physical through enlightenment. One recognizes it when it happens.

The Christ event has been expressed in dogmas. Dogmas deal with theological problems raised in particular historical eras. Beliefs differ—as was evident at Assisi—but beneath the differences, there lies the profounder unitive experience of faith. We argue that Christians—as was evident in the cases of Emmaus in Luke's Gospel and at Assisi in 1986—are still on their way. Emmaus and Assisi were faith experiences. At Emmaus, the disciples experienced the risen Christ. Assisi was a sharing of a faith experience in a way appropriate to our age. Since the early days of Christianity, Jesus' mandate to first seek the Kingdom of God has been incumbent upon his followers. The Kingdom (a concrete reality in search of justice) is "within us." It is in our concrete striving or in a lack of it that each Christian or the Church as a whole becomes authentic or inauthentic. We now set out to try to help reconcile the various threads just indicated by mediating a global mysticism on the model of a global ethics. For Christians, this includes practicing the justice of a Kingdom, which *is within* a person. For non-Christians, mediating a global ethics with an implicit or explicit global mysticism may be helped by Marcel's understanding of Mystery or by implicit notions of faith in non-Christian traditions. Mystery characterizes the basic nature of human consciousness vis-a-vis the temporal, contingent nature of human existence. One expresses some form of ultimate connection with all that we are or can become in the face of our own mortality through beliefs. The monotheistic faiths call this ultimate connection God or Allah but Buddhism refers to it in other ways such as Buddha consciousness or being enlightened. In this sense, we can be confident that our expressions of faith are rooted in God as well as in the Cosmos. We are children of the earth and of the universe. We should reject nothing that is good, true and beautiful within the domain of one's consciousness.

To understand the nature of faith today we must reflect deeply upon our lived experience and plumb its depths in ways that may help guide our complex lives. The touchstone of a relevant lived experience lies in our ability to bridge "lonely fiefdoms" with the cultural contexts of the world around us. Faith helps one discover the good, true and beautiful in all dimensions of life rather than just affirming a set of contingent beliefs. All language is contingent upon the historical context in which it is evoked; it must not be universalized beyond its applicable realms, nor become ossified, hardened into untenable dogmatic positions. Each one of us has his/her own life narrative which remains a deeply personal reality but which can also be shared with others despite the possibility of misunderstanding caused by ethnocentrism, ideological self-interest or bias. This is true not only for the personal experience of individuals but also for that of families, communities or nations. Such experiences occur in cultural situations and historical contexts. It is up to us to discern, interrelate and mediate these uniquely personal standpoints and limited community perspectives with global insights and values. We shall often refer to how mystical experiences help people reach the deeper unitive potential of the human spirit. We seek to balance a global mysticism with the realities that face human beings in an unfaithful world. We explore ways of developing an incarnational spirituality in preparation for a possible Vatican III Council that could help the global Church address the radically new types of problems facing our modern societies. We examine, in this chapter, some of the ways the Church has tried to reconcile humans to God and to one another— even while failing in certain aspects of that mission. We seek to establish theological parameters informing cultures so as to help defuse historical misunderstandings now exacerbated by extremists and terrorists.

OUR GLOBAL VILLAGE: THE MARGINALIZED LIVES OF MANY PEOPLE TODAY

Many people in today's slums live a marginalized existence. The Church is in principle committed to reaching out to the marginalized. How can it guide its faithful to help oppose injustices? Our aim is to seek a middle-way path of virtue that would allow Christians to truly listen to one another through intra-faith dialogues with a view to larger interfaith exchanges that address the world's complex problems. The Church has found models for intercultural communication in some of its saints and theologians. Vatican II asked it to reach out to all persons of good will. The Church, in dialogue with other faith communities, can identify pressing issues so as to devise ethical policies to help heal the human community. A Vatican III would bring the expertise of the world's bishops and theologians along with lay experts in social issues to set up new avenues of approach to the problems of marginalized communities lest discontent lead to open violence as happened in Los Angeles (1965), in France (2005, 2019), in Chile and Bolivia (2019) and in other areas of the world. Such riots show that cultural and economic issues intermix.

One must stress the importance of spirituality and theology. We are incarnated spirits who can do good or evil. Moltmann's theology of hope would impel us to look for a better type of future. Hoping to address dilemmas of a world fraught with violence, we aim to draw out the historical lessons that liberation theologians have given us to foster community. If these theologians expose divisions between the Church's conservative and progressive voices, we aim to avoid polarizing approaches as well as the overly hierarchical organizations such as Opus Dei, which have adopted some of the secretive methods of cults. On the other hand, some liberation theologians may have taken over Marxist views in an insufficiently critical manner.

Intra-Church developments coupled with pressing world problems led Pope John XXIII to call a Second Vatican Council. Is not the Church now facing problems of a magnitude as great as those assessed at Vatican II? If so, believers (including lay people who confront the world's problems on the front lines) must examine new models and structures adequate to our tasks today. Even though the Church has provided extensive commentaries on its relationship with the modern world through papal encyclicals and involvement in many international commissions dealing with global poverty, racism, injustice and peaceful solutions to regional and international conflicts, it has not been able to fully grasp and transform the new modern mindsets that pervade the modern world particularly those of urbanized sectors. Such mindsets find the Church's hierarchical nature to be an anachronistic leftover from the medieval world. Democratic structures which stress universal participation are becoming the standard for most of society's educated sectors, both in the developed and developing parts of the world. New social movements usually involve some form of face-to-face contact with like-minded members of an organization—often using the Internet to facilitate meetings at the local level with agendas determined democratically by all members. To prepare for a Vatican III, the Church could utilize modern technology to facilitate participation by its members including those who were previously marginalized.[2] By issuing a call for broad forms of consultation and collaboration, the Church, using advanced technologies, could return to the spirit of Pope John XXIII who was recognized as a universal pastor for the world community—one who effectively reached out to all persons of good will.

THE CHURCH'S RECONCILING-BRIDGING ROLES IN ITS 2,000-YEAR HISTORY: THE EVOLVING ROLE OF THE LAITY IN THE MODERN WORLD

Throughout its 2000 year history the Church has built bridges between its own self-understanding and the cultures in which it lived. Saint Paul, the first Christian "bridge-builder," explained Christ's message to the Greeks and Romans. The New Testament writings of St. John provided another bridge to the Greco-Roman world. His teachings on the *Logos* and Christian love are a form of incarnational theology. God became human flesh and thereby sanctified all of creation. The bridging efforts of St. Paul and St. John provided solid foundations upon which Christianity flourished in the next three centuries. Origen, a pivotal Christian theologian from Alexandria, introduced the allegorical method in interpreting Scripture. Others framed Christian doctrines using categories derived from Plotinus' Neoplatonism—an ambiguous movement that included eclectic influences from Eastern mysticisms. Following the adoption of Christianity by the Emperor Constantine, the Roman Empire was faced with the migrations of tribes from the East. The first Ecumenical Council of Nicaea had to a find a way to link basic Christian beliefs with the Greek philosophical tradition prevailing in Constantine's time. In his writings, St. Augustine sought to bridge the City of God and that of Man in the crumbling Roman Empire. As he contemplated the fragile existence of Rome and of all earthly kingdoms, he showed that no earthly city can contain the mystery of Christ. It needs a spiritual foundation on which to rest. In the wake of the destruction that followed upon the barbarian[3] invasions, St. Benedict wrote the Benedictine Rule for living in community. The rule centers on *orare et laborare*—to pray and work. St. Benedict's balanced spiritual discipline modified the strongly ascetical bent of the desert fathers. During the Middle Ages, Francis of Assisi and St. Dominic effectively built new bridges between the medieval world and the emerging urban environment. During the Counter-Reformation, St. Ignatius of Loyola and St. Francis Xavier developed ways to preach the Gospel through forms of inculturation appropriate to both modern and non-Western audiences. Xavier and others also developed modes of spiritual life adapted to audiences in the New World and the Far East. Ironically, this inculturation process played a role in enslaving many native peoples in Africa and the Americas. Bartolomé de las Casas attacked such practices, but the Church failed to follow through on many of his recommendations. Consider the mentalities that informed the convening and reception of the last three Ecumenical Councils, those of Trent, of Vatican I and II. Trent reformed the Church in a time of crisis. It did much to guide the Church (ever on its way to encounter Christ). It defined three sources of revelation, (1) Old and New Testaments, (2) Tradition and (3) the magisterium (the pope and bishops as sole teachers in the Church). This teaching was strongly enforced in Catholic seminaries until Vatican II, but it had begun to be modified due to Cardinal Newman's writings that argued for "the development of doctrine." This led theologians to clarify their interpretation of Church teachings so as to stress that the faith of the Church partly depends on the *Sensus Fidelium* (the Sense of the Faithful). This means that Church teaching arises from and is verified in the ways ordinary Catholics understand and live the faith.

After Vatican II, the erstwhile friends and collaborators, Joseph Ratzinger and Hans Küng became leaders of the two opposed views of Catholic self-understanding. From 1968 on, Ratzinger focused on Catholic community and basic forms of Catholic self-understanding. Küng deepened his notion of

Catholic life committed to Jesus' command to love all irrespective of affiliation. We respect Pope Benedict's option, but we favor Küng's broader vision. That requires that we study how Pope Francis has been helping the Church transform the theological aspects of the faith in ways that can help it address, for example, relevant Islamic and Buddhist teachings in grounding a global ethics. Vatican II's document on "The Church in the Modern World" (*Gaudium et Spes*) defined the Church as the "People of God." It points to Catholics' important role in presenting the Church's faith to the world. The People of God expresses the faith of the Church in their everyday life and not just in the pronouncements of the Church. Vatican II's "Decree on the Apostolate of the Laity" recognizes the laity's indispensable role in evangelizing today. St. Thomas More was one shining example in past centuries. Lay persons come in direct contact with the earthly realities directing human societies. We have to differentiate between top-to-bottom hierarchically organized lay societies and more informal, flexible initiatives. Catholic movements such as Focolare (that promotes universal brotherhood) and Opus Dei (which won Pope John Paul II's ardent support)[4] are examples of hierarchically organized lay societies. The National Center for the Laity, on the other hand, boldly supports lay initiatives in health care, business ethics and other fields. Its newsletter, *Initiatives*, exposes abuses in industry. Unlike Opus Dei, the Laity Center has not drawn the media's attention, but it has undertaken many initiatives, which coordinated with the teaching authority of Church, can indeed be effective ways to help heal our broken world.

A GLOBAL SPIRITUALITY TO HELP UNITE HUMANITY

Our world lacks spiritualities that can unite humanity rather than divide it. The faith traditions of the monotheistic religions, Judaism, Christianity and Islam often disagree or clash. Eastern religions, such as Buddhism, have become fashionable in the West over the past half-century. Many educated Western youth have rejected the monotheistic traditions as patriarchal and exclusive. The rise of fundamentalist religious ideologies that misconceive political realities has become a hallmark of our time. A gulf separates the scientific and literate cultures of university life and urban centers from the more naïve belief patterns found in the world's less developed regions or even in US governmental circles motivated by Christian fundamentalism. Interreligious dialogue is now a pressing need due to such terrorist assaults in 9/11, 2001 and the US-led invasions of Afghanistan and Iraq. We aim to explore guidelines for developing a global spirituality that can unite rather divide humanity. We shall draw from the rich resources found in both the monotheistic traditions and those of the East. "Interfaith" and "interreligious" differ. For us, "interreligious" refers to religious bodies' official initiatives; "interfaith" means interactions between persons of different faith traditions. "Interfaith" is thus a broader term that includes but is not restricted to religious bodies' official initiatives. The interfaith-interreligious distinction helps clarify how the "Church from below"[5] can sensitize the hierarchy on ways the Church can better be a Gospel leaven renewing, synergizing the world. This, we argue, has been one of Pope Francis' policies.

On the basis of the Church's time-proven bridging-building ability, we want to focus on three developments within the Church: 1) ongoing forms of renewal, 2) an extension of its teachings on social justice and 3) new forms of ministries that would broaden the laity's role in the Church. These three developments are interrelated. Social justice is one of Jesus' main teachings to be reapplied in every generation. Such a re-application stands in need of constant reflection as to how new ministries might assist Christians live justly. Pope Francis has excelled in reflecting on these realities and current needs. Vatican II opened new paths for lay ministries so as to help the Church more effectively sow seeds of justice in societies wherever it can. We argue that new roles for the laity can enrich and complement the Church's traditional diocesan-parochial structures. Renewed forms of ministries would seem to be crucial to the Church's larger mission of helping unite humanity by promoting a just peace. Such a peace must tap the sources genuine spiritualities in all religions so as to help ethically unite humanity. Historically, the

Church has been marked by both conflicts and the deeds of saints who responded in outstanding ways to the challenges facing the Church. In its early history, the Church had to deal with tribes, many of which it converted. It faced threats to its unity through various dogmatic definitions. Spurred by the Protestant Reformation in the sixteenth century, it undertook a Counter Reformation. Nor was it spared the moral dilemmas caused by colonialism from the 16th to the twentieth centuries. New problems have beset humanity since the Industrial Revolution such as those of the rich-poor divides, secularism and environmental crises. The Church has no choice but to update its teachings on such issues—topics we touch on later. First, we call attention to needs for intimacy.

THE NEED FOR INTIMACY AMONG THE CLERGY AND LAITY

We stress the need to rely on personal experience to situate larger issues facing the Church and humanity as a whole. We therefore explore enriching ways of fostering a needed intimacy among friends such as within small Christian communities (SCC's). As authors, we do not claim that married priests' lives would be more authentic than that of many faithful consecrated persons active in official ministries. The love of God motivating Christians is an intimate experience reaching out to the transcendent. We argue on the basis of our extensive experience with SCC's that these help its members find intimacy with others, even with God. We do so to highlight some of the important issues we discuss below—including why we recommend some basic changes in Church policy. Such changes must, of course, be evaluated at the highest levels of Church authority. But Church authorities can only be effective when they base themselves on reality and are able to anticipate future needs. Since the post-Vatican II Church now faces new crises, Church leaders are again called to give workable answers. There is a great need for true intimacy today. In many cities, people go from the extremes of stress in the workplace and other demands of life to a numbing sense of trivialization.[6] People have little time to communicate in any depth with one another. They rely on gadgets to get through the complexities of life. Alienation from self and others easily occurs.

People crave intimacy but they find it difficult to find friends with whom they can share the intimate details or the problems facing them. Cherished ones often live far away. For believers, the parish should be a place of community, but all too often churchgoing is limited to a Sunday morning experience. Meaningful contacts with others are quite limited. Unless parochial leaders are particularly adept and the parish not too large, many find it difficult to worship in a setting that fails to help believers find intimacy with God and with one another. Many Hispanic Catholics who did not experience intimacy (such as is found within the charismatic movement or SCC's) within their parish have converted to Pentecostalism. Only by establishing vibrant communities, will the Church touch human hearts. By "vibrant communities," we mean those faithful to the Gospel and able to resonate with diverse populations such as youth, ethnic minorities and the mobile, urban professional class. To attain viable forms of intimacy so that persons can feel at home within responsive communities, we need to recognize the obstacles now facing us. To make some of the world's problems less intractable, we need mediating organizations (groups) that can foster values rather than foment ideologies. We must also take into account possible prejudices within our hearts or in our attitudes.

Priests and sisters might be expected to establish an atmosphere where intimate forms of worship and fellowship occur, but many factors undermine such a hope. Not only are most parishes too large, but many priests and nuns have not themselves been adequately trained in intimacy. Even if a priest reads books on intimacy, his training may prevent him to be on intimate terms with his parishioners. Henri Nouwen's books did have an influence in helping people foster intimate forms of contact with God. But writers and teachers like him are far and few between. Many of Nouwen's books seek to foster deep personal relationships in our spiritual experience and in the ways we relate to one another as Christians. Yet, his own testimony as to how he was able to arrive at intimacy is itself controversial. Much of Nouwen's inspiration came from his own felt sense of loneliness. His *The Wounded Healer* is a telling sign of this. The devastating revelations of sexual-predator priests, the forced closing of a seminary in Austria that openly encouraged homosexual behavior offer further evidence of the crisis of intimacy in Church ministries that might be alleviated by recognizing some forms of married clergy. A married clergy would solve only a part of the Church's ability to supply enough ministers to tender to the Catholic faithful. But married priests would not be exempt either from the tensions and demands of marriage or the temptation to live an egoism-of-two-persons in married life.

A CLOSER LOOK AT THE CLERICAL AND LAY STATES IN OUR POSTMODERN WORLD

Vatican II's decrees and documents provide for ecumenical and interfaith engagements as ways of applying evangelical principles to the modern situation. The tensions between initiatives advocated by Vatican II and those not approved by that Council have affected the projects in which the authors have been engaged for over 30 years; they also reflect realities which we explore below. Some say that priests and sisters leaving their "calling" to get married touches on the issue of faithfulness. They quote Jesus' teaching that "no one who puts his hand to the plow and looks back is fit for service in the Kingdom of God (Lk 9:62). Many married priests still want to be servants of the Kingdom. They do question interpretations that impose celibacy as a precondition of serving as a priest. Jesus' use of the symbol of a plow meant that he who plows should not look back lest crooked furrows be the result. But it may be well to realize that in our lives, we often have to "look back." We must look back to the teachings of history lest we repeat past mistakes. The use of 'excommunication" as a tool to stifle diversity in the Church no longer works. New forms of ministry for both men and women need not be a threat to the Church; properly sanctioned by the Church, they could help nuance and expand existing types of ministry and make them more inclusive. If the Church has lost much of its credibility because of its inability to integrate women fully into its official leadership and ministries, it must adopt gender-inclusive structures. One example that it is moving in this direction is that in some seminaries more women are now studying theology and taking new positions of pastoral leadership in the church. The decline in priestly vocations and vocations to religious communities indicates that the Church needs to adapt itself to the culture of a modern, pluralistic, society. In past ages Catholics lived in self-contained communities that promoted the role of the priest and nun as integral to the life of the Catholic community. In most parts of the world, Catholics now live in secular societies and the sense of "vocation" can take many new forms other than that of priest or nun. Many of our youth now seek a spiritual identity broader than that defined by the title "Catholic." They want to bridge Christian approaches with other important spiritual disciplines found in Buddhism, for example. The Church must help our youth realize that the Christian faith can be compatible with some eastern spiritual paths.

The notions of a vocation to the lay, religious or priestly life have all undergone deep changes. Pope Benedict XVI questioned the appropriateness of so many young priests in the developing nations choosing this state to get educated so as to find a way out of poverty. Formerly, a similar rationale may have been responsible for many vocations in the West—but economic prosperity has radically changed this. The young now mostly opt for the lay state. Rome has also tightened regulations regarding gay men aspiring to the priesthood. Such a state of affairs calls for much reflection and difficult decisions. Small Christian Communities are providing new contexts in which the Church is redefining the nature of ministry by incorporating both single and married men and women as liturgical and community leaders and facilitators. If this new paradigm of ministry were developed further, it could help solve the crisis in priestly ministry facing the Church across the globe. We believe that the Church should broaden the forms of ministry to include many types of specialized ministries relevant to today's secular culture. A Vatican III could legitimate such ministries if they were proposed as new forms of service able to address present needs. We seek to establish bridges between Catholic liberal reform groups in the Church and the Church hierarchy. The American Church's long experience with the democratic process gives it a potentially pivotal role (one distrusted in the Vatican prior to Vatican II). A Vatican III could take the Church into the new millennium using input from reform groups. A bishop's excommunication of the Call to Action group in Nebraska (2006) was a sign of the Church's inability to engage in serious dialogue with its critics. We need new ways to foster dialogue among l those belonging to the Catholic tradition. The hierarchy needs to be more pastoral rather than juridical to win back the allegiance of many Catholics who have left the Church. John XXIII represented the pastoral and ecumenical approach needed in the Church of the future. Pope Francis has insisted that the laity of the Church should be consulted in regards to future Church structures that would include outreach to the disaffected. The small Christian communities movement and some support groups for married priests such as CORPUS and Married Priests Now! have become part of the Catholic landscape. They should, we argue, be better integrated into the Church of the future.

STRATEGIC CONCLUSION TO CHAPTER 1

We have examined some of the evolving historical realities that a Vatican III would have to address. Following Vatican II, bishops from the Third World acquired a status much beyond what had previously been theirs. Some of these bishops began to serve in the Curia. But under Popes John Paul and Benedict recentralization in the Vatican took place. Pope Francis has reversed this latter trend. He knows that an isolated Curia cannot come to terms with the cultural-religious dynamics of globalization. He is convinced that the diminished roles of local bishops in guiding their dioceses and the dearth of permissible ways for Catholics to minister to one another must be redressed. Chapter 8 studies the effectiveness of SCC's whose history actually goes back to pre-Constantinian home churches. In the post-Vatican II Church it was liberation theologians who began reemphasizing the importance of SCC's in helping Latin American Catholics live their faith more authentically. SCC's are an experimental ground for evaluating forms of ministries appropriate to the twenty-first century. They provide intimate contexts for faith-sharing, for mentoring youth and other forms of ministry wherein men and women, single and married, lay and priestly members can interact. A Vatican III Council could help discern how new inclusive and ecumenical forms of ministries might play important roles in the Church of the future. The 2019 Amazon Synod paved a way for further such developments. Francis reinforced this, for example, by appointing the Philippine Cardinal Luis Tagle as head of the Congregation for the Evangelization of Peoples—which has increased Tagle's chances of succeeding Pope Francis. The pope might now appoint more cardinals to the Curia who would strengthen his strategy of change while avoiding conservative manipulations to roll things back. Tagle has written on episcopal collegiality developed at Vatican II. An important, perhaps *decisive* question is whether collegiality can best be helped through synods or by convoking a Vatican III Council so as to help the Church effectively tackle the many challenges it faces.

NOTES

1. W. Johnston, "Has Mysticism a Future," *Japan Mission Journal*, Summer, 2006, 82.

2. Having benefited from modern science and technology, the West has used advanced technologies to control and manipulate nature and other non-Western civilizations. Christians in the West have had limited impact upon the growth of the military/industrial complex and international corporate capitalism.

3. The Church's complex history is exemplified in the early Church controversies between Arians (who rejected Christ's divinity) and what became the official Church orthodoxy at Nicaea (325). The Vandals who sacked Rome (410) and parts of northern Africa were Arians. Vandalism is now a byword for desecration. Africa was home to St. Augustine who had begun his The City of God. Mixed forms of orthodox Catholicism and native customs have continued to co-exist. Catholicism in many parts of South America and Africa is marked by its adaptation

of "pagan" rites. Even in the West, the major Church feasts of Christmas and Easter adapted local customs and traditions that appealed to the popular mind. Our efforts for a global ethics that considers the rights of migrants today must be seen in the light of mankind's perennial migrations. While Catholicism has traditionally adapted the customs of the tribes it christianized, Islam has tended to "compromise" less. If, for example, arabesques were originally a style of decoration characterized by a naturalistic setting featuring animals, the Arabs, for religious reasons, forbad the representation of birds, beasts or humans. Arabesque became a style of decoration characterized by intertwining plants and abstract curvilinear motifs. Vatican II set Catholicism on an ambitious plan to dialogue with persons of good will—one that faces practical limitations when dealing with fundamentalists.

4. Over a thousand persons attended the first World Congress of Ecclesial Movements and New Communities in 1998. Yet some movements such as Opus Dei and Focolare are accused of cult-like brain-washing methods. A website is devoted to help "recovering" members of Focolare. Focolare has aspects complementary to SCC's, but its ecclesial, hierarchical links are stronger than that of SCC's.

5. There are conservative and progressive churches from below; our focus is on middle-of-the-road ones.

6. The dominance of today's media leads to trivializations. It is no mean feat for a person to keep a proper sense of balance between the essentials in life and the marginal. Today's media-inspired reversal of Christian values calls for a deeper appreciation of spirituality of the spiritual persons' needs. We seek to address such persons.

Chapter Two

The Challenges of Globalization, Migration, and Religious Fundamentalism

Aristotle's *Ethics*, Book 1, Sec. 2, describes politics as the most authoritative, master art. This chapter argues that Vatican II has offered believers a chance to transcend their differences.[1] We first briefly examine the tragic Middle East situation where Pope Francis has practiced the delicate art of candidly addressing perennial Christian-Islamic conflicts. We then touch on the implications of globalization, cultural and migration problems which have intensified Christian-Islamic conflicts during the past century.

CONFLICTING ASPECTS IN THE HISTORY OF CHRISTIAN-ISLAMIC RELATIONS

Globalization was foreshadowed in the Middle Ages when Jews, Christians and Muslims created a scientific-technological culture that influenced the formation of Western universities in the twelfth and thirteenth centuries. The Church is now well poised to help the West realize that from the Middle Ages through the Renaissance, cross-regional elite interactions provided a basis for the global transformation, which led to the Industrial Age. This initial period included the transfer of scientific knowledge from the Islamic civilization of the Middle East and North Africa to the Christian West. It led to the intellectual revival of the West through the new model of university-based scientific and philosophical education. Interestingly, until the rise of Erdogan in Turkey, it used to be difficult for a Muslim in Turkey to study Arabic. Seminarians in Rome, however, have long been given the chance to study Arabic. The Vatican now invites Muslims to come to the Gregorian University not to convert them but to have them study interfaith relations. We seek to emulate this spirit of Catholic openness. Unfortunately, such a spirit of openness has not always been the case. Pope Urban II's call for the First Crusade (1095) is still a source of tension and misunderstandings between Christians and Muslims. The crusades ended in failure. What is often overlooked is that after plundering Palestine, the Crusaders brought back many physical and spiritual treasures that helped transform Western philosophy, medicine, and spirituality. Humbly reassessing the West's debt to the Middle East and acknowledging the historical ties between Islam and Christianity in shared scientific and philosophical enterprises could help blunt today's all too sectarian nature of encounters between the Christian West and the "foreign" cultures and religious beliefs of Muslims. Muslims' historical memory of the Crusades has led them to refer to the recent Western invaders of Iraq and Afghanistan as modern day "Crusaders."

Vatican II opened the Church to the modern world. It broadened its understanding of its role as a potential catalyst in mediating pressing global problems such as global poverty, racism and political oppression. Its document, *The Church in the Modern World*, insists that the human divisions based on economic disparities between the rich and poor, North and South, must be addressed if the Church is to help humankind realize its fundamental unity. Pope Francis knows that this requires vigorous actions to ensure that the demands of justice be met—without violating the rights of persons or endangering the environment. Societies must remove as quickly as possible the present, huge economic inequalities.[2] Since Vatican II, economic and social disparities in the world have been exacerbated by the growing power of large global corporations that transcend national boundaries and rely on cheap sources of labor to manufacture their products. In the meanwhile, new sources of conflict have emerged based upon sectarian differences as evident in the dramatic events of 9/11. Globalization and cultural encounters have in many ways brought the world closer together, but this has also served to accentuate fundamentalist claims that have led to terrorism. It has bred both fear and hatred in many sectors of the world. The Middle East has been at the center of the many conflicts that have embroiled the three monotheistic religions of Judaism, Christianity and Islam—all of which claim Abraham as father in faith. Although these Middle East conflicts have much to do with politics, religion has played a large role in either uniting or dividing the people of that region. In order to better understand the nature of such problems and formulate strategies for bridging divides, we now turn to examine views on culture and civilization that might help lessen conflicts by pointing to possibly viable solutions.

THE IMPORTANCE OF DISTINGUISHING BETWEEN CIVILIZATION AND CULTURE IN STUDYING CHRISTIAN-ISLAMIC RELATIONS

Because of the interconnections between Islamic and Christian thinkers during the pivotal Medieval Ages, Richard Bulliet refers to a single historical Christian-Islamic civilization. His conciliatory approach to the relationships between Islamic and Christian cultures stands in contrast to Samuel Huntington's thesis of a "clash" between Christian and Islamic civilizations. Bulliet rightly argues that the resurgence of Islam in many parts of the world is due its reaction to Western secular values that tend to do away with religious values. Huntington associates Christianity with Western civilization in a highly debatable fashion. The central theme of his *The Clash of Civilizations* is that the "cultural identities which at the broadest level are civilization identities,"[3] shape the patterns of world politics. We believe that cultures are not to be compared in this way. Huntington's book contains many good insights about the transformation of the world since 1989—as well as many fallacies that need to be analyzed and contrasted with more nuanced views. It argues that Christian-Islamic conflicts going back to the seventh century are due to their claims to be the only true faith. Huntington views the twentieth century conflict between liberal democracies and Marxist-Leninism as having been a "fleeting and superficial historical phenomenon compared to the continuing and deeply conflictual relations between Islam and Christianity." He adds that for Muslims, Islam is a way of life transcending and uniting religion and politics. This is opposed to Christian notions of the separate realms of God and Caesar. "Both are missionary religions believing that their adherents have an obligation to convert nonbelievers to that one true faith" (209–11). Huntington does not mention how the three monotheistic religions collaborated closely during the Golden Age of Islamic learning when hundreds of key Arabic texts in philosophy, theology and science were translated and then assimilated by Christian scholars. The Islamic world recognized Christians and Jews as "people of the Book" sharing a common tradition going back to Abraham. In the Middle Ages, Western universities relied upon key Islamic authors such as Averroes and Avicenna. This continued until the revival of classical culture in the West in the fifteenth century. In many Middle East countries such as Egypt and Lebanon, Christians and Muslims lived peacefully side by side for centuries until well into the twentieth century when politically-motived conflicts began to play a much larger role. Huntington emphasizes the latter to the detriment of the former. Unlike Huntington, Bulliet chooses not to accent the clashes that did occur between the two religions. He recognizes that the fall of the Shah of Iran and the detention of American diplomatic personnel in Tehran in 1979 were a prelude to the 9/11 terrorist attacks on New York's WTC and on the Pentagon.

Previous turning points such as Saladin's conquest of Jerusalem in 1187, the fall of Constantinople to the Ottomans in 1453, and the nearly successful Ottoman siege of Vienna in 1529[4] also had historical repercussions. Still, Bulliet shows in detail that Christianity and Islam share a common heritage rooted in the cultures of the Middle East, North Africa and Spain. For eight centuries, their parallel paths at times virtually overlapped (Bulliet, 15). A fundamental restructuring of Western thinking about their mutual relations calls for a fresh look at history due to the fact that the two faith communities can be thought of as two versions of a common socio-religious system—just as Orthodox Christianity and Western Christendom are two versions of the same socio-religious system.

Christians' failure to stop the Iraq War is an indication of their impotence in today's political realm; it is another way to refute Huntington's clash-of-civilizations thesis that assumes that there is still some form of Christian civilization in the West. To differentiate between Huntington and Bulliet's views, one must distinguish between civilization and culture. Civilization involves the exploitation of nature through new technologies. Culture affects the heart and mind of society. Referring to the inner person including the religious dimension, it helps define civilization but is distinct from it. While Bulliet stresses the cultural commonalities in Christian and Islamic thought that held sway during the Middle Ages, Huntington underplays these facts. The radical changes in Western culture since the Enlightenment are part of the problem. The core Christian values that transcend power politics such as love of neighbor and sharing of resources now play a lesser role in American political life than when Woodrow Wilson attempted to instill Christian ideals into American foreign policy. After WWI, US foreign policy was motivated by national self-interest and fear of Japan, Germany, Russia.

Today, we need a global ethics that transcends purely national self-interests, one that can affirm common values. We argue that the monotheism of Christianity and Islam can help buttress a global ethics able to engage the peoples of the developing world with the wealthy sectors of the Western world. Pope Francis realizes this. We seek to give more weight to the pope's outreach to Islam by helping develop a global mysticism and a global ethical framework rooted in monotheism and in eastern spiritualties such as the Buddhist ethic of compassion. Hopefully, this could help religious leaders cooperate with political and business associates in addressing the economic and educational imbalances now exacerbating the divide between rich and poor nations. The various ethical traditions of the world should be enlisted to find peaceful solutions to the world's most unyielding conflicts connected with national "sovereignty." The way Christians and Muslims cooperated in the Middle Ages is a model for healing today's global rifts. Bulliet's cultural approach is more promising[5] than Huntington's stereotypical view, which ignores some of the positive achievements of the past. Why has the cooperative approach of the Middle Ages been abandoned? Politics and culture have played their roles in this. Bulliet's focus on the inner aspects of culture can reinforce our attempts to dialogue with Islam. Unlike Huntington, we focus on the power of symbols and rituals in expressing and transforming cultures. Huntington's identifying contemporary Western civilization with Christianity is far-fetched given the fact that Christianity is now often relegated to discussing private morals. It is praiseworthy that Pope Francis uses Catholic tradition in his attempts to reverse the trend to privatize if not denigrate religion in the West.

WESTERN SECULARISM, MUSLIM PIETY AND MYSTIC ENLIGHTENMENT

The growth[6] of the feminist movement[7] in the West has had little support from either Catholic or Evangelical Christianity. In both traditions, women have long had marginal roles. The Civil Rights Movement did more to liberate women than did Christian groupings. Christian values are now often ignored or are in flux: women have children out of wedlock, homosexual partners claim the same rights as heterosexuals. In many Western nations, the divorce rate now exceeds 50 percent. In-depth studies of religion, culture and ethics are needed to make both Muslims and Christians realize their commonalities and differences so as to help correct undue historical antagonism. With the rise of science and technology, Western politicians distanced themselves from Christian values. *Laissez-faire* capitalism now threatens the West's communal nature by prioritizing consumerism. In Europe, Christianity has been on the decline since the French Revolution. Various forms of secular-atheist humanism now dominate European ethical discussions. The Enlightenment philosophy of Deism,[8] which has influenced many Western theorists, relegated religious belief to a personal matter while disregarding its social concerns. The European Union's proposed Constitution of 2004 fails to mention Christianity.

Recent popes have argued that modern efforts to separate religion from public life are old-fashioned in that they are rooted in the so-called Enlightenment of the eighteenth century. Pope Benedict and Pope Francis have alleged a flawed double standard in the ways Europeans respect the sensibilities of secularists more than that of Christians.

In the USA, the link between Christianity and American culture is stronger than it is in Europe. Lately, the Republican Party has tried to capitalize on this with an ethics that opposes homosexuality and abortion, but it fails to address social injustices. Mainstream Christian opposition to Middle East adventurism has been largely ignored by Republican administrations. The USA is a global superpower; yet, under Bush Jr. and Trump, Christian moderates have played only marginal roles in international policy-making. Trump's delusory individualistic Gospel betrays Jesus' message and ignores the well-being of all but the rich.

Catholicism stresses a believer's incorporation into Christ's Mystical Body. Its social justice teaching is more compatible with Islamic views on justice than with most of the individualist Evangelical Christian traditions. True, Fundamentalist Islam such as Wahabism does not share the West's concern for human rights. But for Islam, in general the whole body of Muslim believers is responsible for the quality of life in Islamic society. Becoming a Muslim is to become part of the whole Islamic body of believers, which transcends any nation or region of the world. Catholics also claim a universality for their faith community. The Catholic and Islamic traditions both seek to integrate personal and social ethics. Decision-making must not lose sight of public life or of the community. The *Sharia* (Islamic law) is not just a legal tradition. It is based on the principles of Islamic beliefs based on Muhammad's way of life as recorded in the *Hadith* (traditions). In some ways we could compare the *Hadith*'s role with how papal social encyclicals apply the principles of faith to social issues. Christianity and Western values are no longer in sync; we cannot simply equate Western cultures with secular humanism. In fact, many of Western societies' key ethical values such as universal human dignity, the sacredness of human life, and the protection of children's rights are rooted in the values of biblical traditions. The monotheistic faith traditions hold very similar views about the need to address social injustices and provide adequate mechanisms for sharing the social good. Concepts of distributive justice owe much to these faith traditions; they may be one of the strongest bases for ecumenical dialogue in the contemporary world.

Today's glaring inequalities are largely the result of global forms of capitalism in which privileged elites have benefited from present economic systems. The societies that took advantage of the technological developments of the Scientific Revolution are now controlled by capitalists. This has been done without regard to religious affiliation. The Western world's dependence on Middle East oil is one of a symbiotic relationship among the Western powers and their oil suppliers. To protect their vital economic interests in the region, the Western powers have intervened in Middle-East affairs over the past two centuries. The collapse of the Islamic political power in the Middle East created a power vacuum replaced in part by new states that were dependent upon Western nations for much of their economic and military operations. Islam's resurgence in the Middle East is partly a reaction to the attempted Westernization of the Middle East by leaders such as Kemal Atatürk in Turkey and the Shah of Iran. Leaders who sought Western patrons were viewed as puppets dependent upon Western powers for their survival. This pattern of dependence that carried over in the Afghanistan and Iraq wars has fueled much of the hatred toward the West by the insurgents in both lands. The source of this antagonism lies not in any particular religious belief but rather in a sense of alienation spawned by cultural and economic imperialism. Just as the Native Americans and African Americans were subjugated and economically exploited, so many in the Middle East view their present conditions as due to economic and political exploitation by Western interests.

EDWARD SAID ANTICIPATED BULLIET'S MODERATE VIEW TOWARDS ISLAM

Edward Said's classic book, *Orientalism* (1978) revolutionized the study of European influences in the Middle East. Palestinian by birth, Said spent much of his early life in Cairo. Having earned a PhD at Harvard (1963) he joined the faculty of Columbia University. He criticized European and American studies of the Middle East as being biased with presumed notions of Western cultural superiority. The "otherness" of Middle Eastern culture is a fictional construct of the Western imagination exemplified in films such as Lawrence of Arabia. Said argued that Europe and the USA misunderstood the Middle East. The USA alliance with Israel led it to tolerate the latter's expansionist claims in Palestine following the 1973 Arab Oil Embargo. The caricature of Islam and Arabs became part of the media fascination with the Middle East, replete with stereotypical images of Arabs. Said also argued that most Americans saw Muslims as either suppliers of oil or as terrorists. Very "little of the detail, the human density, the passion of Arab-Moslem life has entered the awareness of even those people whose profession it is to report the Arab world (Said, "Islam through Western Eyes," *The Nation*, April 26, 1980). Said opposes the "series of crude, essentialized caricatures of the Islamic world presented in such a way as to make that world vulnerable to military aggression" (ibid). Even though some of Said's claims about Orientalism proved to be inaccurate, his writings on American attitudes toward the Middle East were on the mark.

The Arab view of the West was shaped by post WWI events and the dissolution of the Ottoman Empire that had sided with Germany. Osama bin Laden frequently referred to this event as a source of his hatred of the West. The United States' failure to understand Arab culture led to the Iraq War and has aggravated sectarian conflicts in many parts of the world. One of Said's opponents was Bernard Lewis, a historian of the Ottoman Empire. Like Huntington, Lewis espoused a theory of inherent conflict between Western and Islamic world views. As an advisor of the Bush administration on the Middle East after 9/11, Lewis participated in the American culture wars. He dwelt on Muslim rage against the West. He and Said became intellectual proxies with such neo-conservatives as Victor Davis Hanson backing Lewis against Said's followers.[9] In 2007, Lewis made the provocative statement that soon the only important question regarding Europe's future would be: "Will it be an Islamized Europe or Europeanized Islam." Compare this statement with Cardinal Ratzinger's 2005 argument that "In order to survive, Europe needs a critical acceptance of its Christian culture. Europe seems at the very moment of its greatest success, to have become empty from the inside, as it were."[10] The statements of Ratzinger and Lewis point to various identity crises in Europe that have given rise to rightist political parties. How best address such crises? We believe that our cultural-bridging approach might help defang some European-Muslim tensions. Understanding one another's cultural identities is a way to build peace rather than dehumanizing others through misunderstandings. Another source of Muslim hatred for the West has been its support of Israel's removal of Palestinians from much of their historic homeland.[11] Fundamentalist Christians tend to support Israel unequivocally because of their literal interpretation of the messianic prophecies and a presumed central role of Jewish people in end times (*parousia*). Jimmy Carter, on the other hand, has advocated the rights of Palestinians but his pleas have fallen on deaf ears. Until after WWII, Iran had cordial relations with the US; many Americans were involved in Iranian business and cultural affairs. Following the nationalization of the Anglo-Iranian Oil Company by Mosaddegh in 1951, the US backed Shah Reza Pahlavi's coup. With CIA support, the Shah eliminated all opposition to his rule. His ouster by the Iranian Revolution of 1979 led to Ayatollah Khomeini's theocratic regime. That year's American hostage crisis has come to symbolize the impotence of the US, the "Great Satan."

THE ARAB SPRING AND THE CONCILIATORY POLICIES OF PRESIDENT SAIED AND POPE FRANCIS

The Arab Spring was a series of anti-government protests, uprisings, and armed rebellions that spread across much of the Islamic world in the early 2010s. It began in response to oppressive regimes and a low standard of living, starting with protests in Tunisia. Although the Arab Spring soon led to conflicts in Syria that have destroyed much of that country and to the reimposition of a dictatorship in Egypt, it has had a more fortunate outcome in Tunisia where President Kais Saied, a constitutional law professor and outsider, was elected with the help of young voters. Saied has charted a democratic process that responds to present realities. Saied's leadership has embodied much of the practical, realistic ideals Pope Francis has also lived as priest, bishop and pope. One must let God and one's faith be relevant to one's political strivings. Reaffirming our common historical-ecological roots rather than ideology is most important.

We noted above how the Arab world lost control of its own destiny after WWI while the victorious European powers made key decisions regarding its future. The present configuration of the Middle East stems from these decisions. If a nation or a group of nations attempt to impose its will on others, the latter will rise in opposition. The flip side of such a scenario would be one in which the actors would remember their common Christian-Islamic roots. Judaism, Christianity and Islam should reaffirm their common heritage for the benefit of all mankind. It would require a conversion process to replace the limited perspectives found within one's own faith community. The need for global solutions that can transcend the limited perspectives of the past whether cultural, ethnic or religious, has never been clearer. The environment is an integrated system affecting all life forms on our planet. Ecological theologies can help the monotheistic faiths and eastern religious traditions develop a common understanding of the earth as our mother and benefactor. When we root our language in earth-centered metaphors, we begin to grasp that all forms of life are interdependent. The alienation of much contemporary thought needs to be transformed by new organic patterns of thought centered in life-giving biological metaphors. A creation spirituality can unite rather than divide humanity. As we enter a critical juncture in humans' journey through time, we need both a global ethics and a global spirituality that can inspire and orient our youths into the future. Many in the West have lost their sense of connection to the earth, to the cosmos and to the whole human family. Pope Francis' *Laudato Si*, "On Care for our Common Home" (2015) helped reestablish this connection. Overall Francis' charism has been his ability to discern. When he was asked, in an interview what it means for a Jesuit to be elected Pope, he replied with a single word: "discernment." The value he places on this practice is evident from the way in which he continually returns to the theme. For him, discernment is a dying followed by a rising: it implies letting go of one's own plans and agendas, and allowing oneself to be guided into new life by the Holy Spirit. Following his advice, we focus on mystic enlightenment, which greatly differs from the notions of the French "intellectual" Enlightenment. Mystics speak of being enlightened through a certain darkness of spiritual encounters. Pope Francis has been able to pierce through the darkness and discern how the depths of religious teaching should not be ignored if the world is to be rescued from many threats. See also http://global-spirituality.info/

RELIGIONS' POTENTIALLY IMPORTANT ROLES IN RESCUING HUMANITY

A culture of individual pursuits of happiness has dominated much of Western thought over the past two centuries. Buddhist and Christian spiritualities of compassion—which remind us of how ephemeral the world is—both transcend limited notions of a pursuit of happiness. One needs a converted heart to be open to all—even to those who differ from us or are our "enemies." The Catholic Church is well situated to contribute to a global, "mystic" spirituality and to a global ethic. Nonetheless, a book exploring the possibilities of a Vatican III Council must ask whether the Church as whole is adequately addressing the needs of the contemporary world. We cannot turn back the clock to another age in which a dominant Church institution partially controlled the Western agenda. We must accept the world as it now is but also learn how to transform it. Pope Francis realizes that the twenty-first century needs an "active-in-world" type of spirituality compatible with traditional spiritualities. But if formerly, the Church was tempted to neglect some earthly realities, today the Church must adequately respond to global ecological crises. Western colonialism and capitalism exploited the earth and its peoples as they sought to attain economic and cultural domination. Americans must recognize the role that "Manifest Destiny" played in "legitimating" the subjugation of other peoples. On the 200th anniversary of the abolition of slavery in Great Britain, the Archbishop of Canterbury called for repentance on the part of Western countries and their churches for having allowed slavery. Christians must realistically deal with the problems of impoverished nations in Latin America, Africa and Asia. The world's present economic-political structures have mostly failed to rectify social injustices denounced in the Church's social encyclicals, in Buddhist teachings of compassion, or in the Koran.[12] Men and women of good will must join together in challenging Western individualism so as to share the earth's wealth equitably. Islam enjoins its believers to contribute yearly 2.5 percent of all of one's assets (*zakat*). Such a solidarity, if also practiced by others, would help stabilize the world economy. A fund could be established through the UN to distribute such contributions to assist projects throughout the world's poorer areas. The ecological crisis and fear of terrorism present us with opportunities to reduce inequalities. These should be central topics for a Vatican III to promote the Kingdom of God here on earth. All of the resources we need to accomplish such laudable goals are already here, but we do need to learn how to use them. Everyone should be invited to the marriage feast—believers and unbelievers, rich and poor, conservatives and liberals. The bounty of this earth is to be shared by all. After noting the mixed blessings of growth in the United States, various environmental and migration problems as well as the responses of religious groups,[13] and after alluding to how countries, including China, have been transformed by capitalism, we shall then evaluate the roles of a creation spirituality and of global ethics in living the Gospel today. This will bring us back to how Christian-Muslim social justice teachings could jointly help transform the human heart.

THE AMBIGUOUS NATURE OF THE UNITED STATES' IDEALS AND ITS ROLES AS A GLOBAL ECONOMIC POWER

America is known as the "New World" because immigrants from all continents have sought to begin life anew in the USA. The ideal of welcoming newcomers is expressed in Emma Lazarus' poem now emblazoned on the Statue of Liberty in New York Harbor:

> Give me your tired, your poor, Your huddled masses, Yearning to be breathe free.

Her poem epitomizes the challenges America has faced in assimilating millions of immigrants. Foreign students coming to the USA from the Middle East and other areas of the world engulfed in violence or hatred should be welcomed with understanding and encouragement. Fear of youths from the world's "hot spots" is often overdone. Such youths should be welcomed. Some will become future leaders. The USA's educational system, one of its great strengths, is complemented by many Catholic institutions of higher learning. Both confessional and secular universities in the US have offered scholarships to youth from the Middle East, Africa and other developing areas of the world. This practice should continue so as to ensure that the ideals of a responsible freedom are honored. Such a reaching out testifies to Americans' beliefs in a legitimate freedom of action—exemplified in John Courtney Murray's leadership in drafting Vatican II's "Declaration on Religious Freedom" which helped move the Church toward larger horizons of mutual acceptance. American ideals have played their role on the world stage but this has to be seen against the background of other stark realities. Our brief survey of the USA's mixed record on the international scene will serve as background for our later assessment of the role that a global Catholicism should play to alleviate problems—a role that Pope Francis has been prophetically reassessing.

The USA did not remain exempt from imperialist drives which began in rather innocuous ways with the Monroe Doctrine and claims of Manifest Destiny. US expansionism increased due to its involvements in Panama, Cuba and the Philippines toward the end of the nineteenth century. The USA's rise to superpower status stems from its alliances following World War II. The USSR's disintegration in the late 1980's reinforced US hegemony in the midst of globalization trends. Today, instantaneous communication links the world. The profusion of satellite-based networks enable us to witness events taking place across the globe. This was dramatically exemplified in such events as the Student Revolt in Tiananmen Square in 1989 and the Middle East wars. The growth of the Internet and low-cost international phone services provide endless ways for people to communicate with each other and bypass more traditional sources of information such as newspapers, magazines or government reports. National boundaries are being blurred due to the continual movement of peoples seeking better economic opportunities in developed lands—or to the outsourcing of jobs abroad. International air travel continues to expand despite terrorist threats. A great irony is that democratic and moral ideals are being offset by a problematic consumerism and by repression in many authoritarian countries.

The US population has grown by over 100 million persons since 1980; it now exceeds 320 million—having more than doubled since 1950. Largely fueled by immigration over the past 50 years, it is expected to reach 438 million by 2050. The US is now the third most populous country in the world after China and India. Its consumer lifestyle has led to increasing levels of deforestation, pollution of rivers, a rapid decline in biodiversity and increasing suburban sprawl. The U.S. uses about a quarter of the world's fossil fuel resources—burning up nearly 25 percent of the coal, 26 percent of the oil, and 27 percent of the world's natural gas. Over-consumption has also expanded in other developed nations—giving rise to ethical concerns since this is an unsustainable process. The growth in production and pollution has had a catastrophic impact on the environment. Over the past few decades humans have altered natural resource ecosystems more rapidly than in any comparable period of time in history in their effort to meet the growing demands for food, freshwater, and fuel.[14] Some pertinent ethical questions are what are legitimate "demands" in our present epoch? How can Buddhist-Christian spiritualities help clarify such quandaries.

CHRISTIAN AND BUDDHIST RESPONSES TO ENVIRONMENTAL AND OTHER PRESSING CRISES: FINDING A BALANCE THAT TRANSCENDS MERE ECONOMIC SELF-INTEREST

Alfred Crosby has shown how Western conquests and migrations led to increasing types of rationalization in production and finance as well as to increasing secularization.[15]

Globalization has integrated global markets, but it has had cultural-religious dimensions that have led to sectarian violence. Nations are now ever more interdependent. The world's booming economy has enriched many while leaving others to struggle. With a view to discern how a Vatican III Council might enlighten the world, we stress that poorer nations will be destabilized if they cannot meet their populations' basic needs. Forty percent of the world's inhabitants get most of their drinking water from the summer melt of mountain glaciers, which are now rapidly disappearing. Such a situation will lead to further migrations from vulnerable nations. It may also provoke violence. In a way, scientific progress has destabilized the world since it has provoked climate changes. All citizens have roles to play in this. In 2005, the US Catholic bishops pleaded for dialogue on the crucial topic of global warming now threatening the world. The Evangelical Climate Initiative (2006) addressed this issue from a biblically-inspired standpoint.[16]

The USA's failure to sign the 1992 Kyoto Declaration on the Environment and Trump's rejection of the 2015 Paris Agreement Paris Agreement on climate change have isolated the nation. The industrial economies have produced the highest emissions of greenhouse gases causing global warming. On the positive side, entrepreneurial creativity has made it possible for the world to better address such problems. To avoid looming catastrophes, energy-use adjustments must be made in both in the policies of both developed and developing nations.[17] Reversing the global climate crises must involve all nations. Poorer nations will need assistance from wealthier ones if they are to adequately address the looming crises. Thomas Merton, besides addressing problems of his time such as racism, war and peace, also promoted inter-religious dialogue with the Dalai Lama and Thich Nhat Hanh.[18] Having anticipated some of our pressing environmental problems, the two men urged Buddhists and Christians to jointly seek solutions. Pope Francis followed suit while visiting Asia in November, 2019. Despite differences, Buddhists and Christians should jointly support those wounded by divisions. Francis asked Catholics not to forget how early missionaries had labored in announcing the Good News to Asia.

How balance our sense of identity with the welfare of all amidst globalization? Too often, globalization proponents ignore the spiritual dimension that transcends economic self-interest. Religion must not be exploited to defend the status quo. Old Testament prophets were persecuted for exposing the unfaithfulness of the Chosen People's leaders. Religious leaders can and should exercise a prophetic charism by alerting people on justice issues. In 1980, right-wing activists killed Archbishop Romero of San Salvador. A former conservative, his conscience had rebelled when he realized the human causes of human poverty and saw some of his priests assassinated for defending the poor. In 1995, the Vatican appointed an Opus Dei member, Fernando Saenz Lacalle, a former military chaplain, as Archbishop of San Salvador. Some allege that his appointment as primate of the El Salvador's episcopacy was a rightist coup. Until his retirement in 2008, Saenz Lacalle used his influence to have the Vatican reprimand Jon Sobrino, a former Romero advisor and author of two influential books on liberation theology. While praising Sobrino for his concern for the poor,[19] the Vatican maintained that his Christology was unorthodox. The reprimand of Sobrino shows how complex it is to reconcile the claims of orthodox Christology in the face of social injustice. Upon being censured, Sobrino called the process "not honest." Honesty is the cornerstone of a global ethics. *The Catechism of the Catholic Church* warns us against duplicity. One must communicate honestly: "The truth shall make you free" (Jn. 8:32). Was the Vatican's criticism of liberation theology justified? Certainly, it should be faulted for having supported rightist militias violently opposing Gospel principles. Christians have often been caught between the demands of war, politics and conscience.

During the World War I, French and German soldiers would exchange greetings on Christmas but would then resume their attacks on the following day.[20] Would soldiers— pawns of the powers that be—not gladly act in more human ways? Many areas of life in all parts of the globe are crippled by corruption. All too many politicians the world over betray people's trust. It is not easy for those with principles to achieve their laudable goals. Fortunately, there are people of good will such as those involved in non-profit organizations. Amidst the changes and pressures of life, "idealists" must join hands with politicians in transcending self-interest. An alliance of those seeking non-violent solutions to sectarian conflicts is necessary to holistically heal the earth. With Pope Francis we listen to the cry of the poor for this cry is also the hope of the Church.

GLOBALLY ADDRESSING THE PROBLEMS OF IMMIGRATION WITH JUSTICE

Tracing the path from Vatican II to the present makes it clear that a possible Vatican III should consider recent changes within global cultural contexts. We contextualize such problems in the light of immigration. Immigrants from Africa and the Middle East living in Europe and the communities hosting them have to deal with great cultural differences. On the other hand, many well-to-do Westerners think it their "right" to go and settle in whatever country they choose; they often live in the plush, secluded areas of poorer nations. New integrated communities willing and able to transcend cultural, religious and economic differences must be established in various parts of the world. Even virtual communities linking people through the Internet and other forms of communication and interaction such as teleconferencing or video conferencing could be of help. Since Vatican II, globalization has led to the outsourcing of many types of employment outside the United States and to a continued deceleration in the US industrial sectors such as the production of wearing apparel, automobiles, cell phones, and computers. This has influenced the underlying population structures of the United States and other nations. It has led to the migration of millions of people from Asia, Africa and Latin America in search of employment either in their own country or outside their borders.

Many of the economic patterns in the West run counter to the Gospel. The Church must help Christians deal with rich-poor divisions and illusions about Western hegemony. In a sense, the churches in the West have been all too beholden to the well-to-do. The Church in the suburbs is expanding but the Church's presence in poor urban core is diminishing. As more and more people from many nations leave rural areas to seek jobs in urban areas, social malaise is the predictable outcome. Many immigrants live in poverty or are forced to take low-wage jobs and to live in subhuman conditions in segregated sectors of society. On all continents slums abound. Cities are fragmented between rich and poor. The income-and-cultural gaps between the highly educated and technologically proficient populations, on the one hand, and the immigrant populations seeking employment, on the other, has continued to expand. We now live in very fluid and dynamic cultural contexts resulting from the emergence of new economic and cultural structures that transcend national boundaries and affect the lives of workers and their families all over the globe.

Confusion reigns in many areas of life. Both Buddhist teachings of compassion and Christian views on human solidarity could be applied to alleviate the present rich/poor divides that have been accelerating in Asia as capitalistic principles take hold. The Buddhist philosophy of peace could help nuance the religious claims of the monotheistic religions and help grassroots actions in fostering peace. Catholicism's genius is to "navigate" the shoals of confusion so as to help antagonists and protagonists of all stripes resolve their differences. Vatican II helped us develop strategies that would not stress differences but rather ways to reconcile humans. The Church should increase both its ministry of presence and its efforts to counter the severe problems afflicting the world. Catholic social justice teachings include a transnational approach to problems occasioned by the continued migration of peoples from rural settings to urban metropolitan areas. Diversity requires that we move beyond entrenched interests. The Civil Rights movement helped blacks to move into the mainstream of American life. Still, in many parts of the USA, racial interchanges are limited. Hispanics and Asians have trailed in many Southern states in attaining leadership positions. The same might be said for European nations where a backlash against immigration has led to the rise of rightist political parties.

THE CHURCH, THE RIGHTS OF IMMIGRANTS AND POPE FRANCIS' EVOLVING STRATEGY

Marginal persons are those who live in two worlds without being integrated in either—a recipe for an alienated attitude. *Mestizo* means one of mixed racial ancestry, but Latin Americans call *"mestizo"* one who is involved in a process of "homogenization" yet has to "hide" the reality of being racially excluded. There is a need to integrate marginalized or *mestizo*-like persons in larger contexts. We explore structures that could help Church leaders and ordinary faithful achieve this. For the theologian Virgilio Elizondo (1935-2016), Jesus was a prototypical *mestizo*, a borderland reject from a region of mixed people and caught between hostile forces.[21] The support of the US Catholic Church for immigrant rights in the USA is a positive sign of the Church's involvement at the grass roots level in this important justice issue. The US Church has taken a prophetic stance against populist appeals to "seal" the US-Mexican border and to criminalize illegal aliens. It has defended migrant workers from Latin American countries against many forms of alarmist opposition. The Church is often at the center of US immigration debates. The election of an immigrant, Archbishop José H. Gomez of Los Angeles, to be head of the United States Conference of Catholic Bishops in Nov. 2019 is a sign of the US Church being opposed to President Trump's inhumane stance on immigration.[22]

The rights of immigrants need to be better understood in the light of the UN Declaration on Human Rights (1985). This document clarifies the rights of groups such as migrant workers who live in a nation for a considerable time period without being citizens of the country where they work. The International Convention on the Protection of Migrant Workers and their Families (1990) laid a moral and legal framework for protecting migrant workers and their families. Its Preamble sets forth the context in which many migrant workers find themselves as they seek employment that will support their families with a livable wage and under the protection of state and federal labor laws:

> Employing migrant workers who are in an irregular situation will be discouraged if the fundamental human rights of all migrant workers are not widely recognized. ... Granting certain additional rights to migrant workers and members of their families in a regular situation will encourage all migrants and employers to comply with the laws and procedures established by the States concerned. Convinced, therefore, of the need to bring about the international protection of the rights of all migrant workers and members of their families, ... (we) have agreed as follows:
>
> 1. The present Convention is applicable, except as otherwise provided hereafter, to all migrant workers and members of their families without distinction of any kind such as sex, race, color, language, religion or ... economic position.
> 2. The present Convention shall apply during the entire migration process of migrant workers and members of their families, which comprises preparation for migration, departure, transit and the entire period of stay and remunerated activity in the State of employment as well as return to the State of origin.[23]

The Convention insists that migrant workers and their families have basic human rights even if they lack a legal civil status. Most of migrant workers in the US have a Catholic background. The Church is often the only institutional refuge for many such migrant workers. In his message for the 105th World Day of Migrants and Refugees, September, 2019, Pope Francis recalled the mysterious way the Kingdom of God is already present here on earth. "Yet in our own time, we are saddened to see the obstacles and opposition it encounters. Violent conflicts and all-out wars continue to tear humanity apart" fueled by economic and social imbalances.[24] Against this background, one may detect the evolving pattern of Pope Francis' overall strategy for adequate global policies on migrants. This may be juxtaposed to the 2019 Amazon Synod on the rights of indigenous people which to our mind could form an important part of a Vatican III Council's agenda—a need pointedly depicted in the 2006 film Babel. The film addresses the issues of migration and cultural diversity. Depicting the vagaries of life and of legal "justice," it poignantly illustrates how humans react to tragedies. Set in Morocco, Mexico, Japan and the USA, it intertwines the lives of unsuspecting protagonists in telling ways. The film's heroine is an illegal migrant worker, a Mexican nanny who has worked in the USA for decades. Despite her fidelity to family and friends, she is the film's main victim. Babel brings out in an uncanny manner how chance human actions can take a great toll on some. Another victim, an American tourist, is shot while riding on a bus in Morroco; she is subjected to a very painful stitching of her wound to save her from bleeding to death. Co-passengers on the bus react in a callous manner, but Moroccan families act in kind ways. Other protagonists in Japan are also affected by the complications that had led to the shooting on the bus. The lesson is that the heart should take precedence over money. Babel illustrates how the human family is inextricably related across the planet, but stands in need of an ethic of the heart that transcends national boundaries.

People take many steps in life without knowing where these steps might lead them. Our own intent is to trace a broad outline that may be useful in preparing for a Vatican III. Looking back upon history, we examine migration patterns and cultural diversity. Our hope is that people like the Mexican nanny will not be victimized in the future due to their goodness. Such a hope will be more credible if we can draw out some of the ethical implications of such past evils as colonization. Colonization, made possible by the West's superiority in technology and resources, has in turn fueled migration from former colonies and exacerbated interfaith problems between Muslims and Westerners. Globalization is now an irreversible reality with religious dimensions. This means that ethical people have to learn from history so as to empower the poor. It is necessary to span the centuries to adequately understand the spirit that guided the founders of the three monotheistic religions. Simply put, one could say that the "three religions of the book" profess these core teachings:

- Judaism stems from the Law of Moses found in the first five books of its Scriptures.
- The truth of Christianity respects the Law and the Prophets, but love is paramount.
- The truth of Islam is the reinterpretation of what was taught by Moses and Jesus.

Vatican II touched on such questions but a Vatican III should address them in more detail in the face of the terrorism now haunting the planet. The Gospel's ideals should guide the universal Church as well as each Catholic. Yet, many ideals prescribed in both public and Church documents fail to be implemented. In this age of crises, the Church must make its domestic policies more pastoral, less protective of its own self-interests. Failing that, it will not be taken seriously. The Church's alleged silence during the Nazi holocaust is still a source of contention with the Jewish community despite recent popes' efforts to help reconcile Jews and Catholics. Its silence during the priest pedophilia scandal has hurt it. Another area that touches on basic human rights is that of marriage. Marriage should not alienate one from one's religious tradition. Nor should the Church lose contact with the priests and nuns who have embarked on another vocation. Former nuns and priests can be a vital source of outreach to the modern world in areas now closed to the Church. The Church has the responsibility of defending the moral and legal rights that all humans have as proclaimed in the 1948 Declaration of Human Rights and the various Conventions stemming from the Declaration. The Declaration stressed that migrants have a basic right to a fair wage for the work they do. Most migrant workers who have entered the US in the past few decades have Catholic roots in Central or South America. The Church should work closely with the key agencies of the United Nations and international human rights organizations such as Amnesty International and with the US Congress to develop more just policies toward these migrant workers.

THE RISE OF CHINA, GLOBAL CAPITALISM, AND FREEDOM OF EXPRESSION

Global capitalism has been shifting much of the "means of production" from the industrialized West to the emerging nations of Asia. With a combined population of over two billion (close to 30 percent of the world's total) China and India are now prototypes of global capitalism. The twenty-first century promises to be "The Chinese Century." Such shifts entail many geopolitical questions—seen that all nations have a growing need for sources of energy. Energy-producing nations have formed their own economic and political structures independent of the West. One dramatic instance of new geopolitical tensions is China's increasing efforts to exploit Africa's resources. China is now a focal challenge to the global economy. It retains only remnants of its prior Confucian and Taoist cultural heritage. It has increased controls over its inhabitants through the authoritarian structures of a centralized, totalitarian state; communism is a mere veneer. China has overtaken Europe in economic might, but it lacks adequate moral and environmental safeguards. In 2019, Human Rights Watch declared that the Chinese government poses a global threat to human rights. How mitigate such dire situations?

The Church's social justice teachings can be helpful when assessing the Chinese economic model now fueling the world's economy. Although China does not have a sizeable Christian population, it is concerned about how the West perceives it. Chinese authorities still consider the Church as a "foreign" religion with a political agenda. The Church will need to learn how best adapt its message to the psychology and culture of the Chinese people. Some have faulted Pope Francis for conceding too much to the Chinese Communist government when in 2018 he pledged that the Church would remain loyal to that regime. The Church and the Pope face the delicate balancing act of advocating public policies that do not provoke the Chinese government while insisting that the human rights of people in China be respected. Consider that the recent uprising of young activists in Hong Kong demanding that their rights be respected has run into a brick wall. The young activists fear Chinese reprisals. Worse are the brutal "re-education" camps in which over a hundred thousand Uighur Muslims have been interned in NW China. Indeed the doings of a totalitarian China point to the dilemmas facing freedom advocates. On the other hand, the Church should also help correct the abuses of capitalism by advocating the ethical dimensions of world trade and global finance. Has it sufficiently critiqued the moral decay found in corporate business practices? If not, this must be addressed by revitalizing its teaching on social justice in the workplace. Some people become workaholics, lead over-scheduled lives and find it hard to even share family meals. Many executives of US-based corporations are "practicing" Christians. Yet, their behavior often lacks ethical integrity. The Church should join the forces attempting to influence business practices of transnational corporations such as Walmart so that employees' lives are not hurt or destroyed. Walmart, the largest employer in the US and one of the largest corporations in the world (based on global earnings and profitability), has resisted workers' attempts toward collective bargaining. Already a major corporate force in China, it has accepted the reality of state-sponsored labor unions in China but opposes them in the USA and Canada. The Church can act within the framework of the policies of the World Trade Organization, the International Monetary Fund to the extent that these would join efforts advocating debt relief for poor countries.

Recent contacts by the authors with leaders in East/West medicine indicate that Integrative Medicine may provide an access point for spiritual practices such as *Tai Chi* that resonate with Catholic spirituality. Given the complexities of the Christian situation in China, the Church could join coalitions of progressive environmental and human rights organizations that might provide direction for global corporations operating in China. Such corporations often have a greater power over the future of nations than do their own governments. In September, 2016, the Chinese government praised the pope's *Laudato Si* which might be a sign that it, too, can appreciate some aspects of Gospel values.

CARING FOR THE EARTH: CREATION SPIRITUALITY AND IMPLEMENTING *LAUDATO SI*'S VISION

Christians are called to join other religious leaders to build the earth in collaboration with all those wanting to bring global peace to the world. Current economic conditions provide great leverage to those countries with large reserves of oil and gas. Because of global warming, these sources of energy need to be quickly supplanted by renewable sources such as solar, wind and geothermal power. Some evangelical Christian activists, such as the best-selling author Rick Warren, have formed a coalition of Christian evangelicals to support the transition of the US from an economy based on fossil fuels to one based on renewal sources of energy. Catholic leaders could participate in that initiative. Al Gore's documentary, *An Inconvenient Truth* (2006) reenergized the environmental movement. Still, the unwillingness of many Protestant conservative groups to face this issue has led many young people committed to environmental stewardship to view their churches as being irrelevant to pressing moral issues of our age. Part of the agenda of a Vatican III should include the development of a creation-based theology in harmony with a sound environmental ethics. Catholic theologians such as Matthew Fox, Thomas Berry and Diarmuid O'Murchu have pioneered work on creation theology and creation spirituality. Pope Francis' encyclical *Laudato Si*, squarely faces such issues:

> We must regain the conviction that we need one another, that we have a shared responsibility for others and the world, and that being good and decent are worth it. We have had enough of immorality and the mockery of ethics, goodness, faith and honesty. It is time to acknowledge that light-hearted superficiality has done us no good. When the foundations of social life are corroded, what ensues are battles over conflicting interests, new forms of violence and brutality, and obstacles to the growth of a genuine culture of care for the environment (no. 229).

The encyclical seeks to lead us into the mysteries of the universe, of creatures, and the harmony of creation. It helps us reflect on the universal communion of nature. Failing a sustainable global ecological policy and cooperative approach, *Laudato Si* warns us, the entire planet will face drastic consequences. Francis' meeting with economists and entrepreneurs (March 26–28, 2020) to discuss a proposed pact for a new economy is another sign of his determination to counteract the asocial aspects of modern business practices. He has discussed some of the most complex problems in today's world—from safeguarding the environment to courageously committing oneself to rethink the economic paradigms of our time. This reflects themes he addressed in *Laudato Si*.

CHRISTIAN AND MUSLIM SOCIAL JUSTICE TRADITIONS AND EXAMPLES OF REACHING OUT

The growth of terrorist attacks and the rise of Christian and Islamic fundamentalism since 9/11 could paradoxically lead to needed Christian-Muslim dialogues. Much of Christian fundamentalism—centered in the USA—has influenced American foreign policy. Islamic fundamentalism, based in such Middle Eastern countries as Afghanistan, Pakistan and recently in Iraq, has also made inroads in many European countries with large Muslim populations. The complicated nature of relations between the West and Islam—evident in the history of the Crusades—is also illustrated in the fact that it was not until 1876 that the Ottoman Empire adopted a constitution. The West's emphasis on human rights, freedom and toleration is often lacking in Islamic lands. The Koran does recognize the rights to life, peaceful living and owning property. Communal structures fostering responsibility and interdependence are quite common in the Islamic world. Yet, areas in such Islamic countries as Afghanistan and Yemen have experienced continual fighting. While it is not easy to bring pre-modern Islamic societies into the community of nations, the historical presence of Catholicism in Europe, the Middle East and the USA gives it the potential to help bridge Christian-Islamic differences. The Church's Peace and Justice tradition has much in common with Islam's emphasis on social welfare for the poor, the oppressed and the mentally or physically disabled. Christianity and Islam pioneered the development of health care institutions in the Middle Ages. Muslim medical philosophers prepared many of the key intellectual concepts for providing proper medical care for the less fortunate members of society. The Koran (4:58) holds that justice is a virtue to be practiced by everyone so as to ensure a balanced social order: "If you judge between people, judge with justice." Muslims are expected to donate a percentage of their assets to charities that care for the poor, widows and disabled persons.

Jews, Christians and Muslims share a vital social justice tradition that could be one of the "pillars" of a renewed relationship among the monotheistic religions. One example of reaching out across the religious divides is how Gerald Grudzen and his wife responded during a period of extensive famine in a predominantly Muslim country. They established the Milk for Bangladesh Project (1974–75)—a people-to-people effort involving American citizens from various religious backgrounds. This experience sharpened Grudzen's global consciousness leading him to respond to human need beyond sectarian differences. If fundamentalist Christian missionaries sometimes cause problems due to their lack of understanding of the deeper aspects of faith, a global consciousness based on compassion can help one overcome the intolerance that pits fundamentalists of various traditions against one another. Other examples of reaching out are illustrated in the various relief projects that occurred after the tsunamis in Indonesia (2004, 2019) and after several hurricanes in the USA. Such reaching out is a sign of a caring humanity. None of us is immune from tragedy. If, as Herman Marcuse phrases it, humans are in danger of becoming "one-dimensional" modelled on how a total empiricism treats concepts,[25] we seek to respond to human needs by awakening the *deeper dimensions of one's conscience*. Transforming our self-understanding into non-ideological modes of genuine, "practical" religious compassion is most important to help counter intolerance.

CATHOLICISM AS A COUNTERWEIGHT TO FUNDAMENTALIST RELIGIOUS INTOLERANCE

The rise of religious intolerance throughout the world is a mirror image of another aspect of globalization we must address. The West in the past few years has witnessed many crimes of hatred. Progressives in each of the monotheistic traditions have to deal with neoconservatives who seek to isolate themselves from the rest of humanity, claiming "unique" authority in interpreting their sacred scriptures. The growing level of hostility toward Muslims in the West makes us pause and reflect on how we got into this predicament. Judaism, Islam and Christianity all have fundamentalist groups among their believers. Turkey's Erdogan has exploited deeds of intolerance to "justify" his ideology. The murder of Hrant Dink, an Armenian journalist and social activist, in Istanbul (2007), did awake many Muslims in Turkey to the need for reconciliation with Armenian Christian communities. The growth of Christian fundamentalism has its roots in the Reformation when Protestants claimed that the Bible was the sole source of revelation. However, if all religious beliefs need to be confirmed by the Bible, it can lead to a denial of authentic religious experience including communal forms of religious life based on contemplation and the transformative power of selfless service. On a philosophical level, it can lead to a false supernaturalism that separates religious knowledge from philosophy and science. The flip side of supernaturalism is that of a philosophically naive skepticism. Skepticism about the truths of religion was exacerbated by the Thirty Years War (1618–48). Enlightenment deists later sought to replace the God of revelation with an impersonal power that had designed the universe but then left it to its own devices with man as the autonomous caretaker of the physical universe. Catholicism and Islam both reject Kant's "autonomous self," but neither has effectively bridged the growing gap between the natural sciences and theology. The scientist Richard Dawkins voices his private beliefs[26] when he rejects faith as a delusion.

Christianity and Islam have both had their share of intolerant fundamentalists. Arabia's Muhammad Wahhab (1703–96) founded the Wahhabiyah movement which attempts to return[27] to Islam's original principles. In 1736, he began to preach against what he considered the extreme ideas of Sufi doctrines; his movement eventually led in the early 1800's to an ascendency of clerics in the Saudi Kingdom. Wahhabi ideology inspired Islamic extremism. It requires mosque imams take attendance at dawn prayers. It prohibits smoking and listening to music in public. Extremists of any kind are not likely to "compromise." Thankfully, Pope John initiated a renewal (*aggiornamento*) that has modernized the Church, but it now faces other pressing problems. It is noteworthy that Wahhab's fundamentalist followers call themselves "Unitarians," while Christian Unitarians are the most "liberal" in their efforts to do away with Christian dogmas. If Islamic Unitarians stress the absolute oneness of God (*tawhid*), and if Christian Unitarians do away with Trinitarian beliefs, Catholics believe that God "emptied" self to share love. Jesus warned us of "wars and rumors of wars." He knew that emptying self can be deadly. Those who advocate absolute notions of God, on the one hand, and those who reject all dogmas, on the other, must nevertheless communicate through a global ethics and forms of dialogue enabling them to address humans needs.

We write with the hope of helping heal a broken world. Jesus was broken on the Cross. The bravest of Christians have always known that they may have to witness for Jesus even to the point of martyrdom. Violence and terrorism are still with us. Too often, these are spawned by fundamentalists. Healing a broken world demands a sound spiritual basis and theologies fostering a healing justice. While Saudi Arabia does not allow Bibles or crucifixes within its country, more and more Western countries must accommodate to Muslim needs and demands. The secular West is uneasy when Muslims want to turn a church in a Western city into a mosque. Due to its complex history and because of its historical presence in both the US and the Middle East, the Catholic Church could help bridge Islamic-Christian differences in several ways. These two monotheistic faith traditions cooperated for centuries during Islam's Golden Age in Medieval times. Today, Jewish, Christian and Muslim scientists work side-by-side to find solutions to global poverty, AIDS and other pressing human problems. A further need is to find common cause with eastern religions such as Buddhism that contain a similar ethic of compassion and for all living beings. The Dalai Lama has been an most articulate spokespersons for a global ethics that can unite rather than divide humanity. The Church—due to its history of integrating the thought of world philosophers—potentially has much to contribute in this area also. It could help facilitate, even host, a "religious summit" called by the pope and other religious leaders to explore the pressing spiritual and social issues facing us today.

REVISITING WITH POPE FRANCIS WAYS OF BRIDGING A DIVIDED WORLD PEACEFULLY

Every faith tradition in the world could be invited to such a "summit" with a well-thought out agenda. Yet, all too often, Catholic meetings with representatives of other religious bodies have tended to be only public relations displays to show that the Church is willing to "dialogue." Such meetings have often lacked a real and concerted effort to deal with pressing problems. In his message to the World Day of Peace at Assisi (1986), John Paul II did suggest ways to help reconcile the world's peoples and to care for planet earth. His messages and that of Pope Francis' 2019 during visit to United Arab Emirates (UAE) all prefigure themes that could be pursued at a Vatican III Council.

There is a growing awareness today that world peace is threatened not only by regional conflicts and continued injustices in many nations, but also by a lack of due respect for nature, by the plundering of natural resources and by a progressive decline in the quality of life. The sense of precariousness and insecurity that such situations engender, has also generated various brands of collective selfishness—a dishonest disregard of others.

On the other hand, faced with the widespread destruction of the environment, people everywhere have begun to understand that we cannot continue to use the goods of the earth as we have in the past. Many leaders are now concerned about this problem; experts from a wide range of disciplines are studying its causes. A new ethical-ecological awareness has emerged which has led to the development of concrete programs and initiatives to address pressing ecological problems. The fact that many challenges facing humanity today are interdependent confirms the need to carefully coordinate solutions based on "a morally coherent worldview."[28] An important task of a Vatican III would be to develop such a morally coherent world view in cooperation with other religious bodies and world institutions. How best foster sustainable development, global peace, economic justice and harmony among nations? Failing action from the Church hierarchy, there would be a need to thoroughly consider intermediate alternatives initiated by believers dedicated to the morally coherent worldview advocated by Popes John Paul II and Francis. One of our guiding themes focuses on the Church's reconciling role. Being engaged in politics in the Middle Ages weakened the Church's spiritual mission. The Franciscans, Dominicans and Jesuits all learned from their founders' charism to refocus the Church upon its essential role. Vatican II stressed that the Church is a leaven, a light to the world. In the spirit of an updated Thomism, it touched on eastern religions that were inspiring the New Age. As a result, Catholics are in a better position to evaluate the positive elements of New Age spiritualties and of traditional Eastern teachings. In the spirit of Pope John XXIII who reconciled his sense of history with the "personal touch," in chapter 8 we argue that a way to guide perplexed Christians today is to focus on communities that gather people to share God's love in intimate ways and to deepen Christian outreach where it is needed. Our goal is not divisive but a unitive one. We must find ways to reconcile divergent claims within viable forms of Church organization. Small Christian Communities (SCCs) help make the mystery of faith more personal. They can integrate the personal search of each member in dynamic, transformative ways. SCCs also tend to be more open to interreligious activities with other faith communities, including those of Islam. They foster a sense of the presence of God in the lived experience of its members. Eastern forms of meditation are often integrated into the spiritual practice of such communities. The Church has learned that simply condemning the world and its secular ideologies can be counterproductive. It has a mediating role in the world—it should not attempt to take partisan positions that identify it with one political party, much less a political ideology. To help transform the world, the Church must learn how to dialogue with the contemporary trends now dominating the global media. The intimate relationships found in SCCs help build participants' faith; they begin to realize that God is not controlled by hierarchical structures. The Church needs to learn how to support such "new" alternative structures that were, in fact, the primary means through which early Christians met to celebrate life in the Eucharist.

Eastern religious viewpoints, and issues in religion, science and politics are among the key issues now at the forefront of Internet discussions and in printed material. Many bestsellers espouse dogmatic, atheist, or simplistic views of religion-science conflicts. The Church must address such issues with a nuanced position that is neither dogmatic nor apologetic. We address some of these contemporary issues in chapter 7. Our irenic, conciliatory approach to Islam advocates a cultural rather than a civilizational approach to societies. We study the internal relations underlying cultures so as to lay a foundation for a spiritual solution to our global problems. Such an intelligent critic of Western society as Nietzsche failed to see this. His "death of God" really means the *atrophying* of the spirit, of spirituality in Western consciousness based on Enlightenment principles. God is quite alive in the mystical traditions of the monotheistic faiths that speak to the heart—and even in Zen Buddhism as Catholic Zen believers have testified. These traditions may converge in an apophatic "dark night" of the soul that transcends the subject/object dichotomy of the Western scientific tradition. The apophatic refers to what one cannot be put into words, the kataphatic, to what can be verbalized such as in dogmas that relate to religious mysteries. One discovers various meanings motivated by values according to one's life experiences. A viable global ethics can arise out of the I/Thou unity found in the embrace of the soul with the divine lover of the Jewish, Christian and Muslim mystics. Such a profound experience of unity gives one an emotional and spiritual connection possible only on a cultural (internal) but not on a mere civilizational (external) base. A cultural, spiritual formation is compatible with scientific interests as proved in the lives of Copernicus, Mendel, Pasteur or Teilhard de Chardin—three of whom were priests, the other, a devout Catholic. God is "dead" only in the hearts of those who have lost vital links to ultimate reality. The teachings of the Church must be taken in their *holistic* perspective; failing this, one gets caught up in divisive "conservative-progressive" stances. The Church is holy because it is spiritual. "Holy" comes from the Old English word *hālig*; it is related to the German word *heilig*, "holy." The words holy and whole are etymologically related; the religious sense of holy may have developed due to its keeping believers spiritually whole. If the Church as a whole does not live up to its spiritual ideals, divisions will recur. It risks going back to a crusading mentality rather than being a humble servant able to catalyze the interface between science and religion. Pope Francis has demonstrated that he understands that the spiritual-cultural-holistic approaches to life found in the monotheist religions and in Hinduism and Buddhism are needed to remedy the deficiencies of civilization-centered approaches to human life.

STRATEGIC CONCLUSION TO CHAPTER 2

This chapter has outlined some of the challenges facing the world and the Church. The mandate that Jesus gave the Church (a mandate re-examined by the assembled bishops of the world at Vatican II) is that of reaching out to the world—beginning with one's neighbor. The Church has a commendable history of addressing social problems—even if has often done so belatedly. Part of the problem of being a global Church is that the Vatican has to take into account the voices of the West and those of the developing nations. Theologians and bishops are not immune from the pressures of their peers, or even their own biases. Because we seek to find ways to bridge the divides, we are seeking a middle ground open to all truth. It is not enough to examine the issues of globalization, migration or terrorism; one must also analyze some of the historical and social influences that have led to today's secularism and attendant alienation. On the basis of such an analysis, we are now better able to investigate how current Church structures have developed since Vatican II. What kind of Church restructurings have been in the offing since that Council? Are they adequate to the future needs of the Church as a herald of God's Kingdom? Such questions provide themes for our ensuing chapters. *Laudato Si* argues that due to humanity's lurch toward a technically-enabled civilization, one must retrieve the religious, cultural roots that can help humanity make the planet whole again.

NOTES

1. To integrate a global ethics influenced by mysticism, the Church has to address all the valid aspects of the world religions did Vatican II—an approach we seek to emulate.

2. *Documents of Vatican II: The Church in the Modern World*, (Abbott, ed. 1996), 274.

3. Samuel P. Huntington, *The Clash of Civilizations: Remaking of World Order* (New York: Touchstone, 1996), 20.

4. Richard W. Bulliet, *The Case for Islamo-Christian Civilization* (NY: Columbia University Press, 2004), 9.

5. We endorse Bulliet's view on historical commonalities but growing cultural differences. Calling attention to the cultural, symbolic aspects that inform civilizations may be a key to healing strained Christian-Islamic relations. To address secularism, we stress, for example, the roles of SCCs, a global ethic and interfaith dialogue—as grounded in the insights of a relational theology and an incarnational spirituality taught by mystics from all continents.

6. Not a few Islamic women now challenge traditional, oppressive interpretations of the Sharia, e. g. Saba Mahmood, *Politics of Piety: The Islamic Revival and the Feminist Subject* (Princeton: 2004); unlike many Islamic political activists who seek to transform the state, she focuses on Islamic women's piety in Cairo. She argues that the ethical and the political are indelibly linked in the contexts of Islamic orthodox practices.

7. Some interpretations of the Koran do lead to the exploitation and degradation of women, but historians generally agree that the Prophet Muhammad elevated women's position within the Arabic culture of his age. It is for Islam to address such problems, but we do suggest mediating structures that could help. We argue that it is not so much the Koran itself that is problematical but fundamentalist misinterpretations of it.

8. See www.catholicculture.org/commentary/pope-francis-on-secularism-terrorism-and-synodal-church. Adorno and Horkheimer noted that the Enlightenment's attempts to do away with myth led to disenchanting nature. Some see this as "bad faith." For Jean-Luc Marion, there is an earnest attempt to "return to God." See John Caputo, Mark Dooley and Michael Scanlon, *Questioning God* (Indiana U, 2001). Consolidation of divergent theological claims occurs in John Paul II's *Veritas Splendor* (1993) and in Jean-Luc Nancy, *The Experience of Freedom* (Stanford U: 1993) stresses life's commonalities.

9. Christopher Catherwood, *A Brief History of the Middle East* (Constable: 2006), 148.

10. Joseph Ratzinger, Values in a Time of Upheaval (New York: Crossroads 2005). In May 2004, Ratzinger criticized the West that protects and values Judaism and Islam but denies the same to Christianity. He detected "a peculiar Western self-hatred that is nothing short of pathological." Polls show that Europeans distrust institutions of all kinds. As long as the Church is identified, in the eyes of people with hierarchy and control, hopes of re-christianizing Europe will have little chance. Our alternative for invigorating the Church through the-Church-from-below initiatives thus has a compelling logic of its own.

11. The Ottoman Empire's dismemberment began in 1916 when George Picot and Sir Mark Sykes, devised a plan whereby Britain, France and Russia would retain control of the Middle

East through friendly surrogates in power. Sykes-Picot gave Britain the two Ottoman provinces of Basra and Baghdad outright, and France the Lebanese and Syrian coastline. Palestine was to be put under international rule which would include Imperial Russia. This was before President Woodrow Wilson came up with his idea of the League of Nations. In the middle was an Arab zone under British and French Protectorate—with the French getting the oil-rich Mosul region of what is now Iraq, and some of the Kurdish area of Turkey. Britain gained what is now Jordan (Catherwood, *Brief History*, 169).

12. We seek alternatives to the arrogant ignorance that led the US into the Iraq War's disastrous consequences. Martin Scorsese finds it a blessing to have Francis as our pope. https://zenit.org/articles/interview-with-martin-scorsese-in-losservatore-romano/

13. The later Middle Ages and Renaissance gave impetus for the voyages of discovery that utilized the developing scientific discoveries in navigation, cartography and weaponry that would enable the West to colonize native peoples around the world from 1500 to 1900. This period was marked by the exploitation of native peoples in Africa and the Americas for the benefit of Western nations. It included the expansion of the slave trade from Africa to the Americas and the destruction of Amerindian cultures by the Spaniards and other European nations. Further excursions into Asia and Africa led to the European colonization of India, Indochina and various parts of Africa. This extended period of colonization involved Church complicity in the domination of native cultures by Catholic powers such as Spain and Portugal in South America and the Philippines. Great Britain and France would later divide much of the Middle East after the fall of the Ottoman Empire, which had governed the Middle East since the late Middle Ages. In such developments, we see the triumph of civilization as technology.

14. US National Report on Population and the Environment, 2019. In *Laudato Si*, 228, Pope Francis notes that caring for nature includes "living together and communion."

15. Alfred Crosby, *Ecological Imperialism: The Biological Expansion of Europe, 900–1900* Cambridge U., 2004). Huston Smith, *The Soul of Christianity: Restoring the Great Tradition* (Harper, 2005) accents science's role in secularizing our world. William Whyte, Jr on *The Organization Man* (NY: Doubleday, 1957) on modernity's imperatives.

16. Evangelical Climate Initiative. Cited November 25, 2005.http://www.Christiansandclimate.org. In 2006, the United Nations Climate Change Conference adopted many decisions to mitigate climate change and help countries adapt to global warming.

17. "Global Climate Change: A Plea for Dialogue, Prudence, and the Common Good. A policy statement of the National Council of Catholic Bishops of the United States," June 2001. Advocacy groups raise our consciousness on global warming which leads private investors to develop alternative energy sources such as biofuels and wind energy. Seehttp://www.usccb.org/sdwp/international/globalclimate.htm/change.

18. Merton and Thich Nhat Hanh affirmed their common views during the Vietnam era.

19. In "Awakening from the Sleep of Humanity" (*Christian Century*, 1991), Sobrino wrote: "The world's poor are practically of no consequence to anyone—not to the people who live in abundance nor to the people who have any kind of power. The First World is not interested in the Third World" except to despoil it. Sobrino cites the Vatican's suspicious methods used against him which could inculpate even saints.

20. Since Napoleon and Hitler, the world has been subject to total war. The two world wars initiated the use of poison gas and of bombs on cities. Such weapons are made possible by economies that can produce weapons on a mass scale. Ideologies seek to "justify" total war by saying that a nation at war should hold nothing back. Faith prompts us to hold nothing back. Gabriel Marcel, Edith Stein and Tillich were some Christians who held nothing back in seeking to counter false ideologies and total war. Such realities are reasons why the Church should thoroughly prepare a Vatican III.

21. Virgilio Elizondo, *The Future is Mestizo: Life Where Cultures Meet* (Colorado Univ. revised edition), 2000.

22. In February 2003, when the 9/11 attacks had pushed immigration off the national agenda, bishops in the US and Mexico released *Strangers No Longer: Together on a Journey of Hope*, calling for a comprehensive immigration reform.

23. International Convention on the Protection of Migrant Workers and their Families. Cited November 25, 2006; it insists that migratory workers and their families have basic human

rights even if they lack a legal civil status. Most migrant workers in the US have a Catholic background—the Church is often their main institutional refuge. The Fifth World Congress on the Pastoral Care of Migrants and Refugees held in Rome in November, 2003 included delegates from 84 countries. Pope Francis has decried all nationalisms.

24. http://www.vatican.va/content/francesco/en/messages/migration/documents/papa-francesco_20190527_world-migrants-day-2019.html

25. Herbert Marcuse, *One-Dimensional Man* (Boston: Beacon Press, 1964), 12. Romano Guardini in his *The End of the Modern World* (1957) had written that moral courage is one of the virtues we need most in these chaotic, crisis-ridden times. Pope Francis quotes Guardini several times in *Laudato Si*.

26. www.richarddawkins.net/2014/03/anti-theism-reason-or-bigotry-2/. For believers, faith is consonant with reason: God is not a blip. Pontificating a la Dawkins is unhelpful. We seek to build bridges of converted hearts in need of the types of faith-enlightenment mediations some Buddhists, Jews, Catholics and Muslims have engaged in.

27. Khalid al-Dakhil's PhD thesis on Wahhab claims that a more accurate reading of Wahhab's "hidden" political agenda of conquest would reduce the role of the clergy.

28. Pope John Paul II, World Day of Peace. January 1, 1990. www.vatican.va/content/john-paul-ii/en/messages/peace/documents/hf_jp-ii_mes_19891208_xxiii-world-day-for-peace.html. Pope Francis, having made dialogue with Islam a high priority, is acutely aware that the scourge of war and displacement of peoples will not stop until the great religious traditions can consolidate effective norms of peace." Seeing it as his duty to defend all persecuted peoples targeted by terrorists or oppressive regimes, he has tried to build bridges with Muslims based on the wellbeing willed by God. Wars and jihadist violence have reduced the proportion of Christians in the Middle East from 20 percent before World War I to 4 percent.

Chapter Three

The Challenges of Secularity, Alienation, Ideologies and Pluralism

Our "on-the-way-Kingdom strategy," outlined in the first two chapters, studies how globalization furthers secularization and urbanization. People of diverse backgrounds and cultures now come into close contact on a daily basis. If politics is an authoritative but debased art, how can people of good will make the world a better, safer place? We seek to deepen a sense of human self-understanding through a global ethics. In outlining strategies that can unite humanity rather than divide it, we seek ways that can help people become more conscious of their own life situations as these are affected by historical events. To tackle challenges of secularity and alienation, we begin by examining how Cartesian dualism led to the Enlightenment and a dubious "pluralism." Of course, we must be "pluralist," but pluralism must be aware of the biases deep at work within the human spirit. Indeed, Jesus with his Kingdom message would strip us of our biases.

FROM DESCARTES AND THREATS OF ANNIHILATION TO RE-INTEGRATING MYSTICAL REALITIES

Descartes' view of mind and extension led to a dualism that lunged the modern world into crises that still affect modern societies. Taking Galileo's lead of using mathematics as the dominant approach to scientific reasoning, Descartes' "ingenious" method left God disconnected from the world as we know it. Existence was erroneously assumed to be given in a "*Cogito ergo sum*" ("I think therefore I am")—a philosophically untenable position that fails to bridge the realities of human consciousness and spirituality with the factual world we live in. Descartes was led to deny that the whole person (body and soul) is involved in the ways we apprehend spiritual realities. His cartesian rationalism opposed the Aristotelian emphasis on sensory experience as the source of all knowledge. It held that scientific knowledge could be derived *a priori* from 'innate ideas' through deductive reasoning. This resulted in the untenable position that mind and matter are two totally distinct orders of being—*res cogitans* (thinking self) and *res extensa* (what is measurable). Hobbes then sought to systematically reduce mind to the material. He granted reality to mind only if it is another instance of matter in motion—an approach still held by many today. If Hobbes reduced all to the "material," Leibniz and Wolf stressed the other side of the Cartesian split, that of rationalism. Meanwhile, Locke and Hume in England resorted to the empiricist method initiated by Francis Bacon. During the Enlightenment, Diderot based his atheism on the "sufficiency" of human reason and natural religion. Kant tried to bridge the rationalist-empiricist gaps; his transcendental method imposed on European thought a new dualism between "pure" and "practical" reason. In the meanwhile, the Thirty Years War (1618–1648) between Catholics and Protestants and other wars had been motivated by political and commercial ambitions. Religious wars were followed by the wars of colonialism and by two World Wars, the second of which pitted Western democracies against fascist and communist ideologies. Present, ongoing wars in Africa and the Middle East and the arm merchants that make these wars possible are a basic challenge to all. The human race is living at a critical juncture of its 10,000-year history during which violence has been a constant. We now have all too many lethal weapons that could destroy life. Since the first atomic bombing of Hiroshima in 1945, the world has been facing the threat of nuclear annihilation. Vatican II, aware of such realities, engaged the Church onto a path of assisting mankind in the ways of peace—as dramatically exemplified in Pope Francis' strong denunciation of nuclear weapons in his visit to Japan in November, 2019. Crucial to the above brief recapitulation of Western dualisms is our insistence on the integrative potential of mystic apprehension. Humans must recover the realities of interior life. We believe that Pope Francis has been motivated by such a conviction. He realizes that spiritual discernment is needed to offset the obfuscations that have marked Western dualist traditions. The latter are ever in need of new *integrations* in a now globalized, threatened world. Interiority *is the mystic link* between our daily lives and ultimate reality as taught in world religions.

THE TWO MAIN FORMS OF CATHOLIC SELF-UNDERSTANDING SINCE VATICAN II

Pope John Paul II strengthened relations with the leaders of other faiths with his ability to open his heart to them. Benedict XVI dealt unevenly towards non-Catholics perhaps due to his keen grasp of how interfaith and secular issues challenge the Church. He saw relativism as the Church's central problem as he made clear in his homily at the Mass that opened the Conclave that led to his election as Pontiff. In his homily, he denounced "vague religious mysticism." We argue that despite secularist-relativist opposition to the Church's belief in a transcendent God, Buddhism does not fall into relativism. Interfaith cooperation depends on prayerful dialogue guided (in Christian terms) by the Holy Spirit. Two main forms of Catholic self-understanding have emerged since Vatican II. The first conservative stance was exemplified in Pope Benedict. The second progressive stance was manifested in Hans Küng's global ethics rooted in Vatican II documents. Küng anticipated Pope Francis in taking initiatives to address world problems such as poverty and the environment. In fact, neither stance on Catholic self-understanding can ignore today's secular mentality or the New Age's inadequate attempts to spiritually-ethically bridge our societal divides.[1] We shall first consider New Age eclecticism, then the reality of evil so as to put the Church's potential contributions in better perspective.

BEYOND THE NEW AGE'S LIMITATIONS WHEN ADDRESSING MODERN ALIENATION

In the "First World," there is inter-generational strife as to who will pay for the growing number of entitled retirees amidst a diminishing working population. Douglas Coupland, influenced by his artistic evaluation of the Japanese "Floating World" coined the term "Gen-X" (generation-X) in 1991 to illustrate the pressures and instability facing people living in a fast-paced, ever changing world. Many young mobile Gen-X professionals now live and work abroad. Yuppies and the countercultural yippies had opposed agendas, but they now face the Gen-X questions. What further burdens will Gen-X have to assume in the face of a catastrophic global warming? Is the Church able to offer future generations an alternative wisdom that can clarify the New Age's eclectic, esoteric fantasies? The eclectic coalition of ideas known as the New Age that became influential in the West in the 1970s may have been inspired by some of the same "dynamics" that gave rise to Vatican II. Many of our Western youth have turned to New Age religious-philosophical ideas because they find Western Christianity intolerant of non-Christian spiritual paths, hostile to gender equality or lacking an integrated approach to the body and sexuality. The New Age was motivated more by a suspicion of traditional Western values than by the hope that inspired John XXIII. Prince Charles of England may have learned to talk to plants, and some women may have worn a pendant to ward off bad vibes in their final days of pregnancy. But in the long run the New Age's eclecticism could benefit from the philosophical-theological consistency, which we find in the historical traditions of the monotheistic religions as these might be consonant with eastern religious traditions such as Buddhism and Hinduism. New Age thought is conscious of human needs, but offers only partial remedies for such global crises as poverty, injustice, and global warming. Other ethical issues related to the life sciences and sexual conduct remain points of contention in need of further reflection. New Age devotees resort to spiritual and health disciplines such as massage, meditation and yoga.

Our understanding of what constitutes human nature must be placed within the context of our present understanding of evolution and the birth of the cosmos. Vatican II touched on eastern religious views that inspired the New Age. Just as Thomas Aquinas reconciled the demands of faith and reason, the Church today must address the positive elements within the New Age as well as what is lacking in it. We argue that a Vatican III could further discern which spiritualities can get us beyond eclecticism and offer youths a viable global ethics in addressing the realities of sin and alienation. "Religious pluralism," now a fact of life, is imprecise in two senses. The first sense of being imprecise stems from the uncertain ways of looking at the givenness of one's situation. Is one's situation authentic? The second sense, however, is ideological if it does not recognize that Judaism, Christianity and Islam each has its own view of the absolute, while Hinduism and Buddhism have contrasting nuanced, immanence-based views of reality.[2]

James Redfield has proposed New-Age energy transformations based on "love." While cautioning us against "having power over someone," he reduces love to "giving each other energy.[3] Christian love is not wrapped up in self; it transcends "power-driven" energy fields. The Jesuit expert on mysticism, William Johnston, clarifies the role of energy or "*chi*" as it is called in China or *ki* in Japan.[4] *Chi* or *ki* is a basic emotion akin to Yogic *prana* (breath, life force) rooted in Far Eastern aesthetic nuances. The holistic *chi-ki* field of medicine focuses on the mind/body/spirit continuum rather than on viewing the body as an object divisible into many separate parts and functions. It helps one center his/her total life energies leading to a healthful way of life. By approaching life holistically, one finds the areas of balance and imbalance affecting the whole person and even whole communities. One's individual existence depends on and is interconnected with our environmental existence. Redfield's New Age slant, on the other hand, reduces love to giving one other energy—discounting the deeper insights of the world's mystics. Eastern spiritualities or ways such as the *Tao* are not to be taken as mere New Age adjuncts; rather, they can complement Jesus' saying that he is "the way, the truth and the life" (Jn. 14:6). John Paul II was aware of this when he engaged in significant interfaith encounters at Assisi in 1986, 1993 and 2002. Those gatherings assembled religious leaders . Unlike early Jewish Christians who forced their rites upon Gentile converts (Gal. 2:14) or Rome's rejection of Chinese Rites, the purgative, illuminative and unitive stages of inculturated prayer in mystical traditions could help integrate New Age views within a unified field of consciousness.

THE DILEMMAS AND AMBIGUITIES FACING PLURALIST, MULTICULTURAL SOCIETIES

Unfortunately, encounters with God or between persons and cultures have their rough edges. In his *Confessions*, 10, 16, St. Augustine realized that "The field of my labors is my own self. I have become a problem to myself, like land which a farmer works." Modernity fears being emptied at its core. Today, people communicate through the internet, but words cannot be as effective or as meaningful as are spiritual encounters through which people learn to give and take. It is not a matter of mere compromise but of learning from what has guided people in various traditions and continues to enlighten them. Nations, tribes and groups are all too prone to acrimony or to settle scores with weapons. Violence only begets more violence. The hope is that faith and religion can help mitigate sectarian violence. There has always been a saintly portion of the faithful who have reached out to the outcast and the ignorant. This testifies to the Church's holistic charism throughout the ages right up to Pope Francis. Compromising when necessary has been part of the spirit of Catholicism—granted that there were many exceptions to the rule. It has enabled the Church to speak to all nations and translate its message in categories that can integrate the native genius of each people.

If Charles de Foucauld gave his life while trying to bridge Islam-Christian differences, we seek to learn from his example of loving outreach. De Foucauld was a man who like Mother Teresa responded to the realities of evil. A transformative faith gives the Church an ever "renewable" leaven (I Cor: 5, 6) that responds to problems with hope.

At present, Christians from the right and left all too often engage in sniping repartee that prevents understanding and clouds the heart. Thankfully, epiphanies come when we least expect it. Such was the case when John XXIII stunned the cardinals and the world with his call for a Pastoral Council in 1959. Since the over fifty years of Vatican II's closing, Postmodernism has complicated our philosophic and theological dialogues. It has led to disjointed, polyphonic debates. David Tracy examined the nature of such ambiguous problems.[5] As we also seek to do, Tracy sought to find bridges between the ambiguities of proud, self-satisfied hearts and the vulnerability of those open to the epiphanies of God and of loving one's neighbor as did the Good Samaritan.

Given today's collisions of pluralist views, can the Church help people bridge the ambiguities tearing at their hearts? If saints like Augustine found their answer in faith and in community, the Church today seeks to transcend, for example, the state Marlow finds himself in *The Heart of Darkness*? Marlow, an introspective riverboat captain, travels up the Congo River on his way to meet Kurtz, reputed to be a capable idealist. Marlow gradually realizes that Kurtz and his employers are brutal. The native inhabitants have been reduced to forced labor; they suffer terribly from overwork and ill treatment. The cruelty of the colonialist enterprise contrasts sharply with the impassive, majestic jungle surrounding the Belgian settlements, making them appear to be tiny islands amidst a vast darkness. The ambiguity in the novel is that Marlow wants us to understand his own story while shielding himself from blame. Conrad is a seer who reveals and veils the truth. Marlow remains in darkness because although he wants to tell his story so that we can understand him, he insists on "shielding" himself.

Our goal as Christians today must be like that of St. Augustine when, faced with the threats of barbarian invasions, he reflected deeply on the core of the Christian message. But unlike Marlow, Augustine did not shield himself. He opened himself to God's grace.

The insights of both Augustine and Conrad into the problematic nature of self and of a darkness-needing-enlightenment take on added meaning today. Multiculturalism is a fact of life in many cities of the world. This has led to the rise of rightist movements. As seen in the cases of both Augustine's conversion and Marlow's darkness, an important task for spiritual leaders is to help proud, perplexed subjects reconcile themselves to God. Only by surrendering to God's epiphanies can God help one find self and enable one to encounter others in ways that might bridge the chasms that often divide human beings.

On the global scale, such bridging includes the need to address historical divisions. In its "Declaration on the Relationship of the Church to Non-Christian Religions," Vatican II recognized humanity's common origin: "men are being drawn closer together" (no. 1). It sought to make up for the alienation between Jews and Christians. Vatican II participants still had the horrors of the Holocaust fresh in their minds as exemplified in Holland—as the *Diary of Anne Frank* and the life of Edith Stein attest. This was due to the Dutch bishops having spoken out against Nazism. The years that followed Vatican II pitted Arab states and Palestinians against Israel. The realities of racism and hatred reveal the complex types of deep alienation that have arisen and divide humans from one another.

The role of theologians is to help bishops and the laity deal with contemporary problems so as to renew Church structures and the "temporal order." The ambiguous nature of our many problems requires secular expertise. Such problems include the claims of neurobiologists who would reduce mind and soul to complexly organized matter. In his introduction to *Jurassic Park*, Michael Crichton says that the revolution in biotechnology is being exploited for profit—unsupervised by ethical concerns. Specialized research centers in bioethics often located at major universities are now necessary to help the average person understand the ethical and theological implications of the latest stem cell research. Questions about the origin of life and methods for manipulating genetic structures are becoming more complex and difficult to understand. Experts in genetics and the biological sciences need to partner with ethicists in reflecting on this expanding field of research. Vatican II invited lay people to help renew the temporal order; they can only do so if the Church trains enough lay people to discern patterns of being alienated from one's true self. Appropriate Catholic responses that understand the scope of the tasks now facing the Church are needed. It is a sobering reality that the Church prior to and after the French Revolution often found itself on the wrong side of democratic ideals. This defect was officially corrected at Vatican II but in actual practice the Church still seems to retain ambiguous attitudes toward democratic ideals and quests for an authentic self. Pope Francis has understood the depths of the dilemmas now facing the Church. He has responded, for example, by reemphasizing the roles of Church Synods to help build consensus in a Church often divided between traditionalists and progressives.

THE "GOD OF THE GAPS" AS PHILOSOPHICAL AND THEOLOGICAL PROBLEMS

The modern age has forced theologians to address the ideological claim of a "God of the gaps." This expression contrasts religious explanations of nature with those derived from science; it claims that any role of God is restricted to the "gaps" not explained by science. We argue that "God of the gaps" is an ideological tenet that can be bridged spiritually and ethically. We appeal to the theologians who have shown that science and faith are complementary realities—not caught in "God gaps." Bernard Lonergan once quipped that the "Church often arrives on the scene a little late and out of breath." Descartes is one eminent son of the Church who got it right in logic and mathematics—but wrong in trying to bridge faith and reason. He left God, the world of faith and spirituality unmediated.[6] It took Pascal to remind us that humans in their hearts have reasons that reason cannot understand. The Church has understood Pascal's point—even if it has taken saints to drive the point home.

During their pontificates, both John Paul II and Benedict XVI insisted that faith and reason can and should be "bridged." Pope Francis has complemented this through his own dramatic approach to the realities of alienation, ideologies and sin in our world. We seek to transform the gaps that "crucify" the marginalized by appealing to the personal, group and historical consciousness of believers. An adequate understanding of faith requires philosophical reflection. Many Protestant theologians influenced by Barth have turned their backs on philosophy. At this juncture of history, the Church is well positioned to make new syntheses for interfaith dialogue based on the insights of traditional or critically modern philosophies as well as Eastern ones. Process thought such as we find in Whitehead (philosophy) and Charles Hartshorne (theology) offers a possible synthesis for faith and reason that has become part of the religion and science dialogue initiated by the Center for Theology and Natural Sciences at the University of California, Berkeley and the Ian Ramsey Centre for Religion and Science at Oxford University. Ian Barbour (1923–2013) whose father was a colleague of Teilhard's during his years of paleontological research in China, was the major figure in the development of this field. Like Teilhard, Barbour attempted to bridge the divide between science and faith. Unlike Teilhard, he drew upon process philosophy and theology in his work. We seek to promote theologies that can link process with Teilhard's efforts, while avoiding the dangers of relativism much feared by conservative Christians.

Terence Fretheim interprets the Old Testament through the lens of process theology.[7] He notes that contemporary interest in creation is not due to the churches' leadership or their traditional theologians. Rather, such interest is due to the ecological consciousness of many today. Fretheim builds a relational theology on the insight that creation exists apart from human history. God is the God of the entire cosmos; all creatures come from God. We underpin our own relational theology with the relational thinking at the core of Buddhist worldviews that insist on the interdependence of all. Lonergan's use of the functional specialties has given us a concrete method to implement that interdependence.[8] Our own relational theology is also inspired by Vatican II. That Council initiated many forms of dialogue among persons of good will; it asked religious and secular leaders to re-examine the implications of the modern world. In the early 1960's, the full dimensions of impending ecological crises were not yet evident. Vatican II did not address the issue as one of its main concerns. But many responsible religious and political leaders now agree that the problems of the environment are one area in which they should cooperate to help ensure that the earth be irreparably damaged. The Book of Genesis teaches human stewardship of the earth, but Christians have been slow to respond. A relational theology that realizes how closely humans are bound to nature would certainly be a major theme of a Vatican III Council. Faith transforms, but it must first find remedies for our fallen human condition based on the forgiveness of sins.

CONFRONTING THE REALITIES OF EVIL, SIN, ALIENATION, AND IDEOLOGIES WITH A UNIFIED CONSCIOUSNESS THAT TRANSCENDS SECULAR AND RELIGIOUS CATEGORIES

Hate crimes against those of other cultures or another faith do occur; this is evil. For Aquinas, evil is the absence of some good. It is, a "falling short." Often, evil contains a personal element of sin. Sin is a moral evil—an absurd reality which secularists fail to admit. They recognize evil, but fail to see it as sin. Does the Church manipulate people as some claim?[9] To what extent does a false sense of dread or anxiety complicate misunderstandings between believers and atheists? Christians hold that our failures and sinfulness can be redeemed and transcended. They learn the accounts of Adam and Eve's Original Sin; they have rituals to atone for their own sins. But between sin and its atonement lie such possibilities as cure, prevention and ministry. A realization of the implications of evil and possibilities of redemptive action may help progressive and conservative Christians deepen their basis of discussion with secularists who recognize ethical failures and man's inhumanity to man. Modern society and urbanization have complicated societal roles and expectations in many parts of the world.

David Riesman's *The Lonely Crowd* sees persons in the crowd as lonely because they cannot get in touch with their deeper self. Riesman partly anticipated the future shape and ideology of post-war America. Traditional recognition of human interdependency fades when one becomes an anonymous "entity" caught in the cycles of unemployment or of low-paying jobs. Violence and crime in the inner cities lead to communities living in fear. In some nations, people closet themselves behind barbed wire and are ever anxious on the streets—even in their houses;[10] alienation can be cured by a transformed consciousness.

The Vatican II Council recognized valid forms of Christian secularization but rejected dogmatic secularism. In this, it went beyond the trendy ideas of a secularized Christianity proposed by Harvey Cox and John Robinson. Both of these writers referred to Tillich's view of God as Ground of Being but they failed to address how Tillich had partly based his theology on the Rhineland mystics. Let us compare the prescient efforts of two medieval mystics, Rumi (1207–1273), a Muslim Sufi, and Meister Eckhart (1260–1327), a Dominican in a transitional period of history. In his poem entitled "Only Breath," Rumi captured the potential unity of all humans grounded in a deep mystic consciousness:

> My place is placeless, a trace of the traceless.
> Neither body nor soul. I belong to the beloved
> Have seen the two worlds as one and that one call to and know[11]

While Rumi here captured the sense of a unified consciousness that transcends normal human and religious categories, Eckhart built on the Greeks, on Muslim thinkers such as Avicenna and on St. Thomas Aquinas. For Eckhart, even in the absence of sensory content or of mental objects, a mystic "experiences" when he/she "finds" the Ground of Being; this lets one unite the profane with the sacred so as to become fully human. As in the time of Eckhart, so the Church today needs mystics grounded in the reality of God and able to bridge spiritual and earthly realities. By uniting the profane and sacred aspects of life one becomes holy—holistic. Like Tillich, Pope John Paul II proposed Christian alternatives to secularism; having experienced at first hand the evils of Nazism and Communism, he drew upon Christian tradition in warning the West against secularist ideologies. His was an implicit theology of secularization, which, like Tillich's, was partly based on profound mystical insights—one of our own underlying themes. If nation-states, religions or persons attempt to substitute themselves for God, Rumi's unified mystic consciousness contradicts such hubris. Can a theology of secularization help us integrate mystic insights "into" the "Ground of Being" with the realities of daily life so as to yield and integrate holistic transcultural, interfaith categories?

TOWARD AN ADEQUATE THEOLOGY OF SECULARIZATION

To mediate between faith and science, we distinguish between secularism and theologies of secularization. Secularization is the historical process by which humans have been gaining control over their lives—even if has been at the cost of environmental degradation. Secularism is an ideology that promotes the idea that society benefits by being less religious. Some "secular humanists" aim to bring out the best in people without invoking God—just as there are believers who do not "belong" to a Church. God's influence is now *seemingly* diminished, but unlike what happens in secularism, in theologies of secularization God's creative role is not denied. Such theologies know that today's Western societies are now uncertain due to secular states being separated from religion. Friedrich Gogarten, a pioneer theologian of secularization, accepted the desacralization of the world—a process, which Christianity helped bring about! He based his claim on St. Paul's words that" All is permitted but not all is helpful"(I Cor. 10:23) and on Galatians 4:1ff which argues that humans "were under the control of elementary spirits until God sent his Son into the world." Christians are responsible before God for their own conduct and for the stewardship of the earth. In the West today, the separation of Church and State has become a quasi-dogma. If we give secularism free reign, conscience may become captive to the whims of popular culture, to legal systems. In fact, the First Amendment to the US Constitution aims to keep the State from interfering in Church affairs. This was due to Jefferson's intention of protecting religion from the State. "Separation" of Church and State means allowing equal interfaith access to the public domain—not eliminating spiritual issues from public debate or public concern or reducing God to an irrelevant blip.[12] If secularism is an ideology, our theology of secularization rejects fundamentalisms that play into the hands of secularists by claiming too much. Secularists and fundamentalists are both convinced of their "truth." In examining the claims of both sides, we focus on a middle path of virtue guided by faith, hope and love—one that seeks truth in the holistic ways of Hildegard of Bingen and Eckhart. Such a middle path partially coincides with Buddhist teachings. For his part, Benedict XVI in his *Jesus of Nazareth* (2007) probes into capitalist excesses, which have plundered Africa and other parts of the developing world through colonialism. Benedict adds that abusing economic power degrades humans who must now learn anew why Jesus warned us against the dangers of wealth. Fundamentalists rely on written texts. Capitalists rely on their wealth. Only a foundation of love can change hearts.

STRUCTURES THAT PROMOTE LOVE LEST WE FORGET HUMAN VULNERABILITIES

The flip side of a world revolutionized by technology is that people tend to forget human vulnerabilities. We seem to live in an absurd world. Alfred Jarry launched the theater of the absurd with *Ubu Roi* (1896), which satirizes bourgeois life's grotesque contradictions. People alienated from themselves and from one another can barely cope; some cannot cope at all. Divorce and debt become patterns of life. Not a few drift, become homeless. Extraterrestrial visitors would detect absurd elements in our society as surely as Gulliver detected glaring anomalies in Lilliput and Brobdingnag. Love transcends absurdity; it finds meaning in all legitimate forms of endeavor and builds personal bridges. Jesus and recent popes have warned against wealth. It is an irony bordering on absurdity that the Vatican prior to Pope Francis attacked liberation theologians who had taken this warning seriously. Francis has been trying to help humans mediate faith with reason and justice. Following him, we seek the middle path that has guided major philosophies and that avoid bourgeois excesses. On this view, secularization means that believers adopt what is helpful in setting up new intermediate structures. Being in the world but not of it implies that believers accept a certain marginalization. If, for example, some married priests feel doubly marginalized (by the Vatican and in their reinsertion in a world which only partly accepts them) they can best serve Church and world through alternative forms of ministries (to the marginalized, to those genuinely seeking truth) and by reviving forms of intimacy lost in bureaucratic structures. In this sense, a theology of secularization that recognizes the need of intimacy with God can help us in building needed bridges. Chapter 8 on small Christian communities explores this further.

TRANSITIONAL ISSUES IN BUILDING HISTORICALLY-INFORMED RELIGIOUS BRIDGES: POPE ST. JOHN XXIII AND SOME OTHER SAINTS AS MODELS OF CHRISTIAN MINISTERING

A sense of history can help Christians regain desirable forms of intimacy undermined by modern forms of life. As were the early Christians, so Christians today are marginalized. "Christendom" (when the Church greatly influenced Western culture) occurred between the early and present-day forms of Christianity. Trying to build historically-informed bridges to deal with the new situation is part of our overall efforts. During the Middle Ages in Europe, the papacy and bishops often intervened in state affairs. In most parts of the world, the Church no longer has the means to engage in power politics. The Church's holiness has much to do with the holy lives led by many of the faithful. Thomas Jefferson reproached Catholicism for being under the yoke of hierarchic leaders. Our middle-way approach would reinforce the meaning of the Church's four marks—One, Holy, Catholic-Apostolic. We are finite creatures; yet grace can help us bridge the unfathomable ways of God—as attested by many Christian converts. One problem is that the biblical notion of grace is now hardly understood outside of Christianity and Islam. Vatican II has helped believers integrate the marginal aspects of their lives with the deeper callings of spirituality. One is called to live in fuller conformity with the ways of being Church, a Church that does not reject non-believers or those of other confessions.

Some speak of the Church as being a remnant (*anawhim*) among the nations. In the nineteenth century, Marx, Freud and Durkheim postulated that the modern age would lead to a decline in religiosity. Weber called this the disenchantment of the world. But God knows how to re-enchant us. It is to Pope Francis' credit that he is re-enchanting the holy.

When he abolished the Ottoman Caliphate in 1922, Ataturk replaced it with a secular republican framework. When Pope Benedict XVI prayed in Istanbul's Blue Mosque in 2006, he engaged in a "multireligious" type of prayer rather than in an "interreligious" one (a fine distinction allowing intrafaith prayer from being misconstrued as an eclectic interfaith venture). Benedict noted that Turkey could be a bridge of friendship between East and West. He recalled John XXIII's example in fostering closer Christian-Islamic relations during his tenure as Papal envoy to Turkey. Like popes John XXIII and John Paul II, Pope Francis has combined his sense of history with the "personal touch," challenging Christians to regain desirable forms of intimacy now undermined in the modern world,[13] and to help others cope with alienation by following Jesus. Throughout history—before and after Constantine legitimized Christianity—the laity and the religious orders often took steps to renew the Church. St. Francis of Assisi helped move the Church from its medieval mindset toward a modern one. Despite the violence and political maneuvering that characterized much of Europe and the Papal States, St. Francis was a model of gentleness and strength. Sin is an offence against God and man, but if God is "dead" in the hearts of many today, the risk is that due to sins, a sense of personal responsibility for society can fade—as happened in the Holocaust or is now happening on a lesser scale in acts of wanton violence. St. Edith Stein and Simone Weil—two Jewish women converts to Catholicism prior to WWII—were heroic examples of Christian life. These two mystics who opposed Nazi evils, embodied types of Christian courage needed in our era. If violence or a sense of powerlessness continue to haunt our societies, it is necessary for believers to take initiatives "from below" as has often been the case throughout Christian history.

Prior to Pope Francis, the Vatican often trivialized initiatives it opposed. The Synods of Bishops was often stage-managed. The bishops discussed issues under the watchful eye of the Pope and wrote down their conclusions. But contrary to Vatican II's spirit, under popes John Paul II and Benedict XVI the Vatican head of the Synod of Bishops, edited the conclusions before officially publishing them. An assembly of the world bishops, given the necessary freedom of expression at a Vatican III, could once again sort out present problems so as to come up with solutions that would prevent the Church from falling out of touch with the world's needs. Pope John XXIII's convening a Pastoral Council was influenced by his encounters with worker priests in France as well as his admiration of St. Augustine and St. Francis de Sales. If Augustine remained a pessimist even after his conversion from his wayward life,[14] and if his theology of grace led to conflicting interpretations such as that which influenced Calvin's theory of predestination, Francis de Sales' spirituality of gentleness guided the Catholic Counter Reformation.

In the spirit of Vatican II, we speak of the Church as a sign to the nations, a moral beacon to the world. The Church has begun to atone for past mistakes such as its condemnations of Galileo and of the Chinese rites—both due to clerical misunderstandings. In an age of an educated laity, clerics must "learn to learn" from experts so that the Church be not a backwater of outdated, erroneous opinions. The laity, religious orders and the hierarchy must ever reappraise the realities of sin and self-deception. Revelations of collusion by high-ranking Church officials with the Communist secret service in Poland, for example, indicate that the Church hierarchy is not immune from duplicity. At its June 2018 meeting, the US bishops voted not to revise *Faithful Citizenship*, their document on forming one's conscience in view of better responding to the authoritarian nationalism of rightist politicians. The bishops did indicate that a theology of conscience should be connected to Pope Francis' views on mission and to what was stressed by Jesuit theologian John Courtney Murray. For Murray, the freedom of the church "stands or falls" with the freedom of the people. It is clearly connected with the *sensus fidelium*, an ancient doctrine renewed by Pope Francis. Can the *sensus fidelium* help the Church discern needed forms of wisdom in the wake populist excesses? For Pope Francis, *sensus fidelium* does not mean 'majority opinion'; rather, it is a "spiritual instinct, enabling us to 'think with the Church' and discern what is consistent with the apostolic faith and the spirit of the Gospel."[15]

THE POLARIZING DIVISIONS THAT ENSUED AFTER VATICAN II AND SOME ALTERNATIVES

The post-Vatican II Church was not spared polarizing divisions. Addressing the divisions should involve the whole Church—not just the hierarchy. In the face of human ills, one must begin where he/she is in promoting "we-are-the-world-thinking." We are to grow in experience and understanding so as to reach balanced judgments in the challenging situations confronting us personally and the Church as a whole. Only by doing so, can we jointly pursue actions that can bridge cultures and preserve civilization for the future. Lech Walesa founded the Polish Solidarity Movement that helped put an end to Communism in Europe. Later, as a statesman, he had to face politicians' wiles. Likewise, we must have both the courage he showed when he climbed the fence in Dansk in support of striking workers and the wisdom to combat the collective egoism that tends to be a hallmark of many sectors in "free" societies. Walesa had the courage of his Christian convictions underpinned by theological virtues of faith, hope and love. Non-believers denigrate these virtues, but proper reflection will show that they can underpin the other virtues and can lead to a Walesa-like type of heroic action that can change the world.

Not all of us can be heroes. But as Christians we must be judicious and prophetic. Surely, we must uphold Christian heroism of the type Bonhoeffer and Niemoller exemplified in resisting Nazism. We are to follow in the steps of the apostles Paul and John who both acknowledged the good wherever they found it. Vatican II was an effective pastoral council guided first by a saintly pope, then by a diplomatic one. However, the Council's spirit of renewal was severely limited under popes John Paul II and Benedict XVI. We are all tempted to be "As snug as a bug in a rug." This aphorism captures what happened after Vatican II when both traditionalists and progressives retreated into their own interpretations of the meaning of the Council documents. Many "live-and-let-live" compromises between the two protagonists were hammered out.

Compromise involves give and take. The sad reality is that after Vatican II there was more taking back than giving on both sides of the ideological divide. As Vatican II initiated the Church onto a path of helping mankind in the ways of peace, we argue that Pope Francis' view of Synodality, expressed in the Synod of the Amazon (2019) may be a prelude to a calling of a Vatican III Council. The Pope is helping the Church refocus on needed priorities and providing a new ecclesial template in which the Church from below would interact in more positive ways with the hierarchy. Such a template would be based on bridge-building criteria such as the following:

- Insights into how reconcile cultural, linguistic and ideological differences.
- Understanding one's own culture and history and that of one's interlocutors.
- Good will, a converted heart, a sense of values and of virtues.

Such basic conditions for bridge-building cultural differences imply that dialogue is conditioned on a willingness and an ability of the concerned parties to change as needed[16] so as to overcome false perceptions and set aside troubling differences. False perceptions are partly reinforced by the fact that our thought patterns begin to break down when we try to fathom and go beyond the realities of the Internet, for example. Scientists have mastered the art of organizing information at "incredible" speed but it takes philosophic and religious wisdom to help humans arrive at true meaning and real values. Interfaith and ecumenical dialogues have to consider the deeper paradoxical truths befuddling humans. The history of Christianity is marked by dogmas on the Trinity. Jews, Muslims, Buddhists and secularists all reject such dogmas. Can the theological virtues of love, faith and hope that motivate Christians find implicit spiritual or ethical "analogues" of these virtues in the other world religions? Our relational theology is based on an incarnational spirituality motivating Christians; but caught in the mystery of God-at-work-in-the-world we must learn to re-center in God—as *mandala*-students are taught to do.[17] The Church must help people experience God's grace. Since the global situation is now precarious, we seek to build pioneering spiritual bridges among people of good will. Pioneers venture into unknown territory. One may think of the great explorers or of the astronauts. Science fiction stimulates our imagination. In both society and the Church, life includes exploring areas of achievement and of marginalization. With Pope Francis, we appeal to the theological pioneers who made Vatican II possible, but we must now go beyond these if we are to adequately cope with the problems besetting us in the twenty-first century. We must try to fathom deeper dimensions of God's gifts to us. Some Catholics debate without end as to how Vatican II read the "signs of the time." The important point is not to squander God's grace. Jesus reproached those of little faith. His parable of a mustard seed illustrates the Kingdom's relevance in our lives. We must first heal our own hearts if we are to help others transcend self-serving practices. The Church is to be in the service of the Kingdom. Jesus cautions us not to hide behind the law. Not those who say "yes, yes" will enter the Kingdom but those who do God's will. Paul Tillich helped modern Christians stand at the boundaries between liberalism and neo-orthodoxy, spirituality and secularism. Whereas Descartes' dualist method separated spirit from matter, with Pope Francis we study various efforts to reintegrate the spiritual and the material in life. We do this by appealing to people's lived experiences.

INTEGRATING RELIGIOUS AND OTHER LIVED EXPERIENCES IN A RELATIONAL THEOLOGY

Christians should help humans reconcile or mediate their differences. With that mind, we contrast the bridge-*building* and bridge-*hindering* functions of communities by analyzing how our lived experience is to be integrated more through cultural than civilizational factors. Pope John Paul II wrote his doctoral dissertation on how one appropriates one's lived experience.[18] If the nature of cross-cultural pluralism seems unbridgeable to some, then one must delve deeper into the horizons of inner conversion. Christians have consistently tried to bridge the cultural and faith elements of their lives as occurs in Pauline, Johannine, Augustinian and Thomistic theologies. These traditional theologies have to be updated in our postmodernist age,[19] influenced as it has been by "nihilism." Bernard Lonergan and Jacques Dupuis both developed lived experience as a theological category. They realized that Christian theology can be better served by relying on Wilhem Dilthey's notions of *lived experience* than on Heidegger's interpretation of Nietzsche[20] (See Appendix 5). Dupuis, an expert on Hinduism, spent much of his life working on a hermeneutic that could validate faithful forms of dialogue among world religions.[21] He argued that since religious pluralism is a clear datum of contemporary historical experience, it must become part of our theological reflection. Catholic theology traditionally used a dogmatic-deductive method. It started from the church's dogmatic pronouncements, based on selected scripture quotes, to develop "precise" theological conclusions. It fancied that its general principles could be concretely applied to today's problems. The danger is that the more conclusions are "drawn from abstract principles, the greater the risk of being cut off from reality.... A methodological advance occurred with the gradual introduction of the "inductive" method (Dupuis, Ibid. 8). Dupuis took into account the historical context of the era in which theological reflection has occurred. Christian existence is everywhere conditioned by the historic context in which it is lived, with its cultural, economic, social, and religious components. A hermeneutic theology continuously traces back-and-forth movements between the present contextual experience and the witness of the founding experience entrusted to the memory of the church's tradition. The ongoing movement back and forth between "context" and "text" between present and past, is known as the "hermeneutic circle" (Ibid. 9). On this view, Christians can learn from Hindus and Buddhists as they did from the Greeks (appendices 2, 4).

As a young theologian, Lonergan studied St. Thomas Aquinas' texts in depth. This enabled him to identify the cognitive structure that Aristotle and Aquinas had discovered but had explained in Greek or medieval categories. He began to develop his own original understanding of how human consciousness works. In his ground-breaking *Insight*, he focused on how we arrive at knowledge. His study of human intentional operations—as dynamically related in their self-assembling patterns—probes into how ordinary folk, mathematicians, scientists and ethicists think and act.[22] Lonergan's method can help us bridge our differences for it studies the four basic operations through which all humans should 1) attend to data, 2) understand the data, 3) make correct judgements so as to 4) take appropriate action. All humans of sound mind are endowed with this fourfold cognitional structure-ability: they experience, know, judge and act on the basis of appropriate decisions. This process gives rise to ever new forms of experience in a feedback reduplicative manner. One's feedback reduplicative structure must be appropriated through intellectual, psychic, moral and religious conversions. Lonergan explains how our dynamic patterns of knowing function and how they give us the self-correcting ability to arrive at true, accurate knowledge. Correct knowing enables us to make true judgments[23] and to take adequate action. This is common to all persons, but linguistic philosophers give priority to language rather than to the insights that generate language. Prioritizing language over our experiential, cognitional operations blurs the commonalities of our lived experience and their bridging potential. We have not the space here to fully go into Lonergan's *Method in Theology* (1972). His method—centered on eight interdependent functional specialties—can be applied to the humanities and sciences. It can provide an ethical bridge for human renewal for it uses humans' four basic operations' feedback character. The main potential of the eight specialties is its enabling interdisciplinary cooperation. Such a cooperation, made possible by the reduplicative feedback pattern inbuilt within our basic operations' four conscious, intentional levels gives rise to a self-corrective process of knowing-doing. This reduplicative process is at the heart of Lonergan's method.[24] The method can enable human cooperation in all fields and help the Church find common ground among people of various backgrounds. This is because the eight specialties ground a theology open to interfaith initiatives. Healing and conversion are basic to the method. All of us are in need of types healing attained through intellectual, psychic, moral and religious conversions. Dupuis and Lonergan can help us 1) understand how human consciousness can transcend false faith-science dichotomies, 2) evaluate the roles of the unconscious and of technology in our lives, and even the residual tribal elements that may subtly influence us. The two Jesuits built bridges between faith, culture and science. Religious pluralism, now a global reality, is a starting point for interfaith dialogue open to people's lived experience. This requires methods that can engage us in interfaith forms of dialogue based on the deeper realities of what makes us "human." Dialogue depends on cultural and historical contexts. The context in the US is vastly different from that of the Middle East—but migration patterns now bring people of diverse cultures and religious backgrounds into daily contact, often provoking misunderstandings, even violence. Lonergan's writings are erudite and profound; this makes it difficult for many to grasp his insights into knowing. Nor does the ever increasing dominance of technology in our daily lives make it easy for young people to understand religious argumentations—even the meaning of their own lives. They are now more influenced by their smart phones than by philosophy or messages from the Church. Pope Francis has advised them to really look at one another—not just at their phone when speaking so that they might communicate in tender ways. In more depth, Francis writes in his *Laudato Si* encyclical on the negative, disconcerting aspects of instrumental reason:

> It can be said that many problems of today's world stem from the tendency, at times unconscious, to make the method and aims of science and technology an epistemological paradigm, which shapes the lives of individuals and the workings of society. The effects of imposing this model on reality as a whole, human and social, are seen in the deterioration of the environment, but this is just one sign of a reductionism which affects every aspect of human and social life. We have to accept that technological products are not neutral, for they create a framework which ends up conditioning lifestyles and shaping social possibilities along the lines dictated by the interests of certain powerful groups. Decisions which may seem purely instrumental are in reality decisions about the kind of society we want to build (no. 107).

SOME OF THE ETHICAL-PSYCHOLOGICAL-SPIRITUAL IMPLICATIONS OF HEALING

Just as integrative models of patient-centeredness seek to heal traumatized persons, so we use Lonergan's approach to healing that parallels how Carl Rogers derived the ethical implications of psychological healing.[25] If the challenge is to heal an ailing world, then all would-be-healers must help persons have the insights required for healing self or communities. Controlling one's desires and troubling emotions is not easy in societies confused as to the foundations of knowledge. Realizing this confusion, Lonergan made it his life work to explain insight's healing potential. When *truly healed* of some of the many dysfunctional aspects in life, persons can reach out to the larger challenges of life such as peace-making. On a broader basis, a healing ethics would need to involve humans in practicing the functional specialties that progressively evaluate past failures and breakthroughs so as to build a viable future. Lonergan's method (if understood and implemented) can help us become more authentically human, more committed to others. Based on our inner creative potential to know and act justly, we can arrive at valid forms of ethics, which help us integrate the internal and external realities of our lives. Having appropriated one's own lived experience, one is able to interface with others—in foundational ways—on personal and societal levels. Relying on Lonergan's method, we recall the middle-way approach that long ago influenced such major "Axial Age" figures as Plato, Buddha and Confucius. Having appropriated one's own lived experience, one is able to interface—in foundational ways—with others who realize the need for one to be inwardly converted. A theology of conversion can help us unite past and present forms of living the Christian life. Implementing such a theology could benefit from the type of spiritual motivations nurtured in SCC's open to Kingdom values. Too many diocesan "communities" have become "parochially" cut off from Kingdom demands. In chapter 8, we focus on how SCC's allow people to associate in structured types of fellowship that complement diocesan structures. They make members more aware of what it is to live the faith authentically. A problem is that the spirit is willing but the flesh is weak. The conversions and the maturity needed to sustain spiritual development are a life-long challenge. Responsible persons do what they can to promote a just peace. Lonergan's method is based on processes of conversion similar to Dupuis' but it can also link theologies with scientific methods and personal conversion. It aims to heal the hearts of those willing to be healed; it can help us link various notions of lived experience to religion and science. Lonergan notes that in Catholic circles, renewal often means a return to olden times "of pristine virtue and deep wisdom."[26] He adds that Vatican II was much more than that for it sought to apply virtue and wisdom in all contexts of modern life. That is a lesson that Pope Francis also learned as is obvious from his ministry as priest, bishop and pope and his understanding of the psychology of youths.

LIFE DEMANDS THAT WE TRUST, THAT WE GO BEYOND MERE WORDS

Raising children and teaching young people the tenets of religion may pit parents and teachers against the secular mentality imposed on the young in many schools. If the Church, for example, in its various modes of instruction refers to the arguments of St. Thomas Aquinas on the mystery of the filiation and spiration within the Trinity, students may say, "If people can 'know' something, it is not really "mysterious." One answer is that a person's horizon is enlarged as one makes one's way through life: it helps one discover various meanings motivated by values. Catholic youth struggle with the mystery of the Trinity, Muslim youth with the Prophet's vision, Buddhists with the various traditions that have arisen in the Far East. In all these cases, adherents of a religion are faced with the limits of words; they may have to resort to *foundational apophatic experiences*. Those raised in secular societies plug into secular values bereft of the supernatural. With a view to develop Vatican II's teachings, we speak of lived experience and conversion to illustrate how non-believers can and have been influenced by grace. The conversion experiences of Gabriel Marcel and Thomas Merton, for instance, illustrate how some non-believers underwent "on-the-way" conversions when least expecting it. "On-the-way" lived experiences in ordinary life are indeed important guideposts as to what is needed for societal renewal; yet, such "renewal experiences" can be and often *are* thwarted in practice. Let us illustrate this with the example of a charismatic parish priest in suburban Virginia who responded to their request for a parish youth group. With youthful energy, the young people met weekly to discuss problems confronting them; they would then turn to recreation. The priest had convinced even a conservative couple in the parish who tended to overprotect their daughter to let her join the youth group. Let's call her "Helen." One Saturday evening while engaging in highly spirited but innocent fun, some of the young men hoisted Helen (whom they knew to be shy and in need of encouragement) tossing her up to her delight. At that very moment, Helen's parents walked in—to their great shock. It was like an "I told you so, you can trust no one."[27] That ended Helen's participation. In this case "lived experience" proved to be an obstacle to a further broadening of horizons; the parents retreated into their doubts.

Amidst the mistrust pervading much of life, the Church is called to restoring trust. Sometimes the "devil is in the details" as one seeks to broaden one's horizon in life. The best intentions are also subject to misunderstandings. Normally, a person's horizon expands. What we do not know can beckon us to further reflection on the unknown, on the mystery of God. It takes a Walt Disney or a J. K. Rowling to appeal to juvenile minds; it takes the empathy of a Karen Armstrong to understand the positive aspects of the world religions. Pope Francis has shown an uncanny ability to speak to young people in a language familiar to them. With him, we study ways that the Church can renew itself through appropriate theological categories open to dialogue. Such dialogue must be aware of the complexities of relating faith to secular minds and of integrating religious and secular experiences. A

Vatican III Council could further explore how secular life styles are to be addressed. Needless to say, we would expect many more women theologians to be involved than was the case at Vatican II. Feminine points of view are needed to complement patriarchal approaches. There is a need to integrate these within Church structures. Pope Francis has shown great sensitivity on this issue. In his "Apostolic Letter addressed to All Consecrated People" (November, 2014), he wrote that men and women are empowered to "love, in truth and mercy, every person" who cross their path. Religious founders shared in Jesus' compassion when he saw the crowds who were like sheep without a shepherd. Like Jesus, who healed the sick and fed the hungry, so religious founders sought to be at the service of "all to whom the Spirit sent them." The Pope urged all the faithful "not to be closed" upon themselves nor to "be stifled by petty squabbles" but to reach out to others. Many government and business entities have taken the lead in promoting the equal rights and roles of women. The Pope knows that the Church should strive to overcome an undue patriarchalism but that this will require the Church to enlarge its horizons. How can humans share enlarged horizons across the divides separating scientific-technical minds from the facts of religious experience?

LIVED EXPERIENCE AND LIVING MYSTICISM ACROSS THE GLOBAL RELIGIOUS SPECTRUM

Wayne Proudfoot helps us integrate religious experience within one's lived experience. Schleiermacher's claim that religious experience is independent of concepts and beliefs was "a protective strategy"[28] to avoid conflict between religious beliefs and science. Arguing that all experience is touched by one's culture and beliefs, we stress how mystical, apophatic experiences influence life. A Christian experiences mystic reality in terms of the Trinity or a personal God while a Hindu relies on a notion of a non-personal *nirvana*. The core of mystical experience transcends language, culture and beliefs. It is *apophatic*. Those trained in Western Catholic-Christian traditions cannot afford to remain provincial in a globalized world—nor can the Church. Mystics of any faith are helped by the way meditation integrates one's normal mental activities. Meditation does so by slowing down one's thinking process while intensifying one's consciousness. An interior stillness abides as one returns to daily activity. Those who experience *such a stillness deep* within encounter the living God whom Nietzsche falsely believed to be "dead." Our relational-theology strategy seeks ways to develop intermediate structures that would help defuse atheist claims. Pope Francis' down-to-earth way of teaching the core of Christian life is tinged with a sense of a mystically-based lived experience. This realistic assessment of the core of Christian faith can help us remedy Cartesian dualism and to counter Nietzsche's claim of the "Death of God" in his *Zarathustra* (1884).

For Christians, an act of love mystically participates in God's depths. Yves Raguin has reflected on such depths. Immersed in Teilhard de Chardin's *Divine Milieu*, Raguin peers into the depths of his own being as a way to structure contemplation and to compare Chinese and Western spiritualities. Psychologically, we first become aware of what is outside of ourselves (compare Cezanne or Van Gogh who imagined themselves as being the landscapes they painted). Although we know that we have "an inside," we do not become aware of it immediately as it is more difficult to penetrate" one's own inside "than to grasp the external world."[29] In negotiating the boundaries between the outside and our inside, what matters is not discovering another world, independent of mine, but being aware of other personalities different from mine. This structure of the world of spiritual experience is intimately connected with a symbolism built deep into our own psychology. Symbols are indispensable to spirituality. What we experience is not perceived outside of our psychic and mental structures. To become aware of my inner life, I first get absorbed in my own thoughts and feelings. Eventually, I begin to discover my own interiority as center of activity and thinking, fully aware of who I am. By turning toward my inner being, I begin to realize the difference between my outside and my inside. Our feelings or emotions are a rich field of negative and desirable impetuses that guide or impede one's ability to appropriate one's "inside." Turning to my inside means that I seek not an object outside of myself, but myself. One's inner self then becomes an integrating *Gestalt*—a unified physical, psychological, symbolic, mystical configuration that cannot be derived from its parts. Raguin's view that mysticism begins with perceiving outer realities goes counter to Western accounts The latter speak of an inner-to-outer movement according to which one first detects one's interiority.

The Western view began with St. Anthony and the desert fathers who "sold everything" and gave it to the poor as Jesus counsels in the Gospels. Solitary spirituality gradually gave way to the service-oriented spirit of the post-Reformation era as typified in St. Francis de Sales and Jean-Jacques Olier. De Sales' influential work on the devout life was schooled in his zeal for his apostolate in northern France. Olier, a pioneer in the parish apostolate (he divided parishes into districts so as to better care for parishioners), founded the Sulpician Fathers to educate priests in the seventeenth century. We stress that Western spirituality has had several stepping stones: the spirituality of the hermit, the monk, the mendicant and the specialized servant.[30] Today's ever more secularized Western societies challenge us to evolve new viable forms of "secular spiritualities" involving the Church from below. Raguin's insights into the priority of outer knowing over self-knowing reinforces Bulliet's argument that the similarities between Christian-Islamic cultural patterns began to dissolve when *the outer* aspects of *civilizational* differences replaced the former stress on shared cultural values. St. Augustine tended toward rigorism in his treatment of the body and sexual ties. Reintegrating the outer and inner aspects of spirituality would help the world share good will. With Pope Francis, we seek to engage people of good will by following Pope John XXIII's trust in the Holy Spirit and by adopting, for example, the insights of the writers on creation spirituality.

CHRISTIAN ASHRAMS AS FORESHADOWING SMALL CHRISTIAN COMMUNITIES (SCCS) AND AS INTERLINKED WITH MORE THAN MERE PSYCHOLOGICAL-SYMBOLIC CONFIGURATIONS

Vatican II taught us to see the good in every religion—making this a basis for interfaith dialogue. Lonergan wrote in his "Future of the Faith" (1997) that the Vatican II renewal (*aggiornamento*) has an unfinished agenda. While Vatican II renewed the liturgy and intensified interest in sacred scripture, there remains a "disarray of catholic writing on dogmatic issues . . . an evil that will not be remedied by ordinary measures."[31] The disarray has not ceased. We address the disarray partly by interrelating people's lived experience in the world religions. Vatican II set the tone for this. It even urged Christian thinkers to continue their dialogue with atheists. It is a matter of people integrating their spiritual lives with the outer realities facing them daily. Christian writers on creation spirituality and others such as Paul Ricoeur and Lonergan and recent popes have been helping Christians do this. Their reflections are helpful in countering specious arguments such as those of Nietzsche who failed to understand the depths of spirituality. A Vatican III may be needed to adequately integrate the partially valid insights of the New Age. Of great interest to us are the conversion experiences of such Westerners as Gabriel Marcel and Simone Weil. Their experiences can and should be compared with those of other Westerners who reached out to the East such as Raguin, Thomas Merton, Jacques Dupuis and Bede Griffiths. The latter two found their faith deepened through their exchanges in India. Overall, the lived experience and writings of such Christian thinkers can help the Church remedy New Age superficiality. Raguin's studies of the symbolism built deep into human psychology help reinforce Dupuis' notion of lived experience as a common human occurrence—one that has been ideologically sidetracked by postmodernists who get stuck in superficial cognitional debates.

People speak of Christianity, Buddhism or Islam with various degrees of ignorance—even fear. A genuine religious conversion can remedy this. Christians are called to practice the ideal of unrestricted love. Interfaith dialogue among informed religious persons of good will is needed. Both informal and formal types of interreligious interchanges are integral to an overall understanding of the Church's mission in the world. As we noted, this has been profoundly demonstrated in Bede Griffith's habit of dialoguing with Hindus while living in an ashram. His life of dialogue is an example of an "on-the-way-Christian" who can help us clarify the differences between faith and beliefs. Faith means living, sharing a life of love that is not constrained by the conceptual limitations of dogmas or beliefs which it transcends.

The future of faith, and the spread of the Church beyond its erstwhile Western frontiers in feasible organizational ways can be helped by Christian ashrams. An ashram is a usually secluded abode where a guru and his disciples practice the austerities of a spiritual life. It embodies a spirit of prayer and occasional solitude such as Jesus asked from his disciples. Ashram can also refer to any of the four spiritual abodes or stages of life that the "twice-born" will ideally pass through. One passes through the stages of student, householder (requiring marriage and family), hermit and finally the homeless mendicant. Buddha underwent these stages prior to his enlightenment. As in Christian asceticism, these stages propose ideals for those in search of spiritual solutions. The Church today must learn to guide its followers through modern societies' complex ways—change them for the better. Hoping for a Vatican III, we delve into possible modes of East-West spiritual encounters inspired by SCC's, by ashrams or Buddhist *sanghas* (spiritual communities). The Vatican needs world-religions experts who should be consulted lest the Church fall into the trap of not honoring its "Catholic" commitments. In this respect, Thomas Merton, Jacques Dupuis and Bede Griffiths all distinguished themselves by learning from non-Western colleagues. Merton read widely. He wrote, during the restless 1960's, on the Vietnam War, the Civil Rights movement and the rising interest in Zen Buddhism. Dupuis and Griffiths both studied the Hindu mystical notion of bliss consciousness, *saccidananda* (sharing in God's life—see Appendix 2). Buddhists in India developed their own notions of how consciousness relates one to ultimate reality.[32]

Such notions could help deepen aspects of Western Christians' spiritual lives. What is common to genuine Christian movements the world over is that they offer a message of hope in an age of radically opposed voices. Pope Francis has called attention to both the potential and limits of the Church in the world. We remind readers as to how the Church as one holy, Catholic, apostolic entity has to dialogue with all of mankind on many levels. A dialogue in depth best occurs when people are conscious of their potentially integrative *Gestalt* that cannot be derived from its parts. This is one way to recapitulate the Church's Kingdom-oriented mission, which a Vatican III Council could discuss in more depth. There are, of course, limits as to how that could be done as exemplified in the antagonisms between Christians and Muslims in the Near East—such as in Khomeini's accusing the US of being "The Great Satan." Building bridges among religions and cultures depends in part on participants' attitudes toward freedom. Many Islamic regimes reject Western views on personal freedom. At stake here is the crucial distinction between the complex dynamics of faith as ignored or rejected by atheists, by many advocates of secularism and by fundamentalists. In principle, humans need and seek the truth. But in our day, truth, including Christian truth, is often co-opted by ideologies of the right and left. Some young Westerners, converted to Islam, become terrorists. Convinced of the power of love to transform both persons and society, we seek to clarify the basic confusions of ideological beliefs. The Church should act wisely in its bridge-building efforts. Part of what restricts intercultural dialogues is the West's separation of science from theology. The Hindu mystic Ramakrishna and Buddhists in general differentiate the two. During the Middle Ages in Western universities, philosophy was theology's handmaid. Today the West has downgraded both. A commonality of Christian and Islamic monotheism is that they both avoid monism. While Western skeptics systematically doubt everything, Buddhists place less emphasis on attaining knowledge and more on being enlightened. If Western skeptics, influenced by Cartesian dualism, are relativists, Buddhism can help stabilize Westerners to the extent that the latter are cut off from well-elaborated philosophical theologies. Thomas Merton, Martin Luther King, Jr. and Paul Knitter can help us here.

THE EXAMPLES OF THOMAS MERTON, MARTIN LUTHER KING, JR. (MLK)

We are addressing ways to transform Cartesian dualism through our lived experience of a unified consciousness as this is hopefully lived in the depths of enlightened humans. By appropriating this deeper consciousness one builds bridges between people of good will. Such bridges depend on conversion experiences. MLK and Thomas Merton are two of the great, inspired prophets of the past century. Living out the implications of a global and mystical consciousness, the two men shared a common perception and understanding that the future of humanity rests upon a deeper understanding of our common human identity. Both realized that we must go beyond what has been handed down to us within the context of traditional religious institutions, nation states and ethnocentric cultural beliefs. These two heralds of God's Kingdom constantly challenged the culture of violence afflicting the world. Merton began to speak out against the just war theory in the early 1960s—beginning with his challenges to the American Catholic hierarchy shortly after end of Vatican II. He entreated them to speak out about the threat of nuclear war and to condemn it specifically. He asked them to apply the teachings of Christian love not just to individuals but to society as well: "What matters is for the Bishops and the Council to bear witness clearly and without any confusion to the Church's belief in the power of love to save and transform not only individuals but society."³³ In his 1964 Nobel Peace Prize lecture, MLK spoke of a 'moral lag' in society. He argued that we had lost our way by confusing the relationship of the internal realm of the spirit with the external realm dominated by technology. The internal is the realm of spiritual ends expressed in art, literature, morals and religion. The external is the complex set of techniques humans have devised to ease the drudgery of life. King called for a revolution of values that would help us shift from a "thing-oriented" society to a "person-oriented" one. Our problem today is that we have allowed the internal to become lost in the external. To the extent that the legal process favors the rich and powerful, it must be confronted.

STRATEGIC CONCLUSION TO CHAPTER 3

Chapter 3 touched on mystical, liberating, responsible aspects of religion that enable humans to address pressing problems. Like Jesus, John XXIII was aware of the dangers of a herd mentality alluded to in the parable of the lost sheep. He hoped that dialogue with persons of good will would renew the earth. Marginalized people should be cared for. Since we now live in a globalized world in which people of many faiths and cultures interface daily—it may be said that Vatican II was prescient in developing new forms of dialogue. Its documents suggest how Catholics should be faithful to both Gospel and Tradition. Theologians should help Christians climb over the fences of egoism as did Walesa in Dansk supported by the future John Paull II. The two men moved the hearts of Polish people leading to Communism's downfall in Europe. We now turn to examine more closely the needs of our global village. How might Christians develop communities able to engage in intra-faith and interfaith projects? This is feasible only when enough people commit themselves to combat egoism.³⁴ A first step in that endeavor is asking whether the Church is out of touch. Since we live in a global village, we need strategies able to translate provincial views into dynamic world perspectives so as to integrate valid post-Vatican II strategies. If Christians succeed in understanding the dynamics in the world religions and in postmodernism, they may be able to devise strategies to help the Church get in touch with people's actual needs while promoting God's Kingdom.

NOTES

1. In *The New Science* (Ithaca, NY: Cornell Univ. Press, 1968), Giambattista Vico (1668–1744) anticipated our modern dilemmas; he advocated a pure heart since our modern age is in danger of reverting to barbarism. For him, moral sentiments are the pillars on which the family is built. If these crumble, we descend toward the bestial state.
2. Ian Hammett, *Religious Pluralism and Unbelief* (London: Routledge, 1990), 6.

3. James Redfield, *The Celestine Prophecy* (New York: Warner, 1993). After kissing Marjorie, the hero says: "I couldn't believe the amount of energy I felt when she touched me. . . . The child makes an easy transition from receiving her opposite-sex energy from her father to receiving it as part of the overall energy existing in the universe at large" (189,193). Robert Redfield's study *The Little Community* (1955) based on Indian and Chinese civilizations views civilizations as systems of interdependent, coexisting great and little traditions. His *The Little Community* (1955) is based on factual research.

4. William Johnston, *Mystical Theology: The Science of Love* (London: Harper Collins, 1995) 50, likens *ki* to Thomistic connaturality; some relate it to Tao's *Ying-Yang* forces. The success of such films as Star Wars suggests that many people tend to believe in a universal energy of life charging the body for a variety of mental and spiritual tasks.

5. David Tracy, *Plurality and Ambiguity: Hermeneutics, Religion, Hope* (New York: Harper & Row, 1987). We emphasize the moral ambiguities affecting moral decisions. See note 168 on how Alfred Shutz and Gibson Winter helped resolve such ambiguities.

6. Lonergan's method can help us transform such gaps because he approached religion through apprehensions of value. He dwelt on how humans reach or fail to reach intimacy and the human good. The fact that Lonergan was both a philosopher and theologian of note adds to his method's ability to bridge many gaps haunting us today. Prior to Kant, most philosophers used theological approaches to God's existence to bridge gaps they were unable to fill by philosophical means alone. Such approaches are reflected in Descartes' assumption that God's existence guarantees against self-deceit. Berkeley argued that objects not perceived by any subject can be said to persist only because they are being perceived by God. Kant removed God from theoretical philosophy, arguing that to have recourse to God in trying to explain nature is equal to confessing philosophy's theoretical limitations. In that case, one is assuming something that cannot be conceived. Replacing traditional metaphysics with his concept of *noumena* (things in themselves), Kant opened a chasm between philosophy and theology but left to "practical reason" the possibility of encountering the mystery of the unknowable God. Upon being awarded the 2007 Templeton Prize for his research into the spiritual realm, Charles Taylor declared "The deafness of many philosophers, social scientists and historians to the spiritual" is remarkable. (*NY Times*, March 15, 2007). Taylor's *The Ethics of Authenticity* (Harvard, 1991) stresses the spiritual sources of the self so as to avoid such deafness.

7. Terence Fretheim, *God and World in The Old Testament: A Relational Theology of Creation* (Abingdon, 2005).

8. See "Integrating Religious and other Lived Experiences" later in this chapter.

9. Richard Fenn, *The Secularization of Sin* (Louisville: Westminster-Knox, 1991). Mere humanism is impotent against evil; ethics is relatively autonomous; it can move us beyond humanism. Hannah Arendt, *The Human Condition* (Chicago University, 1958), 38, on how Rousseau' displaced the moral accent from God to "deep within ourselves."

10. David Riesman, *The Lonely Crowd* (New York: Doubleday, 1950). Paul Ricoeur, *The Symbolism of Evil* (Boston: Beacon, 1967) studies how the elementary symbols of evil, sin and guilt were formulated in the myths of antiquity and how we can access the myths through symbols and guilt. Nazism, Communism, Genocides show humans at their worst.

11. *The Essential Rumi*, translated by Coleman Barks (San Francisco: Harper, 2004), 32.

12. Daniel Dreisbach argues that the Ku Klux Klan invented the wall to silence religion. Justice Hugo Black, a former KKK member "legitimized" the wall with his secular bias.

13. Robert Nozick, *The Examined Life* (NY: Touchstone) 1989 on notions of "reality."

14. In Augustine, *Confessions*, VIII, 12, 28–29, we read that his moment of conversion was filled with tears. "I felt that I was still the captive of my sins." The first passage of St. Paul's Epistles upon which his eyes fell read, "Not in lust and wantonness, not in quarrels and rivalries. Rather, arm yourselves with the Lord Jesus Christ; spend no more thought on nature." Love flooded his heart, but in later years he still felt the weight of past sins.

15. https://catholicherald.co.uk/news/2013/12/09/sensus-fidelium-doesnt-mean-majority-opinion-francis-tells-theologians/ For Pope Francis, *sensus fidelium* is to be consistent amidst diversity.www.americamagazine.org/faith/2018/10/25/its-time-us-bishops-revise-their-catholic-voting-guide?fbclid=IwAR26m5PfgBebu8KbmivS6PTla1cO3WpPP-y-RUhsT2ORhebP7ZR2Dwlu_tM A similar point is made in "Lay community is key to reform-

ing Catholicism," https://international.la-croix.com/news/lay-community-key-to-reforming-catholicism/10838?utm_source=Newsletter&utm_medium=e-mail&utm_content=28-12-2019&utm_campaign=newsletter_crx_lci&PMID= 0964d be689e61e205168552536593154. For centuries Church leaders ignored Jesus' injunction on peacemaking. The reign of Clement XI (1700–21) saw a drastic reduction in papal influence due to his taking sides in European politics. Wishing to keep Italy from being embroiled in war, he backed Philip V to succeed Charles II who was to be Bourbon king in Spain. This led to the invasion of Italy by both the Habsburgs and the Bourbons. Clement XI thus repeated Clement VII's mistake that led to Charles V's sack of Rome in 1527. Conservatives and progressives must not forget that systems remain incomplete amidst the accelerating pace of ever more efficient techniques.

16. Vatican II's "Decree on Ecumenism" (21), cites dialogue as a way "for attaining that unity which the Savior holds out to all men." Commentators on the 2019 Amazon Synod argue that the Church has now embarked on a less clerical chapter in its history. In one of the most important—but often overlooked– addresses of his pontificate, Pope Francis declared in 2015 that we are living in a change of epochs. These words of his were reflected over and over again during the Amazon Synod. Pope Francis knows that the Church needs a lung transplant as it were to adapt to today's radically changing realities. Perhaps, that surgery began with the 2019 Amazon Synod. See https://international.la-croix.com/news/the-church-needs-a-lung-transplant/11393?utm_source= Newsletter& utm_medium=e-mail&utm_content=03-12-2019&utm_campaign=newsletter_crx_lci& PMID=0964dbe689e61e20516855 2536 593154 . Also https://international.la-croix. com/news/from-synodality-to-a-creative-pastoral-approach/11169.

17. *A mandala* ("circle") is a concentric representation of the cosmos used in Jungian psychology to guide efforts to reunify the self. For us, it signifies ethically and spiritually unifying mankind. That, we argue, may summarize Pope Francis' life.

18. In his *The Acting Person*, Vol. X of *Analecta Husserliana*, (Boston: Reidel, 1979), the future Pope John Paul II had used "lived-through experience" to deepen Aristotle's categories that explore the dynamic nature of being but do not adequately address lived-through experience. He found the basis of activity and passivity in human potentialities. By differentiating between how man acts and when "something happens in him," he argued that we transcend ourselves in action. Wojtyla acknowledges how Anna-Teresa Tymienicka helped transform his obscure Polish text into a clear one with "world reach."

19. In *The Postmodern Condition: A Report on Knowledge*, tr. by G. Bennington and B. Massumi (U. of Minnesota, 1984), Jean-F. Lyotard notes postmodernism's inability to integrate denotative scientific and evaluative languages. Postmodern implies incredulity toward philosophy's meta-narratives (xxiv). Science seeks to distinguish itself from narrative knowledge existing in myth and legend. Modern philosophy seeks to provide legitimating narratives for science in the form of "the dialectics of Spirit, the hermeneutics of meaning, the emancipation of the rational or working subject, or the creation of wealth (xxiii). If the computer age reduces knowledge to information, Lyotard argues that the transmission and reception of messages must follow agreed-upon rules.

20. In "Dilthey statt Nietzsche—eine Alternative für Heidegger" (2003), Helmuth Vetter clarifies disputed issues.

21. Jacques Dupuis, *Toward a Christian Theology of Religious Pluralism* (Orbis, 1997).

22. Lonergan appeals to the mental acts humans engage in when coming to know. These acts are of three basic types 1) experiencing the data of sensation and consciousness in one's life; 2) understanding the ways of explaining such experiencing; and 3) judging that such an explanation is either probable or certain. One cannot deny these three types of mental activity without self-contradiction. These three types are capped by 4) coming to decisions and taking actions. Too often, the basic nature of our mental acts are lost in the discussions of linguistic philosophers. One's lived experience depends on how one appropriates his/her four basic mental operations—or fails to appropriate them.

23. Since Lonergan's metaphysics comes after judgments that lead to self-affirmation, it is not subject to Derridean deconstruction aimed at metaphysical views of self-identity.

24. Lonergan, *Method in Theology* (New York: Herder, 1972); the eight specialties can help us refute ideologies and renew Church or societal structures; they include research, hermeneu-

tics, history and dialectically arriving at a consensus. But this is only a first phase in a diphase process in the second phase of the functional specialties, each one must "incarnate" the lived experience of conversion. Communication is possible when scientists or theologians' discussions are based on the unchanging realities within their cognitional operations and the many ways trained persons can use the basic operations. This involves reflecting on the roots of lived experience in all cultures and dialectically interrelating these roots. John Raymaker, *Empowering Philosophy and Science with the Art of Love: Lonergan and Deleuze in the Light of Buddhist-Christian Ethics* (University Press of America, 2006) calls this an inbuilt bridge allowing multi-disciplinary cooperation.

25. Michael Balint, *The Doctor, his Patient and the Illness* (London: Pitman Medical). Controlling desire and troubling emotions is made all the more difficult in a world thoroughly confused as to what "knowledge" is. Lonergan realized this confusion and made it his life work to explain the basis of insights and their healing potential.

26. Lonergan, "Theology in its New Context," in *A Second Collection*, 1974, 55.

27. It is better to take refuge in the Lord than to trust in man; still trust *is* important.

28. Wayne Proudfoot, *Religious Experience* (Berkeley: University of California, 1985) 233. Steven Katz in Forman, ed. *The Problem of Pure Consciousness, in Philosophy East and West*, 50, 2, April 2000, 10. "Language, Epistemology, and Mysticism," in *Mysticism and Philosophical Analysis*, 22–74, ed. by Steven Katz (London: Sheldon, 1978). Linguistic constructivists such as Katz claim that no experience is untouched by one's culture and beliefs. Lonergan helps us "objectify" mystic experiences by formulating insights into such experiences' contents in ways that escape constructivist critiques. His method shows how religious experience, like other experience, is not independent of concepts, beliefs or the judgements we make, the actions we take. There are parallels in how rationalists such as Parmenides, Confucianists, Advaitists or Wolff provoke idealist counter arguments tinged with empiricism as in Kant or Ramajuna's modified nonduality.

29. Yves Raguin, *La Profondeur de Dieu* (Descle de Brouwer, 1973); "The Outside and the Inside" (Internet).

30. John McMurry, "Blueprint for a Spirituality of Experience" in *The Priest*, Nov. 1998.

31. Quoted by Robert Doran in *Il Teologo e la Storia: Lonergan's Centenary* (Rome: Ed Pontificia, 2006), 276. Frederick E. Crowe, *Appropriating the Lonergan Idea*, ed. by Michael Vertin (Catholic University 1989,) 141, notes: a reactionary is right in trying to save an ancient faith, but wrong in merely repeating the formulas of Vatican I; the radical left is "right in critiquing the dogmatic formulations of the past in terms of the horizon in which they were uttered," but wrong in declaring independence from those formulations.

32. Thomas Kochumuttom, *Comparative Theology: Christian Thinking and Spirituality in Indian Perspective* (Bangalore: Dharmaram) 13, 35, 49–52.

33. Gerald Grudzen, "Martin Luther King and Thomas Merton: Prophets of World Peace," *Across the Rim of Chaos: Thomas Merton's Prophetic Vision*, Angus Stuart, editor (Bristol: Thomas Merton Society of Great Britain and Ireland, 2005), 116.

34. Buddhism and Christianity warn us against the ego's deceits. "Besides the egoism of the individual there is the egoism of the group. While the individual egoist has to put up with public censure...group egoism not merely directs development to its own aggrandizement but also provides a market for . . . theories that will justify its ways. It then attributes others' misfortunes to their "depravity" (Lonergan, *Method*, 54).

Part II

Has the Church Been Out of Touch with the Modern World?

Part I noted the globalization contexts now facing the Church. Part II explores how people of faith can respect and reconcile one another's divergent claims. It argues that the Church has been out of touch with modern times to the extent that it has not fully listened to its visionary pioneers who strove to adequately apply the teachings of Jesus to their situations. The wonder of Pope Francis' papacy is that *he has been in touch* with the many pressing issues now facing the globe and its inhabitants to an amazing degree. He *has acted* on his convictions. We restrict part II to chapter 4, which gives an overview of the problems of "modernism." Historically, these problems had been preceded by the realities of Church corruption during the Middle Ages. It took saints to rescue the Church from its corruption. More recently, Vatican II did reform the Church, but Pope John Paul II, despite, all his charisms, opposed liberation theology. He undercut the leadership of the world's bishops by recentralizing Church authority in the Vatican. He was not, of course, as conservative as the Society of St. Pius X, which he excommunicated. As to the problems of adequate Church leadership in an age of vast transformations, the Church has been in need of "catching up." Fortunately, Pope Francis is doing just that. In short, part II examines some of the circumstances and divergent theological views that led to and followed both the Vatican I the Vatican II councils. It asks what still needs to be done.

Chapter Four

Conflicts between the Church's Resistance and Openness to Modernization

Is the Church still "out of touch" with the modern world? If it is to seek God's justice and his Kingdom, the Church must constructively speak with all people of good will. In this chapter, we first comment on Modernism and Postmodernism. Secondly, we note how two popes opposed Modernism. Thirdly, we examine Church reforms prior and subsequent to the Protestant Reformation. Fourthly, we discuss how an ecclesial fortress mentality alienates many Catholics. Finally, we consider issues that theologians and bishops should be asking to lay a groundwork for a Vatican III so as to find adequate answers to the problems and challenges now facing both the world and the Church. Pope Francis, benefiting from the leadership of some of his predecessors, has been laying foundations to adequately form a Church leadership able to face contemporary issues.

SOME LINKS BETWEEN MODERNISM AND POSTMODERNISM UP UNTIL POPE FRANCIS

Postmodernism was rooted in Modernism, a movement that emerged in mid-nineteenth century Europe. Rooted in the idea that literature, art, social organization and even daily life had all become "outdated," Modernism sought to re-examine every aspect of life. The movement influenced some Catholics. It was famously condemned by Pius IX and Pius X. For his part, Leo XIII appealed to Cardinal John Henry Newman (a courageous convert to Catholicism) to give an orthodox interpretation of Modernism. With his deep understanding of the Church Fathers, Newman was able to offset exaggerated modernist claims. Newman helps us separate the valid claims of the three "masters" of suspicion (Marx, Nietzsche and Freud) from their ungrounded errors. As a "radical" philosopher with a gift for dramatic hyperbole, Nietzsche claimed that Greco-Christian thought had a pernicious influence in Western intellectual history. Instead, he idealized a "Superman" (*Übermensch*) who would overcome historical errors. Some postmodernists embraced a Nietzschean nihilism that repudiates former views of meaning and value. Writing a generation before Nietzsche and with great eloquence, Newman had shown how dogmas had evolved. His influence on Leo XIII (himself a scholar) has been a providential event. For his part, Pope Francis keeps insisting that all should contribute to the good of all and that scholars should discern the deep truths of faith.

PIUS IX'S STRONG OPPOSITION TO "MODERNISM"

With the notable exception of Benedict XIV (1758–74),[1] the Church opposed many Enlightenment notions between the sixteenth and nineteenth centuries. This was quite evident at the First Vatican Council and, later, in the Oath against Modernism enjoined by St. Pius X. Pope Pius IX had condemned many key ideas of liberal, democratic states in his *Syllabus of Errors* in 1864. Among the errors he condemned were the following propositions:

- #30 The immunity of the Church and of ecclesiastical persons derived its origin from civil law.
- #42 In the case of conflicting laws enacted by the two powers, the civil law prevails.
- #55 The Church ought to be separated from the State, and the State from the Church.
- #77 In the present day it is no longer expedient that the Catholic religion should be held as the only religion . . . to the exclusion of all other forms of worship.
- #80 The Roman pontiff can, and ought to reconcile himself ... with progress, liberalism and modern civilization.

In his *Syllabus*, Pius IX commented as follows on the twofold order of earthly powers:

> The faith teaches us and human reason demonstrates that a double order of things exists, and that we must therefore distinguish between the two earthly powers, the one of natural origin which provides for secular affairs and the tranquility of human society, the other of supernatural origin . . ., that of the Church which has been divinely instituted for the sake of souls and of eternal Salvation.[2]

The Syllabus of Errors risked putting the Church on a collision course with the modern world. The separation of Church and State embodied in the US Constitution and human and civil rights and the US Bill of Rights seemed to be in opposition to the *Syllabus*. In 1869, shortly after issuing the *Syllabus*, Pius IX summoned Vatican I. That Council's proclamation of Papal Infallibility (limited to specific statements of universal belief). In his *Infallible? An Inquiry*, 1983, Hans Küng strongly criticized such "infallibility."

THE MODERNIST RESISTANCE TO THE *SYLLABUS OF ERRORS*

Vatican I seems to have separated the Church from the life of the modern world. The attempts by Catholic "Modernists" such as the Jesuit George Tyrrell (1861–1909) to mediate the crisis were quickly suppressed. Tyrrell embraced a democratic view of Church governance that was quite radical for his time but which anticipated Vatican II's proclamation of the Church as the "People of God" in its *Lumen Gentium*. Tyrrell claimed that "sacerdotalism" had perverted the notion of priesthood in two respects:

First, in the vulgar way of regarding the faithful "sheep" as purely passive to Church shepherds. This perversion lurks subtly and perniciously in something which exists for its own sake and not merely and purely as an instrument for the spiritual service of those who support it. There is sacerdotalism that forgets that the Sabbath and whole Law is made for man, and not man for the Sabbath or for the Law. Man is master of the Sabbath, the Law, the Priesthood. The sacerdotalism which forgets this has its direct counterpart in the conception of civil and political offices "as being ends in themselves."[3]

Second, Tyrrell seemed to place the final authority of the Church in the community of the faithful and not solely in the office holder whether pope, bishop or priest. His sense of Divine Immanence reinforced his views on the validity of the individual's conscience. Conscience helps one adequately express God's truth and God's will. "It furnishes a standard from which the individual may not fall short. . . . Growth and progress demand that under certain conditions the individual may and even must depart from established forms of belief, law and custom, in obedience to the higher and more ultimate law of the spirit itself" (Tyrrell, *Tradition*, 96—see also Appendix 1).

Alfred Loisy (1857–1940), a French Catholic priest and professor of biblical studies became the standard bearer of a modernist approach to biblical interpretation. One of the first Catholic theologians to embrace the historical/ critical method of interpreting the Bible, he did defend Tradition as a source of Christian doctrinal development. This led him to oppose Alfred Von Harnack, a liberal Protestant theologian, who held that the essential kernel of the Gospels could be derived from Christianity's historical origins. Loisy argued that Christianity's evolving Tradition was part of the content of revelation, a common claim of Catholic theologians. He differed from Catholic orthodoxy, however, by claiming that doctrinal positions could change through time based upon the presence of the Spirit guiding the Church. He argued that Church dogmas such as the Incarnation or the Trinity were influenced by Hellenism and could be modified or changed in the light of contemporary cultural factors as long as the Church remained faithful to the core message of Jesus' preaching about the Kingdom of God. For Loisy, "Though the dogmas may be Divine in origin . . ., they are human in structure and composition."[4]

FARSIGHTED LEADERS:
CARDINAL NEWMAN AND POPE LEO XIII

There are many ungrounded assumptions which must be considered before one can adequately evaluate Modernism. After Vatican I, the Church seemed completely alienated from the life of the modern world. Leo XIII asked theologians to help the Church renew itself through a deeper understanding of Scripture and Tradition.[5] He asked Cardinal Newman to evaluate the Modernist Movement in orthodox ways. Like Nietzsche, Newman had a flair for dramatizing history. A man of faith grounded in apophatic love, he showed how dogmas had evolved. Nietzsche believed in unbelief; he was caught in a pathos of partially true insights. He claimed that Greco-Christian thought had a pernicious influence in Western history. Yet, his "Superman" can hardly overcome the mistakes of history. Before Nietzsche's attacks on Christianity, Marx had denounced capitalism; Freud would soon reduce the psyche to the sexual drive. Given such secularist onslaughts and his pastoral concerns, St. Pius X found Leo XIII's efforts to mediate modernist beliefs with faith to be insufficient.

WEIGHING ST. PIUS X'S CONDEMNATION
OF MODERNISM AGAINST SOME BALANCED
APPROACHES TO POSTMODERNISM AND SCIENCE

In 1907, Pius X issued the encyclical entitled *Pascendi Dominici Gregis*. It attacked modernist theological positions which it sought to refute. For Modernists such as Loisy and Tyrrell, faith and science were two distinct modes of understanding. *Pascendi* insisted that religious dogma is not "symbolic"; it is a true expression of the divine deposit of faith. Pius X opposed theories of Divine Immanence for God is not directly accessible to human intelligence. Divine revelation is needed. Pius X excommunicated Tyrrell in 1907 and Loisy in 1909. In 1910, he required all clerics to take an oath against what he named six errors presumed to be part of the modernist Movement:

1. God cannot be known and proved to exist by natural reason;
2. External signs of revelation, such as miracles and prophecies, do not prove the divine origin of the Christian religion and are not suited to the intellect of modern man; 3. Christ did not found a Church;
3. The essential structure of the Church can change;
4. The Church's dogmas continually evolve over time so that they can change from meaning one thing to meaning another;
5. Faith is a blind religious feeling that wells up from the subconscious under the impulse of a heart and a will trained to morality, not a real assent of the intellect to divine truth learned by hearing it from an external source.

No one could receive a Catholic theological degree or be ordained a priest without first taking this oath. The development of critical biblical studies led some to challenge claims that Church officials have a "divine authority" that can ignore doctrinal development. Arguably, the Church overreacted to Modernism. Leo XIII's papacy was a progressive interlude between the papacies of Pius IX and Pius X that eventually led to John XXIII calling a Vatican II Council. Newman, Tyrrell and Lonergan were all proponents of the development of doctrine with due emphasis on the need for the hierarchy to consult the faithful. From this broad principle, many conflicting views are to be weighed in reconciling faith and reason. Under Leo XIII and John XXIII, the Church welcomed nuanced forms of the Modernist agenda. Leo XIII's *Nova et Vetera* program asked theologians to help the Church renew itself through a deeper understanding of Scripture and Tradition.[6] As Vatican II reconsidered the Church's previous opposition to Modernism, so we study some of the ways in which diversified Church structures might today play their rightful roles in Christians' lives. Catholicism has consistently developed spiritualities that have allowed it to survive and prosper in a variety of cultural and political situations. Pope Francis is an admirable example of such development. While some capitalists resent being singled out by him as being at the root of increasing world poverty, and while others wildly accuse him of being a modernist for not insisting more on Tradition, it should be clear that he is the right Pope at the right time. He is ever joyful as he lives out his simple, down-to earth and humble solidarity with the poor. If narrow-minded "traditionalists" are irritated by this, Pope Francis by taking the name of the great Assisi mystic, clearly indicated that he is a "modernist" only in the sense that he has pursued the policies of Leo XIII and John XXIII in welcoming authentic forms of modern life that reach out to the needy and to scientists. By which theological and ethical perspectives should twenty-first century spiritualities be guided?" Paradoxically, many laypeople go on retreats behind cloister walls so as to find their own identity and plan their lives, while religious orders cannot fully address the problems now challenging them.

The decline of Catholicism in Europe and the exodus of priests and nuns from the clerical and religious states following Vatican II have forced many Catholic institutions to close. Numerous parishes lack a resident priest. Many Catholic religious communities face financial crises. Unable to attract new members, they must support growing numbers of aged and infirm retirees. Catholicism's future may rest, in part, with new forms of non-clerical ministries now springing up on the periphery of traditional religious institutions. The authors have participated in several alternative forms of ministry over the past four decades. We believe that a Vatican III Council, guided by a world-affirming spirituality, might transform the Church enabling it to become a powerful voice for peace and justice. The Church does not bend to modern societies' biases; it seeks to transform these with Christian love. Biases impede us from seeing other people and cultures impartially.[7] Some scientists and philosophers may hold immanence-biased views prodding them to deny the transcendent. Pope Francis invites us to put aside cultural biases as he recalls the Father's care for creation. "Are not two sparrows sold for a penny? Yet not one of them will fall to the ground outside your Father's care" (Matt 10:29–31). Unlike postmodernists, we seek to better address the transcendent revealed in Sacred Scripture. We do so by trying to build bridges through a relational theology that mediates between conflicting claims on immanence and transcendence. We apply modern theological categories to traditional views of a provident God who guides the created order. Soren Kierkegaard pioneered a psychology to help us grasp God's transcending ways. He rejected Hegel's rationalism. One generation before Freud and Nietzsche, he wrote about the paradoxical nature of faith. Faith is the "evidence of things unseen" (Heb11:1). It is the personal apprehension of a mystery not be found in the rational, dogmatic framework of the Danish Church of his day. He wrote about the possibility of faith for those living with doubts and insecurity in an age when science is seen as the only test of truth. For him the substance of faith lies in hope—not in scientific reductionisms. His existentialism is a corrective to Sartre's later atheist existentialism. His Christian existentialism was given an encouraging turn by Gabriel Marcel and Camus. Brian Greene admires Camus for having rightly chosen the value of life as the ultimate question. Camus "separated out physical questions and labelled them secondary," but for Greene, "physical questions are primary."[8]

We argue that life values and physical questions each has primacy in its own domain. An interplay of immanence and transcendence allows for evolutionary processes to occur. "Chance" as understood in contemporary cosmology does not rule out an authentic human spirituality any more than it rules out the reality of a Higgs Field permeating the universe as a remnant of

God's primordial creative "Big Bang." Saints are those who turn to God as their basis for trusting. If our orientation toward the divine can be snuffed out, trust in God re-orients us. The God "question questions questioning itself" (Lonergan, *Method*, 103); having found God remedies our restlessness. It helps us relate life's realities within their many emerging contexts as grounded within the emergent spiritual realities of life. A key proponent of an emergent view of humanity was Arthur Peacocke (1924–2006) founder of the Ian Ramsey Centre for Religion and Science. He held that the immanent laws of science are compatible with a transcendent understanding of God. If God—as a scientifically sensitive theology affirms—is creating immanently through the evolutionary process, it is consistent with such a theology to affirm that moral awareness originated in sociobiological ways.

> Humanity could only have survived and flourished if it held social and personal values that transcended the urges of the individual, embodying "selfish" genes—and these values are closely related to belief in a transcendent Ultimate Reality. The existence of such values points to the nature of that unsurpassable Ultimate Reality and then enriches our own sense of values.[9]

Believers do not have to try to be "super-persons."[10] Rather, they should accept God's gentle ways and help unbelievers accept God's love. Claudel's conversion experience upon his visit to Notre Dame in Paris exemplifies this. In his ministry, Abbe Pierre (1912–2007) revealed humans' ability to find the depths of the sacred within the secular and despite misery. His ministry to the homeless and marginalized illuminated the Gospel message so clearly that even in a secular culture such as France, people could not help but recognize his witness of intense, selfless devotion.

A HISTORICAL PERSPECTIVE: CHURCH REFORMS PRIOR TO THE PROTESTANT REFORMATION

Many of the great historical movements for spiritual renewal in Catholicism have emerged from outside the hierarchical, clerical culture that ruled the Church after its accommodation with the Roman Empire in the fourth century. The monastic spiritual culture in Western Europe was largely due to St. Benedict of Nursia (480–547). His Benedictine abbeys existed somewhat autonomously from the hierarchy for many centuries. The abbeys provided a spirituality rooted in daily reading of the Scriptures (*lectio divina*), prayer and work.. They preserved and expanded Christianity's intellectual heritage through libraries and *scriptoria*.[11] In some cases, the abbeys became the focal point for the economic and spiritual life of medieval Europe with extensive land holdings and magnificent churches and liturgical celebrations. In the eleventh century the Benedictine Rule of the Monte Cassino Abbey helped implement Pope Gregory VII's, reforms[12] meant to liberate the Church from lay investiture and simony. The Abbey did lose much of its spiritual vigor as it became politically involved as an ally of the centralized papacy's attempt to assert hegemony over Europe. Later, the Mendicant Friars, led by St. Francis (1181–1226) and St. Dominic (1170–1221), initiated non-clerical spiritual movements. Friars had a more direct access to ordinary Christians inasmuch as they gave up the right to own property. From its inception, this renewal movement was opposed by many bishops and secular clergy. After Pope Alexander IV approved this way of life in 1256, it was replicated in other congregations such as the Carmelites which engage in specialized ministries. The Brethren of the Common Life, founded in fourteenth century Utrecht, helped lay people better live their Christian calling. The Brethren stressed meditation on the life of Christ and sharing one's meditations in small faith communities. Their founder, Geert De Groote (1340–1384), was a mystic who lived a semi-monastic life as a lay person. Although never ordained, he had license to preach. His condemnation of clerical abuses led to his loss of this license, but the Brethren continued to support him and his way of life. Groote helped make the interior, mystical life a viable option for ordinary Christians. Influenced by the Brethren, Thomas A. Kempis (1380–1471) wrote *The Imitation of Christ,* the classical expression of the *Devotio Moderna* calling for apostolic renewal through the rediscovery of pious practices such as humility and simplicity of life.

CATHOLIC REFORMS SINCE THE COUNTER-REFORMATION AND PERSONAL CONVERSIONS

The Catholic response to the Protestant Reformation took many forms, some of its most significant being the spiritual renewal that occurred in Spain under the direction of Ignatius Loyola (1495–1556), Theresa of Avila (1515–1582) and John of the Cross (1542–1591). Ignatius underwent a profound spiritual conversion at Manresa in 1522. His spiritual insights are embodied in his classic text, *The Spiritual Exercises*. The Jesuits (Society of Jesus) began in 1534 when six members jointly pledged themselves to a life of apostolic labor but without the restrictions of traditional forms of the religious life. John of the Cross and Teresa of Avila, two of the greatest mystics in the history of the Church, met resistance to their reform movement. John was imprisoned in the Carmelite monastery at Toledo by order of his superior general for almost nine months; he never seemed to gain the trust of his superiors despite his role as the author of such mystical classics as *The Ascent of Mount Carmel* and *The Dark Night of the Soul*. In their ministries, these Spanish spiritual masters sought to bring a new form of spiritual life to their communities; their efforts marked a new era for Christian mysticism.

Conversion, both personal and ecclesial, is key to our overall argumentation. If one studies how great twentieth century converts have described their conversion process, we note similarities in their experiences. Thomas Merton's *The Seven Story Mountain* and Clare Booth Luce's autobiography clarify how they moved from previously taken for granted realities to a new, deeper grasp of how God fits into their lives. Dorothy Day, foundress of the Catholic Worker movement, lived a radical, spirituality rooted in apostolic poverty; her way, hearkening back to St. Francis, is a clear antidote to the growing challenges of racism, consumerism and militarism that have dominated contemporary American life.

Many of the leaders of the Catholic Peace Movement of the 1960s were lay men and women. Among them, there were many who had resigned from the clerical ministry or left religious orders so as to pursue a more radical kind of Christian lifestyle. Two of the most famous members of the Catholic Peace Movement were Philip and Liz McAllister Berrigan, founders of Jonah House in Baltimore. Members of this small, activist Christian community, which included Phil's brother, Dan Berrigan, were among the leading opponents of the Vietnam War. They provided a model for a resistance-based understanding of Catholicism in the midst of a militarized society. Theirs was an alternative model of religious ministry not unlike the spiritual activist model lived by Martin Luther King, Jr. which called for peace based on social justice.

A PERSONAL INSIGHT ON TRADITIONAL, ALIENATED CATHOLICS

A personal insight into the plight of modern parish life may illustrate some of the aspects of learning and living the Gospel and its message today. While serving in an inner-city parish in Boston, a priest noticed that a devout Irish-American parishioner had stopped coming to Sunday Mass. His wife was seriously handicapped and for years he had brought her in her wheelchair to attend the worship service. Because he had been so dedicated, the parish priest asked him why he had stopped coming to Mass. He replied said that he was "not getting anything" out of the service. This was food for thought. Yes, the parish was full of minorities. The Irish, the mainstay of the parish for many years, had moved out. But he and his wife had stayed. Upon retirement, he had no choice but to care for his wife. Still, he was forced to confess that he no longer found participation in Sunday Mass meaningful for his personal life. Would this parishioner not have benefited from meeting in a small community where he and his wife could discuss their problems and hopes with others? That is one of the reasons why home masses are encouraged in some dioceses. But there are not enough priests around to celebrate home masses. Communion services are another alternative, but these too require a theologically trained leader, such as a deacon to properly address the many complex issues now facing the average Christian. These issues include those of living the social justice requirements of the Gospel—which is not always done in rich suburban parishes. Rather, suburbanites often indulge their fantasies in editing movies with superfine digital means. The Church seeks not be left behind in the technological world, but the Gospel of transformative renewal to which it is bound is not one of mere self-preservation. Some inner city Catholic parishes in the USA have been able to recreate a sense of community by establishing a variety of outreach ministries as did Old St. Patrick's Church in downtown Chicago. This parish, located in the heart of downtown Chicago, is the oldest Catholic Church in the city. At its low point approximately 25 years ago the parish only had three registered members. Today the Church's 3,500 members reach out to the surrounding community. St. Patrick's attracts people from throughout the Chicago area with its inspiring liturgies and its numerous programs serving downtown communities. Its annual block party draws thousands. It has helped revive Irish American liturgical art through its numerous arts activities in this area. Many of its activities promote intimate human interactions, which in turn affect the community at large.

WEDDING THE PERSONAL, THE MYSTICAL AND THE COMMUNAL IN LIVING THE FAITH

We have seen how Cartesian dualism or a Nietzschean claim of God's "death" point to their own limitations. Such limitations have been overcome by those able to experience or at least appreciate the deeper truths of mystics. Mysticism is an inkling of God's depths; it is often experienced in a dark night of the soul—one that begins by peering into one's own depths in need of "enlightenment." Saint John of the Cross had a mystical belief in a loving Being, outside of the realm of feeling, thought or imagination but knowable through a love that passes through a "dark night." This dark night includes a process of purgation of the senses and of the spirit; it leads to an intimate union with God. The process involves keeping a delicate balance between inner and outer activities. With Nietzsche, one can rebel within the uncertainties of an existence where God seems to have disappeared. On the other hand, dedicated parishes and communities manage to wed the personal and communal dimensions of living the faith; they possess the necessary leadership and sensitivities to meet personal and communal needs. We insist that Christians must have realistic ideals. This can be fostered through the personal and communal synergy that arises when cultures meet. Vatican II sought to make Catholicism "relevant" in our complex age. Philosophy gives us categories which theologians develop in ways appropriate to the times. The third millennium is now calling us to learn from the middle ways discovered by the great philosophers of Greece, India, China. While Aquinas adapted Aristotle for the Middle Ages, an analogous task now awaits today's philosophers and theologians. Asians do not distinguish between philosophy and theology as sharply as do Western traditions. As we noted, Yves Raguin who peered into mystical depths is an example of this. Having studied Taoism as well as Teilhard de Chardin, he was able to reconcile Chinese and Western spiritualities. Since faith is the "evidence of things unseen" (Heb11:1), we need the courage to pursue what may yet be unseen but can possibly build bridges between people alienated due to modern realities. Pastors worthy of that name implicitly understand the need of such bridges and they proceed to build them on the local level. Bishops and the Church as a whole must build such bridges on the global level. It is not enough to know one's shortcomings, we must examine our own motivations that may keep us too focused on personal interests.

Christian wisdom may seem the height of folly to those unable to follow the way of Christ. Jesus remains an enigmatic figure to those refusing to yield to him in faith. The Church is saddled with an ambiguous legacy, one of saints—and sinners. In the gospels, Jesus often alludes to the lack of faith that led many to "go away."

From the sixteenth century until Vatican II, the Church was torn by divisions. Pius IX, initially a liberal, led the Church into a fortress mentality codified at Vatican I. We saw how Newman helped Leo XIII turn this situation around by re-examining and synthesizing old and new truths and how this laid a viable path for Vatican II's breakthroughs. Such a synthesizing ability is part of a Middle-Way path that could help the Church enlarge its vision in adequately responding to the needs of both faithful and alienated people.

VATICAN II'S COURAGEOUS MIDDLE-WAY: A MOVE AWAY FROM THE FORTRESS MENTALITY

In our view, a fortress mentality is self-defeating. It runs counter to Jesus' teaching on the Kingdom and openness to the Spirit. Traditionalists want to turn back the clock. If a bishop alienates those interested in greater lay participation or in social justice, the alienated ones should be free to follow Vatican II's middle-way directives. Christian theologians such as St Paul and St. Thomas of Aquinas adapted the middle-way wisdom of Socrates and Aristotle. In our day, Vatican II has helped us meet halfway the sound teachings of Buddhism, Hinduism, Taoism and Confucianism and modern thinkers. It courageously moved away from a long-cherished fortress mentality and toward an openness to all truth. Like Jesus, who did not want to do away with a dot or an iota of the Law or the Prophets, some Christians, encouraged by Vatican II, try to see the good in their own tradition and that of others. Some conservatives forget that the Spirit guides those who try to live the faith in ways that meet the demands of the present and the future. Not unlike a growing chorus of Protestant evangelists who preach a la Trump that striving for wealth is praiseworthy, reactionary Catholics betray the Gospel under the pretext of defending tradition. Avoiding inner-city problems does not impinge on their consciences. Some with authoritarian instincts are trying to undermine Francis' papacy by voicing their preference for Benedict XVI's traditionalism. Vatican II's *Gaudium et Spes* asserted that the Church no longer regards the quest for human rights and social justice as marginal to Church life; yet, some traditionalists dismiss the pursuit of rights and justice as "leftist." They contradict Jesus' teaching that personal conversion and reforming sinful realities are both needed. Vatican II laid important benchmarks for involving the Church in such issues as religious freedom and respecting the rights of women, children, and refugees. *Gaudium et Spes* addressed the whole of the human family, not just Catholics. It recalled that man's history carries the marks of his energies, his tragedies and triumphs. It asked the international community "to regulate economic relations throughout the world so that they can unfold in a way which is fair" (no.86).[13] Christ entered the world to give witness to the truth not to sit in judgement, to serve and not to be served. *Gaudium et Spes* spells dilemmas facing our world which is wealthy enough to alleviate most of the human suffering brought on by economic dislocations. It speaks of people still tormented by hunger and poverty and of how the Church interprets the signs of the times in the light of the Gospel. It seeks to recognize and understand the world in which we live, its expectations, its longings, and its often dramatic characteristics. *Gaudium et Spes* noted that since the 1960's ethnic and national boundaries are no longer adequate to solve global migrations of people. The pace of change has so accelerated that historical divisions prior to and following WWII have taken new dimensions. "History itself speeds along so rapid a course that an individual person can scarcely keep abreast of it. The destiny of the human community has become all of a piece, where once the various groups had a kind of private history of their own. The human race has passed from a rather static concept of reality to a more dynamic, evolutionary one" (no. 5). The impact of today's evolutionary changes upon the modern world has led to a questioning of the traditional modes of belief, particularly among our youth:

> Today's spiritual agitation and the changing conditions of life are part of a broader and deeper revolution. As a result of the latter, intellectual formation is ever increasingly based on the mathematical and natural sciences (which) are transforming the face of the earth (no. 5).

The Council adds that the denial of God or religion, or the abandonment of them, are no longer unusual occurrences. It is not rare for such denials to be presented as requirements of scientific and humanitarian progress. The Council, however, does not mention that, for centuries, the Church had not adequately addressed such problems when they arose.

TWENTIETH CENTURY CHALLENGES TO THE CHURCH'S OPPOSITION TO "MODERNISM" AND TO ITS STANDS ON OTHER SENSITIVE ISSUES

Pierre Teilhard de Chardin (1881–1955) seemed to challenge many of the underlying principles contained in the Modernist Oath. His famous *The Phenomenon of Man* (posthumously published in 1955), proposes an evolutionary human progress toward the Omega Point—a process leading to increasing levels of human interdependence.[14] Teilhard spent much of his professional life doing paleontological work in China, which culminated in his interpretation of the discovery of the Peking Man in 1936. Teilhard's most important spiritual writing, *The Divine Milieu,* emphasizes the spiritual nature of human efforts to transform the earth and build just and humane civilizations. St. Augustine had separated the City of Man and the City of God. Teilhard's spiritual vision unites the earth with the divine presence as a form of the total transformation implied in the Christ event. Teilhard calls the process by which the earth and humans are transformed *Christogenesis*—a part of the evolutionary process. Teilhard's earth-centered spirituality still inspires some contemporary theologians and spiritual writers who seek to connect the world of the Spirit with Christians' everyday life. For the eco-theologian Thomas Berry, a deep understanding of the history and functioning of the evolving universe can guide our own individual lives. Thomas Moore's *Care of the Soul* (1992) searches for a contemporary spirituality based on the ordinary experiences of life filled with wonder and grace.[15] In its effort to preserve Catholic orthodoxy, the Holy Office issued a *Monitum* in 1962.[16] (reaffirmed in 1981) that cautioned against an enthusiastic evolutionism. Fearing that Teilhard seemed to discount the Augustinian view of Original Sin, the Vatican banned publication of his works during his lifetime. In the Vatican's view, Teilhard's notion of *Noogenesis* (the evolution of thought forms in the brain) seems to provide a naturalistic rather than a supernatural explanation of religious experience. The dividing line between the natural and supernatural realms would thus be blurred or even eliminated in Teilhard's mystical vision.

There are many reasons for the contemporary malaise in European Catholicism—some go back to the Enlightenment. Others include the alleged failure of the Church to speak out forcefully against Nazism during the

Holocaust. These "reasons" have diminished the Church's moral authority among many Europeans who now view the Church as a medieval institution with little relevance to contemporary life. In the Galileo affair, Church officials, relying on outdated scientific views, opposed the new heliocentric paradigm that replaced the Aristotelian geocentric view of the universe, and placed Galileo under house arrest. Galileo was only officially rehabilitated in 1992 when John Paul II and a Commission he established expressed regret for having condemned Galileo. The Commission admitted that the condemnation had been due to a unitary concept of the world universally accepted until the dawn of the seventeenth century. It was also due to a failure to grasp that the Book of *Genesis* uses non-literal language in describing creation: It is in that historical and cultural framework, far removed from our own times, that Galileo's judges, unable to dissociate faith from an age-old cosmology, believed quite wrongly that heliocentrism (not yet definitively proven) undermined Catholic tradition, and that it was their duty to forbid its being taught. The judges' error, so clear to us today, led them to impose a disciplinary measure from which Galileo had much to suffer. The 1992 Commission report led John Paul II to recognize the Church's earlier mistake.[17] Galileo's condemnation took on mythic proportions during the Enlightenment as a symbol of the Church's opposition to the scientific spirit. Unfortunately, Vatican II's recognition of the modern world's achievements in human rights, growth of political and religious freedom, and medical breakthroughs have been compromised by other Church policies. Such policies include its opposition to the use of contraceptives in family planning. Pope Paul's 1968 encyclical, *Humanae Vitae*, crystallized opposition to Church teaching on contraception. It led to widespread dissent by theologians and Catholic laity. The Commission appointed by the pope to help clarify the issue included several Catholic lay couples. The Church's historic opposition to artificial contraception is discussed in great detail in John Noonan's *Contraception* (1965),[18] which advocated a change in the Church's teaching in this area.

In a later book,[19] Noonan shows that Catholic moral teaching has changed on several substantive moral issues such as slavery, usury and religious liberty. St. Paul, had not condemned slavery, but Vatican II declared it to be intrinsically evil. The Church's condemnation of usury by many popes and three general councils as an intrinsic evil is another relevant example. As the nature of money changed from being a medium of exchange to a necessary part of commercial enterprises in a capitalist economy, the Church changed its position based upon historical inevitabilities.

Another example of the Church's changing its position occurred with its teaching on the freedom of conscience. This freedom was rejected both by the Council of Trent and by Pius IX's *Syllabus of Errors*. In the Middle Ages and even later, many "heretics" such as Joan of Arc, Jan Hus and Savonarola—victims of the Church's Inquisition—were turned over to the secular arm for torture or death by fire. Rationalists and Protestants (such as Quakers) defended the freedom of conscience. They attacked slavery and addressed doctrinal change much earlier than did the Church.[20] Noonan has argued that a similar process of change has been occurring in the Church's teaching on divorce. According to Noonan, a development of moral doctrine continues to occur within the Church based upon changing historical-cultural circumstances and due to an evolution in human understanding about religious freedom and the marital covenant.

A crucial problem now facing the Church and other monotheistic faith traditions revolves around their ability to adapt to the intellectual and moral climate of the third millennium while respecting the core teachings essential to their mission. Judaism, Christianity and Islam share many of the same moral teachings about the dignity of human life, the sacred character of marriage and the protections that should be afforded to nascent human life, children, the elderly, the disabled and the mentally ill. These faith traditions are in the process of rethinking issues such as the sexual revolution and the feminist movement. This implies balancing women's freedom of conscience with present understandings of human sexuality for heterosexuals and homosexuals and the duties of raising children.

Many in contemporary medicine, psychiatry and the social sciences no longer consider homosexual relationships as a psychological or moral character flaw. The Church and the majority of the other monotheistic faith traditions often reaffirmed their opposition to gay marriage legislation but this position is quickly losing ground among young adults in the western world. The Church's attempts to influence civil legislation regarding marriage seems to place the Church on the side of opponents to what many perceive as a purely civil rights' issue and/or a freedom of conscience issue.

THE VATICAN II HERITAGE HAS LED TO UNEVEN RESPONSES TO PRESSING PROBLEMS: ETHICAL AND INTERFAITH PERSPECTIVES CALLING FOR CATHOLIC REFLECTION

The ambiguities of language and of the human condition affect the lives of all humans. "Give and take" means mutual concessions and compromises. This may include "exerting influence upon others" while submitting to inconveniences of various sorts. But for neoliberal capitalists that often means taking all one can get while giving as little as possible—an unchristian attitude. This led to the concentration of land ownership in the Americas, the importation of slaves into the southern USA and to indenturing serfs in Russia. Juggling between the two exigencies of give-and-take brings us to the dilemmas facing the post-Vatican II Church as exemplified in the opposed trajectories of Benedict XVI and Hans Küng after 1968. Ratzinger turned conservative and began to focus on Catholic identity and the meaning of community rather than on a Kingdom-centered theology. When in 1979, Johann Metz, the leading exponent of political theology was put at the top of the list of candidates for a post at the University of Munich, Ratzinger as Archbishop of Munich refused to confirm the nomination. Karl Rahner strongly objected to Ratzinger's move, saying that, while he himself did not always agree with Metz, his orthodoxy was unimpeachable.[21] Later, as Prefect of the Congregation for the Doctrine of the Faith (CDF), Ratzinger was cool to interfaith and liberation theology dialogues. He "crushed" progressive views or molded them into his Western theological categories. He distrusted theologians who sought to *expand* notions of truth beyond those traditionally expressed in Western theology. He turned Küng into an "outsider," no longer allowed to teach as a Catholic theologian. Küng was more concerned with dialogue among persons of good will than with winning the Vatican's approval. His theology, no longer restricted to traditionally Western presuppositions, went so far as to acknowledge atheists' moral concerns. He developed a global ethics and a Kingdom-oriented relational theology to help transnational, ethical frameworks for economic development and world trade. In our view, these "worldly" sectors are just as important as the personal spiritual issues that dominated previous eras of mission outreach. The "Declaration Toward a Global Ethics" promulgated in 1993 at the World Parliament of Religions was based largely on Küng's *Global Responsibility* and his *A Global Ethic for Global Politics and Economics*.[22] Küng's ethics and Ratzinger's stress on Catholic identity interpret Vatican II differently. We seek to bridge such differences. In the spirit of Vatican II, Küng's global ethics proposal are shared by many Catholic, ecumenically-oriented theologians. Yet, Cardinal Biffi attacked Küng's Project for a World Ethics, which argues that

1. humanity cannot survive without consensus on ethics;
2. there will be no global peace until there is peace among religions;
3. there can be no religious peace without interfaith dialogue.

Biffi claimed that Küng "empties" the Gospel message with a questionable form of ethics.[23] Failing to understand Küng's prophetic vision, Biffi seemed to have forgotten Vatican II. A crucial element of a Vatican III would be to evaluate ethical policies and to adequately distinguish between a problematical relativism and desirable forms of a global ethics. Such a distinction is not unrelated to our positive approaches to Islam and to liberation theologians' commitment to biblical justice. One must give Pope Benedict XVI his due. As a key player in Church policies on freedom within the Church and the limits of theological freedom, Benedict had to collaborate with other religions on such issues as justice, peace and life. His initial encyclical, *Deus*

Caritas Est (God is Love) has a more inclusive understanding of the Christian faith than he previously had. Shortly after his election as Pope, he invited Küng for a friendly chat. One can admire his ability to go beyond some of the stances he had taken as CDF Prefect. Still, a systematic, coordinated approach must be taken to address the problems now facing humanity. It is not enough for Vatican officials to draft policy memos. They must continually re-learn how to compromise when necessary and possible. Pope Francis has excelled in doing so.

The Parliament of World Religions brings large numbers of people to their conferences; yet, they lack grass roots activism to bring about a groundswell of social change similar to that engendered in the Civil Rights Movements of Gandhi and Martin Luther King. We face many global crises today such as climate changes, COVID-19, AIDS, migration of peoples from the developing nations to the affluent nations often done without legal papers, the growth of terrorism, conflict in the Middle East and nuclear proliferation. To address such social environmental, and political issues, the world's religious bodies must refocus their efforts beyond their own traditional faith boundaries and learn how to interact with those who share similar ethical perspectives but not similar religious beliefs.[24] Hopefully, efforts such as these can begin to mobilize the monotheistic religious communities to confront our global crises. Churches, synagogues and mosques must learn how to empower the peace process and reclaim a moral high ground for their beliefs in the service of all.

Postmodernity challenges all three monotheistic religions—none of which can afford to return to the pre-modern era without further loss of credibility. Islamic fundamentalism has damaged the credibility of the Islamic faith in most of the Western world and led to increasing suspicion of Islamic immigrants attempting to enter Europe or the USA. The perceived failure of organized Islamic religious bodies to curtail terrorist influences since 9/11 clouds Islamic claims of its basic peaceful nature. Islam has no central authority such as we find in the Catholic Church. Some attempts have been made to organize the leaders of the three monotheistic faiths to combat terrorist influences and to promote peace and justice in the Middle East and South Asia but most of these efforts have been largely symbolic and ineffectual. In the Western world, religious belief has been confined to the private sphere; beliefs have lost much of their influence other than that wielded by fundamentalist Christians and Muslims. The broad middle ground of religious adherence is moderate, peaceful and willing to respect other religious traditions. Johann Baptist Metz argued with Jürgen Habermas for a moderate post-secular modernity.[25]

Many Muslims and Christians seem to agree that Western secularism is a major obstacle to living a fully spiritual life in today's world. Conservative elements in both religions feel that postmodern secularism must be opposed.

With Küng and Metz, we take an ethical approach, if not to solve this problem, at least to confront the causes of what makes life insecure for so many people today. While many judge institutions and social practices on their ability to maximize profits and power, we seek to go beyond bottom-line considerations. The Vatican once marginalized Küng and liberation theologians. Yet, the Christian call for a loving justice is ever in need of ethical-philosophical input.

THE VATICAN II *AGGIORNAMENTO* AS AN ONGOING CHALLENGE

Unlike his predecessors Pius IX and St. Pius X, Leo XIII did not try to "resolve" the dialectical tensions between the prophetic and conservative voices in the Church. Like John XXIII who succeeded him in the Papacy 55 years later, Leo XIII understood that it was not in the Church's best interest to act[26] as a "juridical machine" operated by the bishop of Rome. Today's Tridentine Catholics want to assist at a Latin Mass sung in Gregorian music. Vatican II helped the Church leave its cultural ghetto. Unfortunately, the legacy of Vatican II has been evaluated in contradictory ways. Progressive-spiritual Catholics such as Dorothy Day, Thomas Merton, the Berrigan brothers and liturgical reformers wrote on what it means to be "The People of God." They realized that on both the local and national levels Christians should help transform the world. Conservative Catholics, however, refused to listen. Indeed, Vatican II and Pope Francis have asked Christians to engage themselves in the world so as to renew it; but to do so, one must have a renewed understandings of self and others. The tensions between the conservative and prophetic forces in the Church have limited its ability to act. How can bishops make more informed decisions on relevant solutions? The Church has continued to lose influence in the West, as recently exemplified in Spain, an historically Catholic country. In 2007, Pope Benedict XVI visited Spain and challenged the morality of the gay marriage legislation the Spanish Parliament had passed in 2005. The reality is that less than 20 percent of Spaniards now participate regularly in Church activities.

Modernism led to a Postmodernism partly rooted in Nietzsche's attempts to reject the Christian heritage. If we cannot escape our fears any more than Thompson could avoid the "Hound of Heaven," Nietzsche was hounded by a caricature of Christian morality of his own making. Rejecting Plato's concordance between beauty and truth, Nietzsche resorted to a negative notion of *ressentiment*. For him, *ressentiment* is an angry belittling of others due to one's felt "powerlessness." Christians have sought to reintegrate the psychic-moral causation Nietzsche confused. They can do so by "trans-valuing" values not through a Nietzschean confrontational view of *ressentiment*, but through the positive meaning Scheler gave it. Influenced by Scheler, Lonergan sees *ressentiment* as a re-feeling of specific clashes one may have had with others. In such a reinterpretation one learns not to belittle others but to "re-feel"[27] clashes as a means of trans-valuing negative feelings with a loving attitude. Rather than castigating love, one learns to translate Nietzsche's intense efforts to transvalue values with an equally intense attempt to live the love of Christ. In this sense, Pope Francis has prodded Christians to help one another recover the meaning of love. He realizes that it is not helpful to silence dissidents on the basis of partisan politics or of a misunderstanding of cultural dynamics. In the post-Vatican II Church, some SCC's helped members reintegrate the psychic and moral dimensions of love that Nietzsche confused. By reinterpreting *ressentiment* as a *loving re-feeling* of specific clashes, one learns to restore Christian courage to its true meaning rather than distorting it. Christians should humbly learn to discern their heart's secrets so as to respond to another's hidden truths. Rather than having a "superman" reinvent ethics, with Tillich, Teilhard, and Gabriel Marcel, one can learn in the trenches. These men's lives were that of a co-creative Christian caring for others. Our on-the-way strategy of love distances itself from Nietzsche's will to power. It reaches out humbly to Buddhists, Muslims, atheists and all people of good will.

If the Internet is a tool for both good and evil, for indifferentism or for caring love, we reflect on how SCC's may be blessed with the lived-experiences of family and friends. When so many people today are estranged from one another, a lived Christian love helps people rediscover themselves. With Nietzsche, one can refuse to judge human action on the basis of "utility." One can even accept his view that Christ was a kind of Buddha "on a soil like that of India."[28] In our effort to help bridge some of the world's conflicting views, we focus on Jesus' revolution of love. While technological revolutions speed human communication skills, these skills all too often remain on the material plane.

Our emphasis on the need for prayer means that we agree with conservatives on this point. We must take time to pray so as not to forget the tested wisdom of the ancients; but this valid insight must also take account of the Church's social doctrine, which is crucially important but often neglected in practice. If Christians honor love in the breach rather than by imitating Christ, the world will produce more critics like Marx, Nietzsche and Freud. To avoid this, we must learn to incarnate love's true meaning which cannot be imposed from above. Jesus taught us how to transvalue values through love. Christian love has had a rough going throughout history. How can the Church help the world implement Jesus' love revolution? Some 100 years after Nietzsche's "Death of God," liberation theology and SCC's began to inspire social and political reforms in Latin America. As bishop, Pope Francis had witnessed and approved of such developments in "his backyard."

Such developments show that Christian theology can evolve and respond to new situations in today's world. Jesus demands courage. Nietzsche's "Superman-claims" challenge us to respond anew to Jesus' calls for a revolution of the heart.

ADDRESSING TODAY'S UNPARALLELED SOCIAL AND TECHNOLOGICAL CHANGES

The US Civil Rights Movement was inspired by the Judeo-Christian ethic. It countered postmodernist claims that Christianity was not capable of mobilizing marginalized and segregated individuals and communities. Pope John XXIII's papacy came at a critical time. Discerning the signs of the times, Vatican II led the Church out of its fortress mentality into a dynamic new era. Its documents teem with suggestions of what is needed in a postmodernist world. It enabled the Church to intervene in a post-World War II divided world. But acknowledging the secular and religious problems confronting the world today has not meant that the Church can give answers pleasing to all. Because Vatican II's renewal agenda was such a breath of fresh air, many were unprepared for its far-reaching views. Paul VI labored to keep the Church from splitting apart due to conflicting reactions to the Council. Christians are in the world but not of it. Vatican II's process of discernment did not always result in the hoped-for fruit of selfless love; human nature keeps reasserting itself. What was meant to be a renewal of the Church often failed due to strident in-fighting. Like Pope Francis, John Paul II was a charismatic leader, open to young people and to non-Christian religions. Both have tried to reverse the decline of the Church's influence in the West. Yet, John Paul II's conservative reinterpretations of Vatican II's documents and his recentralization of authority in Rome ran counter to the hopes of those intent on social justice. He did recognize that social justice is at the core of Jesus' message, but he opposed liberation theologies. This was not a recipe for encouraging realistic dialogue with oppressors. Although he warned capitalist nations against letting the collapse of Communism blind them to the need of correcting injustices in the free market system, he seemed to rely more on spiritual solutions than practical ones. In fact, spiritual measures must be accompanied by ethical reforms lest contradictions keep haunting our world. Needless to say it is not easy to apply the message of love in our own complex situations. Hans Küng and liberation theologians opened many doors which were then shut by the Vatican. Priests and women religious who left their ministry or convents had their work cut out for them to learn what it means to be in this world but not "of" it. The need for discernment is ever with us; 55 years after Vatican II and in the face of unparalleled social and technological changes, it may be time for a Vatican III that would re-adapt the *aggiornamento*. With theologians' help, the pope and the world's bishops could evaluate what has to be done amidst constant change. How can Jesus' counsels of self-giving love be lived in our pluralistic world? Benedict XVI was more moderate than many had feared. His recognition that God is love is important. But how live a life of love today? How can we recognize the good wherever it exists? The faith of Catholics can be that of a simple wisdom such as inspired St. Teresa of Lisieux or Mother Teresa. But it is, we argue, often obscured by many beliefs that have nothing to do with faith's core and that are exploited by one-sided, dubious argumentations that seek domination rather than Christian service. Pope Francis has answered this dilemma from the very beginning of his pontificate by taking the name of the saint he wants to emulate. The Church must be poor in spirit, a Church for the poor. It must be concerned with the environment since it threatens all—primarily the poor. God is only "dead" if Christians are blind to love and fail to distinguish the primacy of faith.

FAITH-BELIEFS DISTINCTION: A KEY TO SOLVING POST VATICAN II CONTROVERSIES

The mysteries of faith are in themselves ineffable-they cannot be expressed in mere words. Yet, believers of different confessions are challenged to build bridges. The important distinction between beliefs and faith is crucial. Faith discerns the value of believing the word of religion. One appropriates one's social, cultural, religious, scientific heritage through beliefs. Scientists collaborate in research and experiments but they cannot repeat all experiments of predecessors. They have no choice to believe what predecessors have published: they believe in their validity. If scientists have no choice but to believe what they have neither the time nor the expertise to ascertain or prove for themselves, the adherents of different religions *believe* particular dogmas of their sect or Church or of an established religion both in intra-faith theologies and in interfaith dialogues. Beliefs are expressed; faith is inexpressible: it *is more* than believing—it involves commitment. Belief resembles the process of following a map. One believes what the mapmaker has outlined. This differs from faith. For Lonergan, faith is the dynamic state of being in love with God.[29] It is "the eye of love." Ordinarily, one loves a person because he/she feels that the person is good or attractive. But with faith, one falls in love with God who is love. Faith is the gift of God's love: it goes beyond and underlies any form of belief. Due to the love that informs it, faith (which transcends beliefs) can unite believers of different creeds prompting them to respect one another. When informed with faith and love, conflicting beliefs can be approached so as to minimize divisions. Only a loving faith can unite believers from different creeds for faith and love transcends human limitations.

Orthodox Jews, Christians and Muslims have conflicting agendas inasmuch as they rely solely on traditional interpretations of their traditions. While many forms of beliefs lead to intolerance—even to terrorism—faith and love are not divisive; rather, they seek to overcome divisiveness. They strive to preserve whatever is good in one's tradition. In the spirit of Vatican II we acknowledge the primacy of faith and love over divisive beliefs. Just as Francis of Assisi enabled the Church to see in nature Brother Sun and Sister Moon and to live the Gospel message anew, so ecclesial structures are now being proposed that might enable us to live our faith in ways that meet today's secularist exigencies. As did the early Church and as did the mendicant orders in the thirteenth century, so today Pope Francis is calling Christians to minister to one another—possibly in small communities. Such communities can lovingly reflect on and address both local and global problems. As we have noted, the modernist views of Tyrrell and those of the postmodernists influenced Vatican II. Implementing a loving justice today demands that we engage in many forms of dialogue. Let us touch on current "faith tendencies" in Christianity that either foster or oppose moderately progressive Christian approaches.

EXEMPLIFYING OPPOSED FAITH-BELIEF APPROACHES TO RELIGION

Vatican II's sixteen documents were all compromises between the progressive and traditional bishops and theologians who drafted these documents. The documents were only approved by John XXIII and Paul VI after much open and behind-the scenes debates. Like the books of the Bible and Church teachings, the Vatican II documents all underwent much editing. Debates and powerplays still occur in the Church. Let us compare two opposed programs, that of the Opus Dei American bishop Robert Finn and that of the progressive Protestant pastor Brian McLaren who admires Catholicism's insistence on Church unity. A leader in the Emerging Church movement, McLaren appeals to those disenchanted with a dogmatic Christianity. *The National Catholic Reporter* (May 12, 2006) reported that when Finn was installed as bishop of Kansas City, he began to dismantle programs fostered by several of his predecessors. That diocese, beginning with Bishop Edwin O'Hara (1939–56) had been a model of progressive Catholicism. O'Hara and his successors had anticipated some of Vatican II's teachings in the liturgy, social justice and involvement of the laity. One of bishop Finn's failures was the disastrous way he handled clergy sex abuse cases. During and prior to his tenure (2005–15) there had been 94 cases filed against the diocese. He was found guilty of failing to report these cases. In 2015 Pope Francis accepted his early resignation. We argue with Pope Francis that Catholicism should foster lay involvement in Church affairs in non-divisive ways. Secularism can indeed be a problem for the Church, but it is an abuse of authority to highjack issues to push a reactionary agenda or to restrict Catholics' legitimate spheres of action.[30] Questionable from the other end of the spectrum are those who would water down the Christian message in the false conviction that this is only way to be relevant today. While faith unites Christians, beliefs can and do divide them. Many Evangelicals fault McLaren for allegedly wanting to integrate postmodernist thought in ways that short-circuit the Gospel. For our part, we do not reject dogmas. The question is what is the role of dogma today? Here the faith-belief distinction is important. Christians should act justly based on their faith. Beliefs should not divide us.

This is why we argue for a middle position between conservatives clinging to their beliefs instead of reaching out in loving faith as does McLaren. McLaren and Finn embody the opposite sides of progressive-conservative spectrum. Non-judgmentally, one may say that both men are earnest Christians driven by their own divergent spiritual journeys. Are Catholics in a given diocese to be forced to live with a bishop's fortress mentality? A Catholic middle way would enable the laity to act responsibly in Church affairs. It would mediate between the past while being open to the future. Can the churches be a salt of the earth, a light to the world? How can individual Catholics who feel rejected by the preponderance of conservative bishops appointed for "toeing the line" continue their ministry of seeking peace through justice? How can they best enlighten the hearts and minds of fellow Christians and reach out to all people of good will—as Vatican II urged them to do? At the beginning of a new millennium, the world is facing profound social, economic and technological changes. How can Christians best respond to the many problems humanity faces? Pope Leo XIII led the way to better understand Scripture and Tradition. Pope Francis has been re-adapting Leo's initiatives to our present situation.

STRATEGIC CONCLUSION TO CHAPTER 4

We speak of faith as informed by love and open to all good as taught in the Gospel and interpreted by the Church. This is what guided Pope John XXIII. Unlike Pope John who trusted in the Spirit despite human weakness and the rise of a materialism, some would like to re-impose a Catholicism entrenched within its traditions—never mind Vatican II. What are Kingdom-Catholics to do in such situations? In our view, John Paul II gave groups such as Opus Dei a decided advantage in the Church. He used the Synod of Bishops to recentralize Church authority. He preached hope but seemed to trust only the hopes fitting his own vision. Part III will examine how Vatican II empowered the Church to implement the papacy's labor encyclicals as well as the means to pursue dialogue with people of good will. Much of Christian morality as outlined in the Gospels cannot be directly applied to public affairs. Christian ideals must be mediated through viable Church structures—not micromanaged by Vatican officials. It is to Pope Francis' credit that he realizes this and has acted on his convictions. How could a Vatican III Council reinforce Pope Francis' initiatives so as to redress missed opportunities? How can new effective bridges be erected that would help meet the needs of the poor in our age?

NOTES

1. Garry Wills, *Papal Sin: Structures of Deceit* (New York, Doubleday, 2000), 241, writes that Pius IX was influenced in his selecting 85 theses to be condemned by a French bishop who had censured Lammenais.

2. www.papalencyclicals.net/Pius09/p9syll.htm. Cited 7/13/06. Pius IX's proclamation of the Immaculate Conception in 1854 was criticized by Protestants as "Mariolatry."

3. George Tyrrell, *Tradition and the Critical Spirit*, ed. James Livingston (Minneapolis: Fortress Press, 1991), 93.

4. http://people.bu.edu/wwildman/WeirdWildWeb/courses/mwt/dictionary/mwt_themes_692_loisy.htm. *Boston Collaborative Encyclopedia of Modern Western Theology*. Cited 7/13/06).

5. Pope Leo XIII's encyclical, *Providentissimus Deus*, (1893) encouraged Catholics to study the Bible in accord with the latest linguistic and historical sciences while still honoring the inspiration of the Holy Spirit in their composition.

6. Popes John XXIII, Paul VI, John Paul II and Francis have all written encyclicals encouraging dialogue with the modern world with its scientific, technological and economic implications. Beginning especially with Leo XIII, the papacy became an agent of mediation in international situations and for humanitarian causes. Today the papacy remains one of the few proponents of multilateralism and of the role of international organizations. This is partly due to the complications of the First Vatican Council, to the Vatican's loss of Rome in September 1870 and the Holy See's being one of the few global actors that remembers the dark lessons of the twentieth century. See "The "Importance of Papal Diplomacy" by Massimo Faggioli, Feb. 4, 2020.

7. On the biases, Lonergan, *Insight*, (1958) 218–44. The "general bias of common sense combines with group bias" to prevent a valid "dialectic of community" (226). See also John Raymaker and Godefroid Alekiabo Mombula, *Bringing Bernard Lonergan Down to Earth and into our Hearts and Communities* (Eugene, OR: Wipf & Stock, 2018).

8. Brian Greene, *The Fabric of the Cosmos* (New York: Knopf, 2004), 5.

9. Arthur Peacocke, *Paths From Science Towards God* (Oxford: One World, 2002), 80. Gaianism grants the Earth (*Gaia*) its rightful place as a center. It denies that humans are the pinnacle of evolution: they are just a small, inessential part of life on earth.

10. Postmodernism has promoted relativism and discontinuity with the past. The Church should help us recover our sense of identity as well as a new viable multiculturalism.

11. Walter Ong, *The Presence of the Word: Some Prolegomena for Cultural and Religious History* (New Haven: Yale Press) 1967, 112, 314 argues that through the Middle Ages "visualism" was important but was raised to a new prominent intensity with the invention of alphabets. This led to conditionings of human consciousness by media that accentuate sound. Ong sought to help humans understand the anthropological functions of *feelings and valuing*—a process much needed in Western culture.

12. With the Protestant Reformation, rulers began to impose their religious views on their subjects. Church influence began to wane.

13. *Pastoral Constitution on the Church in the Modern World*, pages 200–01.

14. *Vedanta's saccidnanda* bliss consciousness "corresponds" to Teilhard's Omega point; see Bede Griffiths, *A New Vision of Reality: Western Science, Eastern Mysticism and Christian Faith* (Springfield, IL: Templegate, 1989) 92.

15. Philosophies of emergence seek to integrate evolution within a transcendent directionality through Teilhard's understanding of consciousness' transformative power within cosmic evolutionary processes. Ian G. Barbour's *Religion and Science: Historical and Contemporary Issues* (Harper, 1997) writes: "Teilhard objects to the separation of sacred and secular realms. Christ is presented not as an intrusion into the world but as the continuation and fulfilment of a long cosmic preparation. For Teilhard, the purpose of the incarnation was not primarily the remedial work of atoning for sin, but the constructive work of uniting all reality and bringing it to union with God" (248). In *The Universe is a Green Dragon: a Cosmic Creation Story* (Santa Fe: Bear, 1984), Brian Swimme argues that the powers of nature such as fire and tornadoes reveal the cosmic dynamic of "self-organizing" activity.

16. Emile Rideau, *The Thoughts of Teilhard de Chardin* (New York: Harper & Row) 1967, 251, examines problems in Teilhard's thought. For Rideau, Teilhard sought the purity of the Gospel with a correspondence between grace and nature but his *The Phenomenon of Man*, does not address sin or the beyond.—only focusing on what lies ahead.

17. *L'Osservatore Romano*, November 1, 1992.

18. *Humanae Vitae* was a turning point in the faithful's acceptance of Church teaching. See John Noonan, *Contraception* (Harvard University, 1965).

19. John Noonan, *The Development of Catholic Moral Teaching* (Notre Dame University, 2005)

20. *America*, April 25, 2005.

21. David Gibson, *The Rule of Benedict* (San Francisco: Harper) 2006, 177.

22. Küng's Global Ethic Foundation, www.weltethos.org/dat eng/index3_e.htm

23. *Japan Catholic News* (Nov., 1991).

24. In par. 139 of *Laudato Si*, Pope Francis writes: "We are faced not with two separate crises, one environmental and the other social, but rather with one complex crisis which is both social and environmental." In par. 161 he says: "Doomsday predictions can no longer be met with irony or disdain." This would be a prime topic for a Vatican III.

25. www.researchgate.net/publication/264579719_A_Post-Secular_Modernity_Jurgen_Habermas_Joseph_Ratzinger_and_Johann_Baptist_Metz_on_Religion_Reason_and_Politics. 9/11 caused Jurgen Habermas to revise his stand on secularism. In 2004, he used the term "postsecular" to describe what modern society ought to be. 9/11 caused him to reflect on society's moral foundations; he argued that religious convictions are not the nonsense that philosophy long portrayed them to be (*New York Times* Magazine, April 7, 2007, 8). If many Europeans view secularism as being anti-Christian, we appeal to theologies of secularization that would offset Islamic objections to Western decadence.

26. After an unfortunate diplomatic stint, Pecci (Leo XIII's family name) had been exiled for 32 years to Perugia as bishop. As Pope, he promoted Catholic Biblical studies and revived the study of Aquinas. Among other Popes named Leo, two had deepened the divide between Eastern and Western Churches. Leo III, alienated Orthodoxy by crowning Charlemagne (800) and by accepting the *Filioque* clause. Leo IX presided over the East-West schism (1054). Unlike the latter two, Leo XIII laid seeds for developments that were mirrored in Vatican II's openness to both Orthodoxy and modernity.

27. Manfred Frings, Max Scheler (Duquesne University, 1965) Ch. 5. Lonergan, *Method*, 33.

28. Nietzsche, *Antichrist* (New York: Penguin, 1968, 31); *Genealogy of Morals* and *Ecce Homo* (one cover: New York: Vintage, 1989) 17. Nietzsche errs in focusing on Christendom, not on a faith, which seeks to free humans. One is often limited to one's perspectival view of things. Since one looks at reality from one's own cultural experience, it is not easy to enter into the equally but diverse limited experience of others. This also applies in all human interactions. Nietzsche, at first a friend and admirer of Richard Wagner, later turned against

him because of Wagner's later embrace of Christian ideals. Nietzsche opposed nationalism and conformism as well as Christianity. We situate Nietzsche within the perspective of love that he misdiagnosed. The first two *Avenger* films directed by atheist Joss Whedon would reverse Christ's redemptive role espoused by C. S. Lewis. The Russo brothers' 2018 *Avenger* film is more balanced; both Russo brothers are proud of their family Catholic heritage and of the faith that nurtured them.

29. We might have titled this book "Mapping a Map of Love" for it maps transformative aspects of Christian love. Being prone to tunnel visions, we often get so wrapped in one aspect of reality that we dismiss other aspects. Virtues that enable to use our strengths so as to deal with our weaknesses can us help transform the world with God's justice. For the faith-belief distinction, Lonergan relied on W. Cantwell Smith.

30. Bishop Gumbleton, long-time auxiliary bishop of Detroit, fought the pre-Vatican II types of control which were re-imposed upon bishops—again diminishing their roles.

Part III

Principles and Strategies for the Church to Help Us Bridge Our Divides

Part I explored the challenges of globalization and secularism. Part II argued that, due to its hasty reactions to the problems of Modernism, the Church was handicapped in responding to twentieth century problems. Vatican II did much to redress the handicap, but the long-ingrained forms of traditional Church structures and teaching almost guaranteed that not all would fully accept the *aggiornamento*. The Post-Vatican II Church's inability to convince all believers occurred despite (perhaps because of) the fact that the Council used scriptural sources to adapt Tradition and recommend new courses of ecclesial action. Recalling how the hearts of the disciples on their way to Emmaus had burned upon hearing the words of the risen Lord, part III seeks to give some answers to the problems posed in parts I and II. It explores interfaith and ecumenical contexts that might rekindle the hearts of today's faithful. It starts with chapter 5's focus on God's Kingdom. It asks how new bridges can be erected to mediate earthly realities. We answer that question, by recalling two of our underlying emphases. The first is our appeal to mystics' deeper views into reality; the second is that of an overarching synergetic potential for human cooperation in philosophy and science.

Religion is controversial, but it can be made less so when common mystic realities are understood and lived. To highlight the human potential for a spiritual synergy across human ideological divides, we appeal to theorists such as Teilhard de Chardin and Lonergan who manage to reconcile the principles of science, philosophy and spirituality. We build on their insights so as to help the Church again transform humanity by devising viable, authentic forms of community. We do so by reassessing the perspectives that have guided both the Church and political entities. A possible Vatican III Council could help people transcend the misunderstandings that arise from human biases, ethnocentrism and ideologies—or due to unexpected changes. The latter can result in people being traumatized as illustrated in *Don Quixote*. The disciples on the Way to Emmaus, on the other hand, had their faith renewed upon encountering the Risen Lord.

Chapter Five

Liberation Theology in the Light of Scripture and Justice Issues

A cause of dissension in the Post-Vatican II Church has been the way liberation theologians interpret the Gospel to overcome social injustices in such places as Latin America. This chapter gives a background for grounding liberation theology in Kingdom-of-God scriptural teachings. It outlines the scriptural sources of social justice issues now confronting the Church—issues it cannot ignore if it is to remain faithful to the Gospel. We examine some biblical texts and teachings of the early Church that may be relevant to how we can minister to the global community today.

SOME HISTORICAL EVENTS AFFECTING CHRISTIAN VIEWS OF CHURCH AND STATE

Were Jesus and the early churches a success story? Answers to this question depend on what one means by success. Jesus brought judgment on worldly criteria of success and was condemned for it. If success is achieving what one plans, then Christians can only say that God is in the planning. Perceptive people have helped Christians discern how to do God's will. Still, questions arise as to how this can happen—based on what criteria?

The search for the historical Jesus is filled with the minefields of theological, historical and factional controversies. Many fanciful theories about Jesus have been advanced. Some purport that he was "married" with Mary Magdalene or that he established a "dynasty." What is certain is that we cannot retrieve Jesus' "real" words; nor can we ascertain what deeds Jesus actually performed. He did leave a large imprint on the sands of time, but we cannot accurately recover the chronology in his life. Controversy also rages about the type of Church Jesus founded and the mission he gave it. What did Jesus say about his own ministry? How did he instruct his disciples on ministering to others including the poor and oppressed? What does it mean that he would be with us "until the end of time"? To answer such questions we must recall the circumstances under which the Gospels and the rest of the New Testament were written and interpreted by the early generations of believing Christians. Today's mainline scripture scholars and theologians tend to agree that the three Synoptic Gospels offer us a credible interpretation of what Jesus said and did. John offers us a profound reflection on how we might live Jesus' message of Christian love—despite political intrigues and unjust social systems.

The first three centuries of Christianity, marked by persecutions, were the time when Christians fashioned the canon of Scripture and the Church Fathers began to interpret the Word of God—giving birth to the Christian traditions still affecting believers today. For more than a millennium after the Emperor Constantine legitimated it, Christianity molded much of European thought and politics. Constantinople[1] broke from Rome only to fall to the Ottoman Turks in 1453. This was followed by Luther's Reformation and other divisions. In the face of religious intolerance, English seekers of religious freedom such as the Puritans and Quakers established colonies in North America. In the meantime, the Renaissance and Enlightenment led to today's secularist ethic. Long before such developments in the Protestant and secular worlds, the Church had been influenced by the personal piety and initiatives of religious orders. Early in the thirteenth century, the Franciscan and Dominican orders helped instill new life in the Church. Committed to the common good, these orders sought to meet people's everyday needs, urging them to return to evangelical ideals and to educate future generations.

The Church has during the past four centuries given birth to new initiatives such as that of the Jesuits in sixteenth century. Saint Ignatius Loyola demanded obedience from his Jesuits but also gave them an enviable freedom in their work. The Jesuits showed great initiative in addressing all sorts of problems. Other religious and missionary orders from the West sent men and women overseas to preach the Good News. The missionary effort gave rise to heroic deeds but also to questionable cooperation with colonial regimes. "Giving to Caesar what is Caesar's, and to God what belongs to God" helped extend the Church worldwide. This involved preparing native leaders in Africa, Asia and in the Americas; but missionary endeavors also embroiled the Church in questionable forms of paternalism. Despite the wars in Europe and the miseries of the Industrial Revolution, the Church began to defend the rights of workers and the common good. Sound Christian policies and effectively implementing them, however, can sometimes clash. One notes, for instance, that nominally Christian nations were often complicit in the evils of colonialism, the exploitations of the Industrial Revolution and the atrocities of the two World Wars. Vatican II was pastoral in nature. It reflected on the complex movements in history and gave us guidelines to integrate the positive movements of the recent past so as to face today's secularist tendencies. It reaffirmed Christians' duty to practice the type of justice Jesus himself preached and modelled in his public ministry. In *Laudato Si*, Pope Francis reflects deeply on such issues. The basic problem, he writes

> Is the way that humanity has taken up technology and its development according to an undifferentiated and one-dimensional paradigm. This paradigm exalts the concept of a subject who, using logical and rational procedures, progressively approaches and gains control over an external object. This subject makes every effort to establish the scientific and experimental method, which in itself is already a technique of possession, mastery and transformation. It is as if the subject were to find itself in the presence of something formless, completely open to manipulation (106).

SOCIAL JUSTICE IN THE BIBLE—POPE FRANCIS' RADICAL EMBRACE OF JUSTICE AND LOVE

Our world is vastly different from that of biblical times; still, Christians must ever go back to Jesus' Gospel. The meaning of God's revelation in the Prophets, in the Psalms, gospels and other biblical writings has provoked much debate. From the Synoptic Gospels and from St. John's prayerful reflection on Jesus' message, we come to understand how radical Jesus' teaching of altruistic love is; he came to set the world on fire. Having understood that God is love, we are to learn to love our neighbor as one's self; we are to share that loving message with non-believers. Such love implies that we be just and that we act justly to bring about a durable peace. There can be no peace as long as structural injustice prevails. Christian social justice proceeds from the ideal of Jesus' all-consuming love. Too often, we manage to forget or tone down the implications of Jesus' radical message. It seems too hot to handle. As has happened throughout history, anyone who truly believes in that message of love and acts on it must be ready to pay a great price. Spiritual writers and theologians help us develop the patience and other virtues needed to love. Ideally, Church leaders are to interpret Jesus' message so that it may bear fruit in our personal lives, in our parishes and dioceses or in the Church as a whole. But as with colonialism or the Industrial Revolution, Christian practice often fails to match not just the difficult ideals Jesus gave us, but even the more practical policies the Church has evolved to bring the ideals closer to reality. We are called to reflect on such painful realities and to offer constructive, prayerful alternatives that can be realized by earnest Christians open to truth wherever it may be found. Christian ministry begins first with one's immediate situation: the Church helps us extend it to the whole world.

Jesus was crucified due to his fearless denunciation of social evils. Pope Francis has shed light on the type of Christian ethical teachings needed today to help us act justly. What would Jesus say and do in the face of a technologically advanced world confronted with pressing ethical dilemmas such as an increasingly unequal distribution of wealth? Jesus enjoins us to love one another and to be willing to pay the price of such love. We believers in Jesus' word have found his pearl of great price; too often, we choose to bury the pearl. The crucifix is a powerful symbol. We cannot escape its symbolic implications. Yet, too often, we recoil from paying the price of love. For many, love remains an ideal; individualism and materialism prevail. Living the Gospel is tolerated—provided it does not rock the boat of the pursuit of wealth. The Church does not reject new technologies provided they do not impede the living of Jesus' message of love. Pope Francis reminds us that genuine Christians know that love must be pursued even in the face of opposition. He has been calling us to live Jesus' radical message of love. He has learned from St. Francis that being rich can impede one's following of Christ. His inviting world leaders and young people to come together at the Vatican in May, 2020 to discuss the theme "Reinventing the Global Educational Alliance" is in the spirit of overcoming human antagonisms and to restore anew the fabric of ethical relationships.

GOING BACK TO JESUS TO RE-CENTER ON THE KINGDOM OF GOD

Joseph Grassi has drawn the implications of Jesus' message of love based on justice.[2] This message was variously anticipated in the Old Testament such as in the Book of Deuteronomy which outlined ways to eliminate poverty in Israel—as illustrated in the great central prayer of Judaism known as the *Shema Israel:*

> Hear, O Israel: The Lord is our God, the Lord alone. You shall love the Lord your God with all your heart, and with all your soul, and with all your strength. Keep these words that I am commanding you today in your heart (6:4–6).

Jesus made these words his own and enjoined them on his followers. As the Jews had to fear the Lord and keep all his decrees, so must Christians honor Yahweh who is mindful of all believers. The prophet Isaiah spoke of God's covenant with the king as "son of God." This theme is taken up again in Psalm 72 that implores that the king's son "may defend the cause of the poor." When the chosen people underwent the great crisis of the exile in Babylon in 587 B. C., the prophet Ezekiel once again examined the implications of God's covenant with his people. He wondered whether God had abandoned his people and worried that some of his fellow Israelites might be tempted to come to terms with Babylon's victorious gods. Then he had the vision of a chariot of fire coming down from the sky propelled by four living creatures which seemed "to symbolize God's presence in all living creatures, whether humans, wild beasts (lion), domestic animals (ox), or birds (eagle)" (Grassi, 57). This was an assurance that God was in all creation, not just in the Temple of Jerusalem. The chariot symbolized that God could move in any direction. Above the heads of the creatures loomed a crystal sky. God's glory dwelt in a fiery cloud (Ez 1:1–26). Ezekiel realized that God's presence was not limited to the Ark of the Covenant. God was also with his people in their exile. Ezekiel heard God's voice commanding him to eat a scriptural scroll which was as sweet as honey. Eating the scroll symbolized that the external sign of God's word would enter his heart and become part of his whole being. Ezekiel helped the people receive God's word in their hearts. Grassi stresses that it is not sufficient to hear the word of God and then "just do it." "The Torah and the Prophets . . . are opposite sides of the same coin of God's revelation and need one another" (73). God listened to the cries of a suffering people and delivered them. The Wisdom literature is in search of a successful life, but it implies a listening-and-observing attitude. God "is the model of one who listens and feels the oppression his people" (74).

When the Bible presents the young King Solomon as an idealized model for searchers after wisdom, it again speaks of a listening heart that informs an understanding mind. It is from this quality that flows Solomon's legendary wisdom such as that the judgment he makes in discerning who is the true mother of a child claimed by two women. All of Israel "stood in awe of the king, because they perceived that the wisdom of God was in him, to execute justice (1 Kgs 3:28). It would be naive to overlook the fact that Solomon's reign is often interpreted in the form of political legitimization. Scholars note that his reign was marked by a great literary movement that wrote down oral tradition in ways favorable to the King. In fact, Solomon rejected much of the earlier covenantal political theology in favor of dynastic power in Israel.

As Constantine later legitimized Christianity at a cost to its core message, so had the era of Solomon legitimized a reign at the risk of rejecting the teaching of the prophets. We are touching here on a constant temptation on the part of entrenched interests to use religion for their own agenda. The documents of Vatican II were all compromises between conservative and progressive forces. Theologians of left and right interpret the Vatican II documents in their own light. A wise reading of the Bible and of Vatican II documents demands that we not overlook the temptation of legitimizing one's prejudices. To be truly spiritual people, we must have listening hearts and be open to the nuances of texts as they apply in our complex situation. The Church can be weakened from within and threatened from without.

Its structures are not an end in themselves; they are legitimate when they help promote Kingdom-oriented policies or when they facilitate the Church's mission of raising servants of the gospel. Churchgoers are tempted to flee from the world's problems—they can even be complicit in abetting political regimes that favor their own interests. Jesus calls all Christians to live out the beatitudes lest they deserve a "woe be unto you" for failing to first seek the Kingdom of God by living just lives.

What makes the New Testament "new" is its return to the core of Torah justice as preached by the prophets. Each evangelist has his own perspective in interpreting Jesus' life. The four Gospels were "edited." The earliest of the four canonical Gospels is that of Mark. It is also the "most naive." Matthew and Luke reflect on Mark, using among other texts the lost "Q-source." John, the last of the written canonical gospels is a studied reflection on the events in Jesus' life. If in Mark, the superior, sinless Jesus lets himself be baptized by the inferior John the Baptist, without any theological explanation, Matthew, Luke and John give theological reflections to account for this anomaly (169).

For Mark, writing shortly after the Romans' violent destruction of the Holy Land when Christians were expecting the imminent return of Jesus, the task was that of breaking down the Roman Empire's walls. The time perspective in Matthew is different from Mark's. By the time Matthew wrote, Christians had ceased expecting Jesus' imminent return. Jesus' parables in Matthew involve delay. In the parable of the ten bridesmaids, they all go out to meet the bridegroom, but as he "was delayed, all of them became drowsy and slept" (25:5). In other Matthean parables, the time of God's future intervention is uncertain. Matthew directs his Gospel to an affluent audience, but he insists over and over again on a more perfect justice than that of Scribes and Pharisees. In Matthew, Jesus makes it clear that he had come to fulfill the Law and the Prophets. God is the liberator of the oppressed. Jesus makes the Shema Israel and the Old Testament's commandment to love God and neighbor cornerstones of his own teaching. The radical core of Jesus' message of love is enjoined in his parting commandment to "go and make disciples of all nations . . . and to teach and obey everything" he commanded (Mt. 28:19–20). If Matthew "has gone as far as justice will go in imitating God's equal distribution of his gifts" (Grassi, 179), Luke goes further. While Matthew tells his hearers to "Love your enemies and pray for those who persecute you (5:44), Luke adds "Do good to those who hate you, bless those who persecute you, pray for those who abuse you" (6:27–28). More than the other gospels, Luke emphasizes *metanoi*a (repentance) as the root of justice. Luke is also associated with the writing of the Acts of the Apostles. In the opening chapter of Acts, the risen Jesus explains how the good news will spread to the world. "You will receive power when the Holy Spirit has come upon you; and you will be my witnesses in Jerusalem, in all Judea and Samaria, and to the ends of the earth" (Acts, 1:8). Luke's parable of the Prodigal Son illustrates a central theme of Christian life beckoning all Christians to reach out to the lost and marginalized.

In the Gospel of John we find ideal models for new relationships (Grassi, 208). John does not emphasize the in-groups among Jesus' disciples. Matthew had made Peter the first among the twelve. In Mark, only Peter, James and John witnessed the transfiguration. John does not even refer to a group called apostles. Jesus sends all his disciples without distinction: "As the Father has sent me, so I send you" (John 20:21). The dominant theme in John's Gospel is love. The first Epistle of John was written to counteract gnostic-oriented Christians who taught that Jesus had only appeared to be really human. That epistle stresses the concrete incarnational reality of Jesus and his love for us. John's writings advocate justice in human relationships. They portray women as active, innovative ministers of the Kingdom. In John's Gospel, Jesus tells us that in his Father's house there are many mansions. Sadly, conservatives and progressives in the post-Vatican II Church seldom listen to one another. There are many reasons why the world today is polarized, including the rich-poor divide, competitiveness amidst the many demands of life, a dogmatic secularism. When too much wealth is concentrated in the hands of a few, Gospel ideals are merely given lip service. Jesus illustrated the Church' mission with such simple parables as those of the lost sheep, a lost drachma which bring great joy when found. His parables tend to set our usual "priorities" on their head.

In studying the various emphases of the four canonical Gospels, the early Church as well as scholars have had to decide what comes from Jesus himself. To answer this question, we must not forget that the four Gospels are all suffused with the Easter faith of the early Church. If these Gospels are a product of faith and of Church approval, we must not go to the other extreme and haphazardly pick and choose what appeals to our fancy (as do some popular books on Jesus). There are criteria of historicity that study the validity of certain passages in the gospels. In his *A Marginal Jew*, John Meier notes that for Judaism, Jesus is "marginal" to its own faith. But, the first Christian believers acknowledged Jesus as the son of God, the one who had come into the world to redeem it. Jesus, though marginal to his own people, instituted a world movement to empower the marginalized and downtrodden. With Pope Francis, we seek to develop the Gospel foundations for empowering others. Locating the privileged or marginal position at which one stands is a first step toward clarifying how one may best live the Christian message today.

NOT IGNORING THE RELIGIOUS-CULTURAL DIMENSIONS THAT HAVE LED TO SECTARIAN VIOLENCE

Globalization has affected both the world's economy and the nature of religious experience in all parts of the world. It is primarily an economic phenomenon, but it has had important religious and cultural dimensions that have exacerbated today's sectarian violence. Thomas Friedman, an influential writer on globalization, has tended to ignore the religious dimensions that affect globalization. On his speaking tours, he is often asked such questions as "Is God in cyberspace?" Or "Where does Jesus fit in?"[3] The best answer he can muster to such questions revolves around the symbol of an olive tree which suggests the rootedness of community that people need and want. In past centuries, the major spiritual traditions of the West such as Judaism and Christianity, existed within a kind of cocoon of their own making. This protected them from the historical forces that developed outside of their protective covering of religious creeds, moral code and liturgy. Many of the strongest Jewish and Catholic communities were centered in ethnic enclaves of Russian, Poles, Irish and Italian immigrants who brought to the New World a fervent devotion to their ancestral faiths. Such communal cultures that newly arriving ethnic groups brought to the American heartland stood in contrast to the more individualistic white Anglo-Saxon Protestant culture. Jews and Catholics were often met with hostility by the Nativist Movements of the nineteenth century. This culminated in the re-emergence of the Ku Klux Klan in the first two decades of the twentieth century. The Church's mission is to reach out to the marginalized and invite them to the table of eucharistic fellowship. If it fails to do so, it becomes countersign of Gospel imperatives.

THE VATICAN'S REACTIONS TO THE INFLUENCE OF LIBERATION THEOLOGIES

We have been arguing that a Vatican III Council could help the Church better live out the message of Christ in the modern world. This would include recalling its humble roots as servant of the poor—a path Pope Francis has clearly advocated. What ideological factors affect the global, local and personal levels of our lives or the attitudes of the proponents and opponents of liberation theology? Biased attitudes often distort peoples' perceptions.

Vatican II was prophetic when it laid paths for overcoming biases—beginning with our own. In adapting the Gospel to today's needs, some modifications in our attitudes toward capitalism may be in order. A central element of the Church's social justice teaching is that "various legitimate though conflicting views can be held concerning the regulation of temporal affairs" (Vatican II, *Gaudium et Spes*, 75). The Church's stance on liberation theology seems to have coursed through the two horns of the capitalist dilemma: one should resist injustice, but most people are motivated by self-interest. Capitalists must be moral as they create jobs and make a profit. Since there are various legitimate, but conflicting interests, the Church strives to mitigate greed in the light of clear evangelic directives on the Kingdom of God. Too often, people are treated merely as consumers—an insidious error in need of spiritual enlightenment. The Church is to be an instrument for ushering in God's Kingdom but it has not always been willing to confront the facts of marginalization in society. In Medieval Europe, it tolerated the practices of a leisured, militaristic aristocracy. Only belatedly, did it denounce colonialist and capitalist abuses both of which influenced socialist criticisms of Western civilization. We shall not try here to address the many tensions between Adam Smith's *laissez-faire* capitalism and Karl Marx's denunciation of such.[4] Popes since Leo XIII and Vatican II have stressed the need for social justice. The Church tolerates capitalism but warns of its excesses; it has defended workers and their right to unionize but condemned a communist ideology based on historical materialism and loss of liberties. On the other hand, the Church's authoritative social doctrine was all too often ignored in "Catholic" South America. This led to liberation theology and the practice of basic communities that reflected on the marginalized poor so as to raise their consciousness as to oppression. The world's bishops assembled at a Vatican III Council in consultation with the many experts on the subject could address distributive justice. What partly gave birth to liberation theology are the appalling conditions of the poor in Latin America's so-called Catholic societies. Why did not that "Christianized" continent give rise to a more just society? Giving more than lip service to the Gospel would have led to more just societies and not necessitated the rise of a liberation theology. In the twentieth century, Latin American liberation theologians found conditions[5] on their continent as appalling as had Karl Marx in Europe a century earlier. Because it sided with the poor but was not clear as to the use violence or Marxist principles, liberation theology was controversial in the Vatican until Pope Francis gave it new life. It has sought to apply the faith by aiding the poor and oppressed through involvement in the political process. Its opponents allege that it ignores liberation from sin. If those of the ruling and leisure classes tout their faith by saying we must first be liberated from sin, how can one help the poor by applying Christian principles to combat the sins that gave rise to unjust structures?

Leonardo Boff, a foremost exponent of liberation theology, argues in his *Liberating Grace* that theology must address social injustices and the fate of the poor. Grace is "the ability to escape the evil that lurks as a possibility in the epistemological status of science. It means overcoming the temptation to self-enclosure."[6] Boff lucidly explains the roles of science and technology in modern society; they are powerful tools in need of grace on the part of users. He sees Latin America's situation of dependence and underdevelopment[7] as due to the enormities of "social and structural sin" (84) responsible for that situation. One must consider both the personal and structural levels at which sin and grace affect the human condition. In 1985, Cardinal Ratzinger issued a "notification" on Boff's book, *Church: Charisma and Power*, alleging that it is "dangerous." He silenced Boff for a year. Already, in 1984, Ratzinger had targeted Boff and Gustavo Gutierrez, the founder of liberation theology, in its first "Instruction on Certain Aspects of the 'Theology of Liberation.'" Boff was supported by Cardinal Arns of Sao Paulo and by other progressive Brazilian bishops who saw strong ties between a spiritual liberation from sin and a liberation from social ills. Ratzinger's Notification denounced liberation theology as "a perversion of the Christian message as God entrusted it to His church." Due to outcries against the Notification, Pope John Paul II directed Ratzinger to issue a more moderate "Instruction on Christian Freedom and Liberation." Ratzinger sought to outmaneuver "liberation theology by providing an orthodox theory of liberation based on personal conversion rather than reforming sinful structures."[8] The silencing of "dissidents" by authoritarian regimes is a nasty business. In the Church, deprived of its former ways of enforcing its views through tribunals, the silencing of dissidents has taken a more subdued form. Yet, such silencing inhibits the Church's primary mission of establishing God's Kingdom. Jesus spoke of the mustard seed to symbolize the spread of the Kingdom. Unfortunately, before the advent of Pope Francis many Church prophets were reprimanded—including Gutierrez, Boff and Sobrino. "First seeking the Kingdom of God" is a Gospel imperative. While the aftermath of Vatican II led to tensions in the Church, it is the Church's duty to help unite the faithful in serving the Kingdom and addressing injustices. Since the Church and individual Christians are ever "on the way," they must take time to reflect on how to share the Eucharistic proclaim the Good News to all. "The Two Popes" is a film that exposes both the antagonism and friendship between Pope Benedict XVI and his successor as they pursue their own notions of being an authentic Christian. Good will has been the touchstone of Pope Francis' ministry but he can hardly impose this on others. This is a dilemma affecting how a possible Vatican III would course between good will and harsh realities.

STRATEGIC CONCLUSION TO CHAPTER 5

We have spoken of how one comes to know oneself and reflect on the circumstances of life so as to take appropriate action.[9] This is consistent with Jesus' message of love. As happened in the early Church, so today the Church is threatened—but in different ways. Often standing on the margins of secular societies, Christians today need divine guidance and a deeper understanding of what a marginalized Christianity means. Being on the margins, the Church must again serve as a yeast leavening the dough, as a light that shines in more than arcane ways. What makes Jesus' message to be the salt of the earth in an ever-changing world is the willingness of Christians to live the core of Jesus' teachings. The Church is called to effectively re-adapt ways of sharing God's love. Jesus assured us that the Church would last until the end of time. The disciples were to preach his message to all nations. But Jesus knew that not all would accept his revolutionary message of love and justice. Our world is all too focused on self-interest. Two millennia after Jesus, the world has modes of communication unimaginable in his time. The world religions engage in interfaith dialogue but many marginalize religion. A further problem is that fundamentalist interpretations of Jewish, Christian and Islamic scriptures have led to terrorism and war. Biblical revelation is interpreted by scriptural scholars and theologians to help the Church's faithful better understand how we are to live the Bible's complex message. Pope Francis has given new, perceptive ways to apply this message today in ways that may remind us of how the two disciples on their way to Emmaus had their hearts opened by Jesus's words. The Church must safeguard what is authentic in Christian history while building bridges for applying the Christian message today. It is a matter of authentically living the Gospel's message. Our last three chapters address such issues with a view to better evaluate how the Church addresses the problems of a globalized, secularized world. Pope Francis keeps reminding us that the Kingdom of God takes its power from the strength of Christ's love—not by violence nor by propagating close-minded, fundamentalist, distorted beliefs.

NOTES

1. Christianity, once based mostly in Europe, now has a world presence. Lest we repeat mistakes of the past, we note some of the cultural-political differences that led to various divisions in Christianity such as that between the Roman and Constantinople Churches in 1054. We contextualize this with such previous events as the legitimation of Christianity by Constantine, the "disruptive" role of Islam on Christianity, and the histories of China and of the Middle East. These events offer some parameters to evaluate the role of Christianity in the world. Cultures and religions, once known to the West in superficial ways, now impact on its everyday life. The Papal role reached its zenith under Innocent III, only to be tainted by Alexander VI, Julius II and others who used the papacy to further their families' interests. The wars between religions have given way in the West to the separation of Church and State. Christian apologists claim the providential role of God that led to Christianity's privileged status in the West. Secularists allege that Constantine legitimized Christianity to further his own interests. His predecessor Diocletian had instituted a tetrarchy, a sort of check and balance among those aspiring to supreme leadership in the Roman Empire. Constantine undid that by declaring himself sole ruler. The history of a privileged Christianity has not always been to its honor. The Enlightenment eventually led to Church-State separation but secularism has brought in problems of its own. All humans have beliefs perhaps false one: faith links us to God.

2. Joseph Grassi, *Informing the Future: Social Justice in the New* Testament (New York: Paulist, 1989).

3. Thomas Friedman, *The Lexus and the Olive Tree: Understanding Globalization* (New York: Farrar Straus Giroux, 2000) 447; his *The Earth is Flat* (New York: Farrar, Straus and Giroux: 2007) later argued that technology tends to level the field among nations.

4. The rise of technology and instrumental reason has been accompanied by a recent increase of authoritarian leaders. This may be the result of the atomization of individuals unable to think clearly. Karl Marx had anticipated some of these developments when shocked by what governments' hands-off policies toward the free flow of capitalism had done to impoverish workers, he and Engels wrote *The Communist Manifesto*.

5. Erwin Krautler, a friend of Benedict XVI since their seminary days, who became a bishop in Brazil's Amazon region contends that Europeans do not understand poor Brazilians' plight. For him liberation theology expresses the people's struggle for life; it helps them become conscious of how they can put food in their mouth. He made his views known to Benedict during his 2007 visit to Brazil. Cardinal Claudio Hummes stressed in 2019 that "the Amazon needs a Church with an indigenous face." He asked: "How can we think of an indigenous Church if there are no indigenous clergy?" https://international.la-croix.com/news/synodality-means-walking-together/10790?utm_ source=Newsletter &utm_medium=e-mail& utm_content=30-12-2019&utm_campaign=newsletter_crx_lci&PMID =0964dbe689e61e205168552536593154.

6. Leonardo Boff, *Liberating Grace* (New York: Orbis, 1988) 62. Grace can help human efforts to escape the evil lurking in societal structures. Freire's conscientization method is a first step toward such a goal. The irresponsibility of Brazil President Jair Bolsonaro is so great that jurists plan to accuse him of ecocide, a crime recognized by the UN, and take him before the tribunal for crimes against humanity. https://leonardoboff.wordpress.com/2019/09/17/the-amazonthe-common-wealth-of-the-earth-and-humanity/.

7. Some argue that multinationals have deepened the plight of developing nations.

8. Gibson, *The Rule of Benedic*t, 195.

9. Paulo Freire, *Pedagogy of the Oppressed* (New York: Seabury, 1970, 75.

Chapter Six

Interfaith and Cross-cultural Implications of Globalization

We have been linking the intra- and interfaith issues facing the Church so as to test how these issues can cross-fertilize one another. Lest people become prisoners of their upbringing, we seek a meeting of minds among those of different disciplines, different cultures. A universal-Kingdom-oriented Church must deal with such realities as it tries to spread the Gospel message in the face of globalization's cross-cultural implications. In giving a bird's eye view of world problems, we stress the Church's fortes in social justice and interfaith dialogue as central elements of its mission. This chapter asks how the Church might engage in meaningful dialogue with the faithful and with representatives of other religions and of society at large. To be effective, intra- and interfaith dialogues on social justice all demand the types of conversion Jesus enjoined upon his followers.

RESPONDING TO THE WORLD'S NEEDS IN A ONE-DIMENSIONAL WORLD: THE INFLUENCE OF TEILHARD DE CHARDIN, TILLICH, AND GABRIEL MARCEL ON THE CHURCH

In the midst of an often simplistic media influence, persons are threatened with being "one-dimensional." Images take over. Television and other media reduce our ability to convey profound and true meaning. "Civilization" triumphs at the expense of culture. In the midst of a one-dimensional globalizing influences, the Church can do its counter-cultural work in both its intra- and interfaith missions. Its intra-faith mission is also a venture into ecumenism. Let us illustrate the nuances of language in mediating some of the profound meanings of Christian life. Learning a new language is a challenge, an opportunity for deeper encounters. If, for example, "compromise" in English has negative connotations, *"compromiso"* in Spanish implies commitment. Consider the difficulty of following up on one's being a sponsor at baptism in a secularized, globalized world. In the days when people lived in the same town or village most of their lives, a sponsor at baptism did not find it difficult helping parents nurture a child's Christian faith. Today, we need to consider anew how to live a *"compromiso*-as-commitment" to a child when distance and other commitments making it hard for one to be a vigilant godparent. Not just in a child-godparent relationship, but also in many other aspects of life, the nuances of a committed-*compromiso* life are important. From a Christian viewpoint, unlike the trivializing influence of the secular media, it is necessary to be multi-dimensional and non-cynical. It is helpful to be blessed with poetic insights into Christian symbols. John Paul II had a poetic-mystical mindset which influenced his relations with others. This immunized him from harboring undue fear. It enabled him to discover in the Koran, a mystic, poetic quality like his own. In *Redemptoris Missio*,[1] he outlines dialogue's guiding principles which demand "deep respect for everything that has been brought about in human beings by the Spirit."

Pope Francis, too, has shown great respect for other traditions. Such earlier pioneers of global theological strategies as Teilhard de Chardin and Tillich both had an indirect influence on Vatican II and a direct influence on post Vatican II theology. Both had had their worlds shattered during World War I as they served as military chaplains—in the opposing armies. Like John XXIII, they both realized that the churches were faced with new challenges which had to be met. Tillich used the biblical notion of *kairos* as the God-appointed time for realizing salvation in this world. He helped modern Christians stand at the boundary between idealism and realism, liberalism and neo-orthodoxy, spirituality and secularism. As Tillich used his correlation method in his *Systematic Theology* to apply the Biblical message to answer modern philosophical and social problems, we are examining the forms of a salvific *kairos* available to us in our post-Vatican II situation. Ours is a "twin *kairos* strategy." First, we consider recent theologies that can unite people of good will. Secondly, in chapter 8, we draw some lessons to be implemented in SCCs that combine intimacy with their societal concerns. The *kairos* of which we speak is that of conversion to which Jesus invites us. A striking example of conversion is Gabriel Marcel who turned to Christ while working for the French Red Cross in World War I—trying to trace soldiers listed as missing. In place of the mere information on file cards, he came to "see" real, though invisible persons. He shared in the agony of grieving relatives. He eventually developed his *Homo Viator* (human pilgrim) philosophy which is quite in keeping with our own twofold "on-the-way" strategy. In his *Joy of Love*, Pope Francis endorses Marcel's pilgrim approach. In this spirit, we seek to respond to present crises as best we can.

Our own on-the-way *kairos* strategy seeks to bridge human differences with a sound ethics informed by a sound spirituality based on Jesus' teaching on the priority of Kingdom values.

When Jesus' disciples tried to prevent others not belonging to the inner circle from casting out demons in his name (Mk 9:39–41), Jesus tells them that such miracle workers are co-workers, not enemies. They cannot turn around and do harm if they have cast demons in his name. Jesus cautions his followers (45–48) that they themselves may be in need of healing. Rhetorically, he tells them that one must "do away" with an offending foot or hand lest one's whole being perish. Here Jesus is practicing intra-faith and interfaith dialogue; Accepting the healing powers of those of good faith, he uses their experience and our own to bring us to God. What preceded this event and Jesus' injunction was the scene in which Jesus had told his followers that they must not strive for pre-eminence. Rather than trying to lord it over others, they must learn to serve others and become the least of all (33–35). Mark, the earliest of the canonical gospels, realized that Jesus' followers are in need of permanent conversion. Christ's teaching, far from being incompatible with the duties of citizenship, prompts every generation to readapt that teaching to the demands of the day. It links persons of faith with all of creation and with those who, for one reason or another, do not believe. Vatican II's documents focus on spiritually renewing the world in their attempts to bridge the ambiguous nature of ideals and realities on the basis of Jesus' "new wine in new skins." This phrase must again and again be re-evaluated as did, for instance, Teilhard, Tillich and Marcel.

HOW POPES HAVE TRIED TO MEDIATE AMONG CONFLICTING VIEWS OF CAPITALISM

Consider the conflicting agendas of the World Trade Organization (WTO) and of the World Social Forum (WSF). The WSF is a gathering of a wide range of progressive organizations and movements around the world. While WTO has consistently declared its intention to privatize all it can so as to open more frontiers for the free flow of capital, the WSF denounces this agenda. The conflict between these two radically opposed views as well as the unstable nature of greedy capitalism can be illustrated in how the Cerberus Capital Management took over Chrysler in 2007. Cerberus knew it was a gamble. When Chrysler went bankrupt two years, Cerberus lost over $2 billion dollars and had to forfeit its equity stake.[2] Can the Church help bridge some of the gaps that provoke such recurring social and economic conflicts?

The reality is that there has been an ongoing shift in the power equation between those intent on making a profit and their socialist critics. For example, Latin America's election of socialists in the early twenty-first century indicates that voters want to overturn a social stratification that has impoverished the majority. Intermediate structures are needed to do so. This is why we are arguing with Pope Francis for a global ethic and a relational theology that can build intermediary bridges between religions and nations. The world community now recognizes the need for a global strategy to combat the climate crises. This cannot occur without an ethics able to mobilize the global will to effect necessary lifestyle changes. Catholicism's traditional natural law principles can provide a basis for the environmental ethic needed for the twenty-first century. To do this, the Church's natural law teachings must be updated within evolutionary biological contexts rather than the more static Aristotelian concepts. Ethics addresses the question of moral rules based on what makes an action "good" or "bad." We seek to link ethical principles to a relational theology applicable to theistic religions, to a secular ethos or to such a non-theistic world view as that of Buddhism (which is relational in its essence).

The social doctrine of the Church—summarized in John Paul II's *Centesimus Annus* recalling the 100 years since Leo XIII's *Rerum Novarum*— is based on an ethics compatible with or complementary to other ethical traditions. Some argue that *Centesimus Annus* condemns capitalist evils, but offers only a "chaplaincy church" that fails to concretely address such evils in depth so as to lessen the excesses of corrupt practices. On commenting on *Centesimus Annus*, Pope Francis stressed that his own *Laudato Si* is not a "green" encyclical: it is a social encyclical. Specifically,

> The common good is placed in jeopardy by attitudes of unbridled individualism, consumption and wastefulness. All this makes it difficult to promote economic, environmental and social solidarity and sustainability within a more humane economy which considers not only the satisfaction of immediate desires but also the welfare of future generations. Faced with the enormity of such challenges, it would be easy to lose heart, giving in to uncertainty and anxiety. Yet, "human beings, while capable of the worst, are also capable of rising above themselves, choosing again what is good, and making a new start (June 8, 2019).

The Church must heed the teachings of the biblical prophets and of Jesus. Refusing to learn from liberation theology's new perspectives on how grace works in today's world and condemning new approaches are not valid "catholic" positions. They are, rather, divisive partial views. God listens to the cries of a suffering people. Christians are heroic when they seek to relieve victims from oppression. Church leaders do their duty when they publicly call attention to injustice and seek to adapt Church structures so as to better serve the people. The South American Continent's electorates, in response, to the neoliberal agenda of many right-wing governments did elect left-wing parties, as occurred in Venezuela. A free rein was given President Hugo

Chavez and his successor Maduro to accelerate changes in broad areas of society; their opponents retort that they have opened a way to dictatorship. The Church must show that it is not merely a "chaplaincy," that it can make a difference in society by helping both left and right mediate, bridge their differences. We encapsulate such bridging as a Middle Way.

A CHRISTIAN MIDDLE WAY AND A RELATIONAL-THEOLOGY-MEAN REACHING OUT

The Church can only make a difference to the extent that its leaders and its faithful remember that she is ever "on the way," that it is beholden to its master. The Holy Spirit helps it ever "rediscover" Jesus anew: she is not merely a "chaplaincy church" but a courageous one willing and able to bridge differences. As it has done in the past, the Church can "make a difference" by reconciling conflicting theological views with the world's needs. But in contrast to the past, Church theologies must now bear *more* than a Western stamp. Seeking to mediate world needs, we endeavor to learn from Asian and African theologians who can help us discover unsuspected parallels between the middle paths of Buddhism and Christianity. Spiritualities based on a middle path of virtue have characterized the world religions. Consonant with a middle path of a virtuous spirituality is the type of ecumenical theology that shaped Vatican II. Balanced theological bridges informed by a global ethics are ever needed to convert the hearts of people.

In 2003, the Japanese Cardinal Hamao reproached the Roman Curia for assuming and behaving as if their role was "to instruct, to teach, and to correct" local diocesan bishops. Rather, Vatican officials should realize that their role is "to listen, to help, and to encourage." Hamao added that he favored convening a new Council to allow the world's bishops to discuss "the necessity of greater autonomy for the local churches."[3] We argue that it is not a matter of either personal conversion or reforming sinful structures; rather, it is a matter of both conversion and necessary reforms. We cannot overlook the facts that it took a Luther to reform the Church's sinful ways in the sixteenth century and a Karl Marx and the socialists to counter the exploitation of labor by the industrial elite in the nineteenth century. It is now its the evangelic duty of Church leaders to help the faithful live as good Christians while reaching out to others. This is indeed the path Pope Francis has trodden. He insists that the Church correct its bureaucratic excesses. As was shown in the devastating facts of clerics abusing children, many Vatican officials and bishops seemed all too interested in getting back to "normal" (meaning that all local decision-making remain in the hands of the Vatican and bishops). This stance led to the formation of the Voice of the Faithful in 2002. Representing a cross-section of traditional and progressive Catholics, the Voice of the Faithful concentrates on sexual abuse and financial issues. Partly spurred by Voice of the Faithful, on Dec. 17, 2019, Pope Francis abolished the use of the Vatican's highest level of secrecy in clergy sexual abuse cases lest it be thought that the rule of 'pontifical secrecy' is used to protect pedophiles and prevent police from investigating crimes. Proposals are now being made to reform Canon Law to help the Church keep pace with the inevitable developments of the modern age.

Other lay-oriented groups such as Call to Action—steeped in the values of democracy and gender equality—are on the cutting edge of Church reform; they advocate the rights of all the faithful. Our relational theology argues for a larger role of the faithful in building and sustaining communities that can help educate children, and adequately respond to today's realities. It seeks to integrate the spiritual and secular aspects of our lives. It presupposes a divine-human synergy which Tyrrell presciently pleaded for some 120 years ago. But, instead of resorting to Tyrrell's law-of-the-spirit type of immanence theology, it enlists, coordinates our lives' supernatural and human components. It reaches out to all so as develop new relevant syntheses as Pope Francis is doing. By definition, Catholicism is holistic; ideally, it can help incorporate East-West mystical traditions and act as an evangelic leaven ready to tackle the legal barriers that impede a just sharing between the poor and rich. If Descartes erred in assuming that philosophy can "ontologically access" God, many thinkers have suggested ways of rectifying Descartes' mistake. In view of this, we ask how might the yeast of faith help effectively synergize the supernatural and human components of human living. The recapitulation theory of the atonement in Christian theology seeks to explain the meaning and effect of the death of Jesus. Our own transformational, relational theology would apply this traditional view in ways consonant with Jesus' counsels of Christian self-giving as reapplied in the nineteenth century by Leo XIII in grappling with the injustices of his day.

THE CHURCH, THE REALITIES OF IMMIGRATION, AND THE MASS MEDIA AND THE LASTING INFLUENCE OF *RERUM NOVARUM*

Opposition to illegal immigrants into the USA willing to take jobs paying minimal wages resembles earlier patterns of discrimination against immigrants often unable to speak English. It also bears similarities to attempts to restrict the civil rights of blacks, women and gays. The prejudices encountered by Jews and Catholics made them even more aware of the importance of their faith traditions. The local synagogue or parish served both a spiritual and civic function for these immigrants struggling to find their way in a hostile culture. The Catholic Church has recently come to the defense of

Hispanic immigrants' rights, but it now lacks the moral authority it had some 100 years ago when Catholic European immigrants were settling in the USA. In his encyclical, *Rerum Novarum* (1891), Pope Leo XIII responded to workers' plight. The encyclical broke new ground in the Church's understanding of the economic conditions found in the new industrial era. Encouraging the right of labor to organize—but without the class conflict espoused by Marxists—it provided a framework for the right of workers to bargain collectively with their employers. It insisted that workers and employers should agree freely as to wages for it is a right more imperious and ancient than any bargain among humans. Remuneration should be sufficient to maintain the wage-earner in reasonable and frugal comfort. "If through necessity or fear of a worse evil the workman accepts harder conditions because an employer or contractor will afford him no better, he is made the victim of force and injustice."[4] Cardinal Gibbons in the United States had insisted on workers rights from an American viewpoint, but some Vatican conservatives misunderstood the cultural differences that had prompted Gibbons and others to defend workers. They misinterpreted American forms of individualism. Overall, the Church's moral authority helped foster the growth of labor unions in the first half of the twentieth century. Some of the recent decline of the Church's authority can be attributed to the clergy sexual abuse crisis; it also reflects a failure on the part of the Church to grasp and confront the processes of secularization and the impact of a global consumer culture. Such realities were inherited by Pope Francis. He has to deal with many world and ecclesial crises as well as with other pressing needs. The media now exert an undue influence on youth; they deluge young girls with images of skinny models. Three out of four teens say that the media make it seem almost a requisite for teenagers to have sex. To bridge the chasms between parental and ecclesial expectations and the deceptive enticements confronting youth, one must examine the realities facing parents. We seek to establish relational theological bridges to link Christians with all of creation, with persons of faith and with those who, for one reason or another, profess to be non-believers. This is why, we outline some necessary conditions for bridge-building such as a need to understand one's own culture and that of others. For Christians, this includes the ability to find the sources of renewal in our own lived experience.

A RELATIONAL THEOLOGY AS A MEANS TO UPDATE THE *AGGIORNAMENTO* IN A DIVIDED CHURCH

The Old Testament initiated a justice-based relational theology and Jesus lived it. We, too, can live a relational theology—if we take seriously Jesus' injunction to strive for the coming of God's Kingdom. In this Kingdom, faith and reason, charity and justice, East and West can all meet. This is so because the self-transcending teachings of Jesus (as these have been lived by holy persons) incarnate, as it were, the deeper aspects of a relational theology. All comes from God; all is interrelated; we need wisdom to recognize this and the courage to follow through. The Buddhist view of enlightenment is a parallel type of relational theology—but grounded in a world view of immanence.[5]

Today's complex issues must be addressed from a comprehensive perspective aware of the pervasive impacts of globalization and of economic competition. The Church must prophetically lead "from the future as it emerges."[6] The trust and cooperation engendered by small, dedicated communities must complement the problems faced by large institutions. In an era of intense conflict and massive institutional failures, conversion is the soundest way of addressing complex issues on both the local and global levels. These two levels are no longer isolated; Internet blogs have immediate impact on the short term. We as Christians must reflect on and involve ourselves in the long-term, ethical implications of issues.

Paul Tillich analyzed Kant's "autonomous self." He argued that "heteronomous" political and religious ideologies had arisen to counter the naturalistic character of modern secular culture. This resulted both in a "super-naturalistic"[7] theology and in totalitarian political ideologies of the extreme right and the extreme left. Such extremes only complicate without solving the spiritual bankruptcy of bourgeois culture. Tillich held that the fundamental change in method for philosophy and science led to a skeptical rejection of the supernatural claims in theology. Beginning with Galileo, the mathematically-oriented natural sciences "banished" the supernatural. Nature was seen as purely objective, rational and technical—divested of the divine. It is now possible to have a concept of the world without any notion of God. One may argue that an egalitarian placing of the individual above community and cultural diversity all undermine religious belief.[8] If supra-naturalistic and heteronomous political and religious ideologies of both right are common today, we argue that in the tradition of Leo XIII, John XXIII, Paul VI and Vatican II, Pope Francis has addressed economic issues from a perspective that does not overlook social justice, the environment or cultural diversity. The latter must in turn be informed by the religious views that have inspired cultures. The Cold War ended, only to be followed by confrontations between the world views informing secularism and the various world religions. If Vatican II laid a groundwork for dialogue between Catholics and those of other persuasions, the avenues that the Council opened have in many ways been closed or narrowed by a recentralized Vatican bureaucracy. We must again make efforts to understand and implement Jesus' Good News focused on the Kingdom of God. In this perspective, Christians must practice justice and be Kingdom-oriented; they form authentic communities when they help persons live Kingdom values, that is, by respecting all persons as interrelated with one another and with nature. By dialoguing with one another in a spirit of mutual respect, they can foster the dialogue implied in authentic relational theologies. Politics left to the spirit of the world are divisive. The Vatican II *aggiornamento* partly failed in that it has divided the Church. What can Church leaders do to rectify the situation?

Teilhard's groundbreaking thesis on evolution sought to reconcile science and faith; it integrated in a single, holistic vision what had previously been separated. His views on evolution and human consciousness have impressed many but provoked much discussion. Not to be forgotten is that Cardinal Ottaviani, prefect of the Holy Office, had proscribed many of Teilhard's books prior to the opening of Vatican II. Ottaviani's attempts to delay the opening of Vatican II and then to co-opt its agenda were thwarted when Pope John insisted that the bishops be given a free hand in discussing issues.

This received a large press coverage. Vatican II became a reality only after the pope was able to diplomatically outmaneuver Ottaviani. The Pope let the Council become a collegial affair featuring the all the world's bishops. He appointed de Lubac, a close friend of Teilhard to the Council's Preparatory Commission along with Congar and other progressive theologians to the Council's Preparatory Commission. The Pope, de Lubac and other theologians willing to consider how the new theology differs from a misrepresented "modernism" won the day. Yet, many Catholics are still asking what *aggiornamento* means. If the issue continues to divide Catholics, a partial answer lies in a deeper understanding of religious paradoxes.

FOCUSING ON THE DEEPER ASPECTS OF CHRISTIAN-BUDDHIST "PARADOXES:" INTERFAITH-INTERRELIGIOUS DIALOGUES AND CROSS-CULTURAL CATEGORIES

It may be paradoxical that reaching back to the history and cultural impact of Buddhism can help clarify the meaning of the Church's *aggiornamento*. Recent popes have guided the Church through turbulent times. Pope John Paul II's philosophical background helped him realize that Buddhism is a philosophy of tremendous breadth and depth as well a religion. Buddhist enlightenment implies letting go of self, not letting the ego distort the relational aspects of our lives and of the cosmos. Before his enlightenment, Gautama—the Buddha—wandered about, like other monks, begging for food. He lived in small communities of disciples, seeking liberation from a purported *samsara*, the cycle of death and rebirth. With his enlightenment, the Buddha rejected Hinduism's notion of *Atman* or "Self" in favor of a non-self (*anatman*),[9] a development of self towards a Selfless state. He trained monks to seek an enlightenment that is as radical as Jesus' invitation to his followers to leave all things behind. Buddhism and Christianity have analogical visions of an adequately lived, shared experience. On such a basis, the two can find common bases for dialogue. From a Christian point of view, human existence is not comprehensible apart from God. For both Buddhists and Christians, the path of enlightenment (overcoming sin and alienation) means grasping the reality of human interdependence and then living a life of service. To the extent that spiritual leaders evolve a community ethic, they will be building spiritual bridges. While Christians view Christ as being complete, Christianity as a historical movement is always incomplete— involved in a dynamic quest inspired by the Holy Spirit. Faith, hope and love bring an element of paradox into Christians' lives. By pointing out how both Christian and Buddhist paradoxes testify to the deeper aspects of reality, Christian thinkers could help the Church, now engulfed in a world of postmodern relativism, update its "perennial philosophy" to buttress a Christian theology in a globalized age abounding with continuities and paradoxical discontinuities. Few persons are able to appropriate their consciousness so as to reach a mystical state. In our day, many Westerners have turned to Zen for a new understanding of what mystical experience may be. For Zen practitioners, one experiences ultimate mystical (or spiritual) enlightenment when one comes to grips with reality's holistic nature. Holistic fullness means that the whole is greater than the sum of its parts. Zen and mysticism in general are possible paths to God; they take us beyond "things" and may lead to one's being grasped by Ultimate Mind. To grasp something complex, one turns to its simple forms. Mystical experiences are such simple forms of human consciousness.

For Robert Forman, a mystical state is a simplified mental activity that slows down the thinking process but intensifies consciousness. One begins to pay less attention to bodily sensations or daydreams so as to become fully silent inside, what may be called a pure consciousness event (PCE) experienced by mystics of many religions. A PCE is "a perceived unity of one's own awareness per se with the objects around one, an immediate sense of a quasi-physical unity between self, objects and other people, . . . (a state one) may call the unitive mystical state."[10] A PCE is a minimally complex encounter with one's awareness. Mystics can be ordinary people who may have experienced a PCE and had their spiritual eye opened by the mysteries of God. Dancing synergizes Sufi dervishes. Some theologians claim that ascetics are inebriated with God's energy. It is an "inebriation" that synergizes one so as to help transform the world through God's grace.

It may be that Western-based spiritualities (that evolved from Egyptian hermit lifestyles) could benefit from non-European spiritual experiences in responding to today's needs for a secular spirituality. Many Westerners now practice Yoga. Yoga practice can be taught as a Christian spiritual discipline. In this case, one uses a mantra (sacred word) to recall one's rootedness in the divine presence. Catholicism has a long history of incorporating legitimate spiritual practices and rituals from other cultures when they help the believer access the deeper levels of spiritual consciousness (See Appendix 2). Part of the reason for secularization in the West is a failure to offer Westerners alternative modes of spiritual practice that can consciously open them to the divine presence. Regular, long-term meditation leads to the empty-mind experience Buddhists call enlightenment. It results in a deep shift in one's knowing structure; one's experienced relationships with perceptual objects change deeply. In some people, this new structure becomes a permanent, inner stillness to integrate the outside and inside into which we divide the world. Such a stillness perdures, even while one is otherwise engaged. It enables one to de-intensify emotional attachments, to progressively sense one's quiet interior and to become more open to a Kingdom ethics and to the virtues and values necessary to course a middle way between the many extremes facing us. The interior life can orient us toward a Kingdom ethic to facilitate dialogue with other religions and with secularists—as Thomas Merton and Bede Griffiths demonstrated so well.

In keeping with our interfaith-interreligious distinction (the latter is more "official" than the former), we have been exploring how intra- and interfaith issues may interact with one another. Intra-interfaith endeavors are helpful to community-building and peace-making. We briefly examined Christian history and some of the competing claims in religion and philosophy. Jesus' disciples launched a movement recorded in the New Testament. Their original message must be re-applied in every generation. Even after Vatican II, the Church has too easily condemned prophetic voices. We shall not try to second-guess the then Cardinal Ratzinger's judgments on individual theologians. But we can point out that he did not understand Yoga or Zen spiritualities which have attracted so many idealist Westerners. In fact, Ratzinger was repeating a mistake Clement XI made in 1704[11] when he condemned the Chinese Rites out of ignorance. What led to the Rites' condemnation involved petty clashes between Franciscans and Jesuits in their approaches to evangelization in China. The Franciscans erroneously denounced the Jesuits' method of adapting the Christian message to fit Chinese cultural sensibilities. The Church's action led to the persecution of all Christians in China.

Today, the Church risks alienating many spiritually-minded young people to the extent that it does not recognize that yoga and Zen are primarily philosophic—they are as compatible with Christianity as Greek philosophy has been. In adapting Greek, Chinese, African or Indian cultural patterns as legitimate ways of expressing and living the Gospel, some adjustments had or will have to be made. Pope Benedict was riveted within traditional Western theology. Both as cardinal and as Pope, his ventures into the interfaith dialogue with Islam and Buddhism were insufficiently informed. It is a problem when a Western theologian fails to understand in depth the cultural and religious histories of non-European cultures. In 1990, Ratzinger, as Prefect of Congregation for the Doctrine of the Faith, issued an official Letter on "Some Aspects of Christian Meditation"[12] claiming that Yoga and Buddhism are incompatible with Christianity. Many experts in both fields faulted the Letter. Zen Buddhists noted the Letter's mistaken interpretations of Eastern prayer. The Letter inaccurately claims that Zen seeks to guide its practitioners toward a "union with God." Mystics know that a mystical "is" copula differs from a logical one.

"Atman is Brahman" or Al-Hallaj's "I am the Truth" are phrases that use *not* a logical copula as in "This boy is John," but a mystic one. Confusing the two, the Vatican Letter misconstrues Zen and yoga. We quote the Letter (left column) and add John Raymaker's response in the *Japan Mission Journal* (1990) that focuses on a relational "oneness" achieved in meditation as stressed in Zen (right column):

SHORTCHANGING-BARRIERS IN VATICAN LETTER A BRIDGE TO EAST-WEST MYSTICISM

Part I. Introduction

3. Christian prayer "flees from concentrating on on-self . . . (Its) essential element is the meeting of two freedoms."	Zen does not concentrate on the self; it disciplines it; it speaks of the meeting of two freedoms but does not insist of two in speaking of the ineffable.

Part III. Erroneous Ways Of Praying

8. "In combatting the errors of pseudognosticism, the Fathers affirmed that matter is created by God and as such is not evil." In opposing another fourth century error, the "Fathers insisted on the fact that the soul's union with God in prayer is . . . mysterious."	The Letter resurrects Western pseudognostic hang-ups (dualist psychologisms). These are not problems with Zen. On the contrary, Zen insists on avoiding such Western errors. Christian Zen realizes but does not stress St. Basil's daring phrase that "we are to become God."
10. Both of these forms of error continue to be a temptation for man the sinner. They incite him to try and overcome the distance separating creature from Creator, as though	Number 10 suggests that Zen is not unlike Western aberrations of the Middle Ages; yet for Christian Zen, there is no question of surpassing Christ. Rather, the Letter contradicts

there ought not be such a distance; to consider the way of Christ as something surpassed.	itself, for while it here denies union with Christ, in Part IV, it legitimizes such Christian union.
11. "However, these forms of error . . . can be diagnosed very simply."	Maybe—but not by simplistically lumping Zen, as the letter does, with obscure Western errors.

Part IV. The Christian Way to Union with God

14. "An absorbing of the human self into the divine self is never possible, not even in the highest states of grace."	True. But Zen in no way claims such as absorption – no more than did St. Basil in his comments on our union with God.

Unlike Pope John Paul II's careful distinctions between pluralist and exclusivist stances in theology and in interfaith dialogue, the CDF Letter legitimizes Christian union with God but attacks strivings for union with God in other religions. It fails to grasp that Zen's "non-self" preserves and enlarges the self in dynamic ways. Zen can enlighten us in ways compatible with Christianity. Catholic Zen teachers (*Roshis*) have shown how Zen meditation can deepen a Christian's spiritual experience. Differences in beliefs can be broached to the extent that enlightened by faith, one silently experiences the apophatic—as does Zen. True, Asian traditions such as Zen primarily help one identify one's inner center. They minimize the importance of grace in the process of disciplining one's body. A balance must be found between caring for both body and soul. Modern exchanges between East and West scholars have been beneficial. D. T. Suzuki stresses that Zen helps one becomes conscious of the cosmic unconscious, but he does not clearly reconcile Zen enlightenment(*satori*) with Christians' stress on the reality of evil; we do face this issue.[13] Rather than "concentrating" on self, a Zen "no-mind self" re-centers us at a deeper level in a self metaphysically distinct from God, yet perfectly identified with God through love. God is so present in one's depths that there seems to be but one Self—one way to speak of God being mystically present. We argue that a Christian Zen can help those seeking God mediate Eastern and Western versions of mysticism.

Key to such an effort is to fathom *prajna*, Zen's most important word.[14] We emphasize (see Appendix 4) that a Catholic *prajna* permits us to develop a notion of a relational self—one that integrates anew a Cartesian ego, Kant's autonomous self or even Tillich's heteronomous self. We do rely on Eckhart and Tillich's Ground of Being that is foundational to relational self. Being This is a base for interfaith and interreligious dialogue. We may go back to Rumi's notion of a unified consciousness that transcends normal human and religious categories or we can even dare say with St. Basil "we are to become God" to illustrate what a mystic relational self implies. To avoid New Age syncretism, one must commit one's self to God—the foundational Ground of Being. The hierarchy, the Church from below and SCCs should all make such a commitment to God—a topic we touch on in chapter 8.

Lonergan's religious foundation (when one accepts God's gift of his love) and St. Basil's spirituality can both be applied to a Christian Zen. The two views can meet upon sufficient reflection. As "the bonds between Zen and the art of calligraphy are rooted in a deep, natural relationship,"[15] so a relational theology is rooted in a deep *kairos* of grace. The creative power of Christian enlightenment or of religious conversion can tap a spontaneous willingness in sincere persons, moving them to engage themselves in our age's complex problems. Our relational theology seeks to help Christians live a Gospel ideal committed to the Good News in deep intra-, interfaith ways. A famous Zen Ox-herding pictures indirectly illustrates this point. In the pictures, the Ox signifies one's deep self; the oxherd is an ordinary human person who, enlightened through practice, becomes one with the Ox. The first picture shows the oxherd who, having lost the Ox, stands alone in a vast pasture. How, we ask, can a human being lose his/her deeper self? The pictures suggest that although the Mind-Ox (grace) helps us lest one's deeper self be overlooked, yet ignorance and delusion do lead one to stray from the Ox; the oxherd then begins a search for the Ox. At first, he relies only on vague intellectual knowledge. Painful Zen practice finally enables him to straddle the Ox; he becomes one with it but in the paradoxical way that having become free by being identified with it, he no longer needs it. The eighth picture shows the two disappear in the embracing nothingness of a circle. The final two pictures show the oxherd return to everyday life as an enlightened one. He bestows goodness to all he meets and seeks to make the world a better place. A verse describes enlightenment in terms applicable to Christians:

> A thought of faith once awakened is the basis of the way forever.
> A spot of white is therefore observed on the Ox head.
> Faith, already awakened, is refined at every moment.
> Suddenly come to an insight, joy springs up in the mind.

The oxherd seeks God as an open question as do some postmodernists. One can reject faith, as many do today; but at a deeper level, it is struggled for within our inner depths. As the oxherd returns to the world, so Christians are urged to counter evil by conquering pride and sin. SCCs that foster intimacy and reflect on the Gospel are a way to help us conquer pride and sin, but even more importantly to discover one's true self.

The previous paragraphs on a relational self, on Rumi's unified consciousness and on the oxherd serve to lay a basis for Lonergan's foundations which underpin his notion of religious conversion. For Christians, all truth originates from the same source. We have distinguished beliefs in karmic reincarnation from a Christian self-transcendent union of love with God. For us, the former can also be explained by the latter. The peoples of Africa and Asia have traditionally, recognized human interdependency.[16] If Western peoples originally understood the interdependency of tribal and national life, individualism began to lead them develop materially. On the positive side, it helped them devise notions of democracy, personal dignity and human rights. But such notions can and have been distorted into a ruthless competition based on self-interest that undermines the common good. Many Asian and African nations, on the other hand, have held on to their traditional tribal or group solidarity. They have not found it easy to reconcile group national welfare with the individualist capitalist mentality driving so many Westerners. This has led to corruption in many developing nations. All Catholics should be faithful to Vatican II teachings that promote forms of interfaith dialogue focused on human interdependency. John XXIII addressed post-World War II crises by listening to the Spirit and trusting his brother bishops. Today, we live in a world threatened by COVID-19, terrorism, nuclear warfare and global warming. Pope Francis has made it clear that Vatican officials, tempted to restore pre-Vatican II ways of doing, must learn to listen to the bishops and to the faithful—and at times to the insights of those of other persuasions.

THE KINGDOM OF GOD, CHRISTIAN IDEALS, AND RESPONSIBLE INTIMACY

For Christians, Jesus is unique; yet, saying "Jesus is the Christ" is a faith assertion not shared by those outside of the fold. Jesus is marginal to Jews. For Islam, he is respected but has been supplanted by the Prophet Muhammad. Where are we to find truth in such divergent claims? If believers insist on their own claims, at least, they must respect the faith of others. We seek to build relational bridges able to reconcile the best elements of all traditions. William of Ockham (1285-1347) initiated in Western thought a denial of a clear link between faith and reason. Lonergan helps us recover the link by appealing, as Jesus did, to conversion. But the reality of how conversion is to be lived must be clarified in terms of modern experience and of the limitations of the scientific method. There are quasi-unfathomable depths within each human person—depths that can lead to great achievements but also to despair or violence. Scientists apply their method to "control" nature, but if they overstep the bounds of responsible freedom, they only complicate the problems of the human situation. Intra-faith and interfaith dialogue are both needed so that the deep insights of the Buddha on enlightenment and of Jesus and of Muhammad on the uniqueness of God may be approached from a notion of our common humanity. All persons should try to understand and appropriate their own experience. For Christians, such an appropriation can lead to an in-depth experience of what Kingdom and community mean and to credible forms of dialogue with non-Christians.

"Be ye perfect as your heavenly Father is perfect," Jesus admonishes us (Mt 5:48); yet we also say "perfection is not of this world." It is virtually impossible to observe all the ideals implied in the commandment to love neighbor as self. There is a type of contradiction at the heart of the Gospel. How realize its ideals? We are faced with the question of how to reconcile Jesus' "impossible" counsel with the reality facing each one. The eight beatitudes in the Sermon of the Mount are ideals we strive to reach as best we can. By so doing, we implement the heart of a theology of the Good News. Conservative Catholic theologians and laity are correct in wanting to build community, but they should not do so through misunderstandings. Nor should they misrepresent Jesus' priorities. In the Our Father, we pray "Thy Kingdom come." Community is intimately connected with but subordinated to the priority that Jesus imposed upon his believers, that of first striving for God's Kingdom and its justice.

We all depend on one another. Recognizing this fact as well as our dependence on nature might be an appropriate first step for understanding the meaning of the Kingdom of God. As we saw, Jesus constantly reminded his disciples that unless their justice exceeds that of the Scribes and Pharisees, they shall not enter into the Kingdom. For Christians, community life and the demands of justice are both important. Christians seek to understand how God is ever revealing Self anew in Trinitarian love. They are to imitate their master in letting community life be a means to establish God's Kingdom on earth. Just communities respect the rights of all members. Such a respect furnishes the proper context for living out Jesus' teaching on the Kingdom. If Christians get their priorities right, they will be able to deepen the type of Christian spirituality and community life that St. Francis or St. Teresa of Avila founded in their generation. Due to the nature of our global village, some Christians youths are now exposed to the claims and lifestyles of various sects of the Hindu and Buddhist religions. Vatican II paved a way for this. A Vatican III Council would establish guidelines for what is allowed or not desirable in such cases. Since faith is ineffable, beliefs have arisen in every religion; but belief "gaps" are often divisive. But behind differences there is the potential unity of faith. Beliefs are to be respected; yet, their gaps (when believers are open to God but caught in verbally-induced or ideological ambiguities) can be transcended in and through faith. One has the power of unrestricted love to the extent that one responds to God's Word mediated in beliefs—a good basis for interfaith dialogue.[17]

Vatican II's "Declaration on the Relation of the Church to Non-Christian Religions" praises Hindus and Buddhists' sensitivity of the heart. As the Church is open to the complementarities between faith and reason, so some Indian theologians seek to integrate Christian spirituality with Hindu traditions. They argue for a complementarily of revelations and try to arrive at essential truths that have been conditioned by particular historical contexts. Raimon Panikkar (1918–2010) called for a mutual fecundation of religions. Defending a Christian interpretation of Hindu sacred texts, he found in the Trinity a solution to all the philosophical and theological problems of India. He argued that Christian Trinitarian faith cannot contest Eastern religions' basic intentionality.[18]

For the Indian Catholic theologian Thomas Kochumuttom, just as Jesus is the *Logos* manifesting the godhead (Jn 14:6), so, in parallel fashion, Indian culture speaks of "Wisdom" (*prajna*); it recognizes the theological significance of *logos*.[19]

Prayer is a form of loving intimacy with God. For a Christian, such intimacy expresses itself when addressing the Father as "Thou"; it has led some Christians to care for people and/or get involved in societal problems. For Indian theologians, intimacy leads to profound dialogue enabling Christians to relate their lived experience to that of non-Christians. Intimacy with God and others is one of the foundational aspects of religion and of community. Without it, people can easily fall into alienated indifference.

A VATICAN III COUNCIL NEEDED TO INTEGRATE ASIAN AND WESTERN THEOLOGICAL INSIGHTS

We have contrasted Catholic quests for self-identity, which appeal to conservative minds, with the fact that many youths seek a spiritual identity that is broader than traditional notions of Catholic self-understanding. If conservative bishops make reforms of the Church unlikely in the short term, we take a longer-term view by identifying with the telling insights of liberation theologians, of Küng's global ethics and other Vatican-II-based approaches. With Pope Francis, we seek a possibly global, transformative self-understanding of the Church—faithful to tradition but open to non-Western perspectives. Most helpful in such an endeavor is the notion of the *development* of doctrine espoused by the eminent theologians St. John Henry Newman and Bernard Lonergan. We explore Buddhist and other Eastern traditions that are compatible with Catholicism. Incorporating kindred Greco-Indian insights can be helpful to deepen and ground Western theologians teaching on *logos*, for instance. "Spiritual life" means sharing in the life of God; but how? This depends on what we mean by sharing in God's life. For Christians, God's life is Trinitarian.[20] A comparative theology asks how Jesus could be the mediating symbol for non-Christians as he is for Christians. Jacques Dupuis (censured by the Vatican and then exonerated for his writings on Hinduism) often quoted Vatican II Documents and the popes. Like some other theologians, he held a "pluralist" view of non-Christian Hindu philosophies; scriptures of other faiths contain some truth. John Paul II taught from a Christocentric Trinitarian perspective, yet he practiced an open form of interfaith dialogue. How do we share in the divine life? This depends on what we mean by the life of God. For Christians, God's life is Trinitarian. Christians in India could speak of our being blissful in God—*saccidananda*—as is the case when we share in Trinitarian life (see Appendix 2). Such deep Hindu insights of bliss in sharing in divine give us a basis for a relational theology to be complemented by one of the Kingdom of God. "Guru" has become a common word in the West. The word has its roots in the Sanskrit *gri* (to invoke, praise, or make an effort). It is cognate with Latin *gravis*, heavy grave or serious. In India, a guru can also signify an "an avatar of God." A local church is the house where its Guru resides and people listen in faith.[21] How may one ground paths of faith through a social justice apostolate with the help of interfaith perspectives that respect other religions' beliefs? Pope John Paul II was open to Kingdom values but he tended to see these values through the eyes of older Church teachings. Pope Francis is reconnecting the Church to Vatican II teachings, prodding some to plead for a Vatican III Council. Vatican II"s *Declaration on the Relationship of the Church to Non-Christian Religions* was a bold initiative opposed by conservatives who argued that it would impede the evangelizing-missionary aspects of the Church. The *Declaration*, a very brief document, lays down principles of recognizing truth wherever it exits, e. g.: "In Hinduism men contemplate the divine mystery and express it through an unspent fruitfulness of myths and through searching philosophical inquiry" (no. 2). The Council praises Hindus' deep meditation and a loving trusting flight toward God. It touches on Buddhism as a path that encourages a search for supreme enlightenment through one's own efforts.

SMALL BASIC COMMUNITIES (SCCS) IN THE AMERICAS

Vatican II and other influences of the 1960's gave birth to new movements in the Catholic Church, such as that of liberation theology and the reestablishment of SCCs which had flourished in the early Church. Liberation theology, for its part, has also reinforced calls for SCCs. The term liberation theology was first used by Gustavo Gutierrez, a Peruvian priest. Such a theology urged that the Church concentrate on liberating the world's poor from their oppression. This is not unlike Yahweh's call to Moses assigning him the task of liberating his people. One may also recall what St. Augustine exclaimed one day when he saw a drunkard go by: "There, but for the grace of God, go I." Grace is necessary for conversion from any kind of oppression. In the face of human ills, each person must begin where he/she is in promoting "we-the world-thinking." We are to grow in experience and understanding so as to reach balanced judgments in concrete situations that in turn call for further understanding, richer judgments and courses of action. Such growth led to the birth of liberation theology. The story of how the Vatican silenced liberation theologians is well known. In 1972, the conservative bishop Lopez Trujillo of Columbia, elected general secretary of CELAM (Latin American Episcopal Conference), sought to dismantle liberation theology. At first, a majority of CELAM had tolerated the new theology that for the most part did not advocate violence. Liberation theologians know that SCCs can help members address the problems confronting them while honoring the Gospel message of social justice. Nevertheless, the Vatican and Trujillo sought to end CELAM's toleration of liberation theology due to its alleged toleration of violence. In his speech at the 1979 Puebla CELAM[22] conference, John Paul II was conciliatory. He praised the Latin American Church's preferential option for the poor and recognized that the message of liberation theology is partially compatible with Catholic social teaching. But he insisted that the Church could not tolerate an image of Christ as a revolutionary figure. Ironically, John Paul II practiced his own version of liberation theology.[23] Previous to Pope Francis, the Vatican did not show an even hand in condemning what it alleged to be Marxist theologies advocating violence. It did little to condemn rightist militias in Columbia or Guatemala that murdered the defenders of a preferential option for the poor. It hardly opposed the trumped up charges that social activists were rebels. A preferential option for the poor led to activists being put in untenable positions with hardly any defense from the one-sided policies of a Cardinal Trujillo (1935–2008) in Colombia. Trujillo had been awarded the red hat although he had led efforts to stem the tide of liberation theology. One should not use claims of orthodoxy to oppose the practice of justice.

The two cousin bishops Lorscheiter in Brazil did stand up to one-sided Vatican views. Both bishops insisted that liberation theology does not advocate Marxism. But after Pope Paul VI, no more progressive bishops were appointed in Brazil until Pope Francis did so. Some 20 years before becoming Pope, Cardinal Ratzinger had praised liberation theology inasmuch as it rejects violence; he had stressed Christians' responsibility toward the poor and oppressed, but he had not gone beyond mere theoretical views as to how poverty is to be overcome. Can we discover a pattern in the Vatican's actions before and since Vatican II? The Vatican's actions on justice issues confirm that, prior to Pope Francis, the Vatican overstressed its being the sole center of unity in the Church. The aftermath of Vatican II destabilized the delicate balance between traditional-progressive views in the global Church. John

Paul II and Benedict XVI took it upon themselves to recentralize. The spirit of openness alive at Vatican II gave way to mutual distrust. The Vatican's appointments of conservative bishops by John Paul II and Benedict led to their dominating policy. On the positive side, many nuanced positions were advanced to refine some of Vatican II's approaches to being a global Church. Our aim is to try to further refine the traditional *sentire cum ecclesia* (to think and feel with the Church) through the eyes of Pope Francis. As the phrase "people of God" became a rallying cry after Vatican II, so we insist that the Church must not think and feel with careerist bureaucrats but with the people of God. Pope Francis keeps repeating that the Church must reach out to the poor and to the marginalized as did Jesus.

HOW FARES POPE JOHN XXIII'S *"AGGIORNAMENTO"* TODAY? WHAT IT STILL NEEDED?

As Pope John XXIII was influenced in his wish to renew the Church by his exposures to non-Christian contacts in Bulgaria and to the priest-worker movement in France, so with Pope Francis we seek to address the challenges of inculturating Christianity in ways that distinguish between the imperatives of interfaith dialogue and spreading the Good News. The Church has a global presence but is in a state of crisis in the West. As did Pope Paul VI, who had to course between extremes, so we seek to mediate between reality and interfaith ideals. Pope Francis has facilitated the possibility of a further Church renewal by appointing a majority of the cardinals who will vote for his successor. This majority now includes a much larger percentage of Third World cardinals. Whether or not Pope Francis or a successor will call a Vatican III, Catholics can assume that the Spirit of Jesus who breathed on his disciples at the first Pentecost still inspires Christians today. Many conservative bishops appointed by John Paul II failed to address society's pressing problems. An issue, at once crucial and delicate, now stares us in the face, one that parallels what faced the early Church as expressed in 2 Timothy (2:15): a bishop must uphold sound doctrine. But Scripture also enjoins us to show solidarity with victims.[24]

In Chapter 8, we focus on the way SCCs live out this delicate balance by organizing networks seeking to empower the poor. The delicate balance between being orthodox and living an authentic Christian life is one that the Church must maintain. It is part of the *aggiornamento* stressed especially by popes John XXIII and Francis. Empowering the poor is to be rooted in valid types of spirituality practiced, for instance, in Catholic ashrams. The experience of the ashrams and of SCCs have shown that it would be well do reintroduce models of house churches that existed in the early Church. This is not to do away with parish or diocesan structures; rather, it a question of empowering believers. Reintroducing valid forms of relational communities focused on Kingdom values and living up to recent popes' pleas for alleviating the poor and oppressed should be a top priority—one that is consonant with the early Christian model of house churches. The Church should be attuned to how the Spirit works among the people of God. As Jesus reacted toward the failures of Jewish leaders, so we have been exploring Jesus' emphasis on social justice. Like Jesus, Pope Francis wants to alleviate the miseries of the poor; he urges planners to find solutions to what divides cultures and religions. Christians are called to religious and moral conversions which should be supplemented with intellectual and psychic conversions as Lonergan and his followers have shown in great detail. Christianity and Buddhism both offer us relevant perspectives in these areas with their respective notions of virtue and of living the Buddha's noble Eightfold Path.

A NOTE ON ANGER, *ANGST*, ANXIETY—HOW SOOTHE THEM

For Aristotle, the truthful man is truthful even when there is "something at stake." He who claims that he has no ulterior motive is a "contemptible" person (*Nichomachean Ethics*, IV, 7). Because most humans have conflicting agendas and some resort to violence or unlawful means (if they can "get away with it") and because great is our ignorance on many subjects, the world needs police, judges, and fences to keep peace. While the capital sins tempt us all, the virtues can help us transmute our faults with a middle path that courses between extremes. Some may quibble as to whether the Buddhist Middle Way or the Greeks' Golden Mean (golden middle way) adequately address the reality of anger. St. Augustine, for one, tended to reframe the ancients' notions of virtue as vices. Augustine and Nietzsche "transformed values" in radically different ways. Vatican II taught us that it is wise to develop ecumenical and interfaith strategies that can reconcile humans rather than to stress differences. If for example, Buddhists can help us turn anger into a source of wisdom that is a laudable goal.[25]

There is much to unsettle one in life—to make one impatient or angry. "Anger" and German *Angst* are both derived from the root "*angh*" (to be constricted). One may think of anger as an impetus that caused basic divisions within both Buddhism and Christianity. One has only to think of Luther's 95 theses and his "Here I stand," or of the fratricidal wars that followed from that stand. Other troubling divisions are those between East and West (Kipling's "never the twain shall meet"), between masculine and feminine sensibilities, rich and poor. Such polarizing differences need mediating. In tune with our overall strategy of anticipating a possible Vatican III, we are engaged in on-the-way mediations. We offer suggestions for theologians, bishops and ordinary Christians which could only be implemented through new mediating, transformative structures so as to break new ground in the Church. In the face of anger, we advocate conversion both in the center and peripheries of Church life. As the poor and disadvantaged feel ever more constricted within putative "freedoms," the manipulations of capitalist and state-guided initiatives call for efforts to allay justifiable anxiety feelings on the part of the oppressed. We can all meet Jesus and one another on the way to a new Emmaus (think of the Emmaus Houses Abbe Pierre set up to care for the homeless in Paris). Being ever on the way toward heartfelt conversion—and possibly toward a Vatican IIII—we are engaged in a mediating process that could open perspectives for such a Council. If enough people—on any side of a divide—learn to translate their fears and anger into virtuous action, an atmosphere for mediating our differences can emerge. Deviations from any religious founder's vision inevitably arise. Can renewed forms of spirituality join together to globally address such deviations so that seeming "trespasses" (viewed from narrow viewpoints) may become sources of intra-faith and interfaith breakthroughs?

COMPARING THE BUDDHISM'S *MIDDLE-WAY* BRIDGING-POTENTIAL WITH THE CHURCH'S ADOPTION OF A THOMIST *GOLDEN MIDDLE WAY*

In our polarized world, there are open-minded persons who love the Church and want to commit themselves to forms of spirituality old and new. We are at one with such persons. With them, we set forth on middle-way paths of virtue, such as that of Buddhist and Thomist teachers. They taught us to avoid the extremes of a situation. Scholars endlessly debate the nuances of these traditions. Perhaps it is due to such endless debates that both spirituality and virtue are attacked by ideological atheist-militant humanists. Such attacks reinforce the poisoned atmosphere that spoils partisan politics today. Those who seek to pursue the path of virtuous wisdom are attacked as "professional moralizers." True, we must beware of the rigid fundamentalists in various traditions who self-righteously accuse others of moral failings. One may think of William Bennet who had his comeuppance when his moral campaign was undercut by his own excesses in gambling.

The example of Gunther Grass, who waited more than 60 years before confessing his own youthful participation in Hitler's SS Corps, illustrates another danger of "holier than thou virtuous" attitudes. We approach the virtues in the spirit of Jesus who at every turn stressed that we his followers must seek not to be served but to serve, that we must see him in the poorest of the poor, the marginalized of society, the blind. The Church has its share of Good Samaritans who earn our respect. Such heroic figures as Abraham Lincoln, Martin Luther King, or the transformed Robert Kennedy (once he truly understood the plight of the poor) are often cut down in their prime. We would do well to emulate such modern heroes who have had the courage to confront society's inequalities. In this spirit, we uphold heroic men and women, known or unknown, who let themselves be guided by the liberating potential of the theological virtues of faith, hope and charity among which charity or love is the greatest (I Cor. 13). Our task is to help mediate between our spiritual needs, ethics and global realities. Such a mediation implies a distinction between arbitrary authority in the Church and the role of leadership. Since John Paul II began appointing bishops on the basis of their allegiance to Church authority rather than on their leadership abilities, there has arisen a crisis of leadership. Jesus' warned against lording it over others. Authoritarianism has had a deleterious effect since apostolic times;[26] it invariably fails. Catholics, committed to both new and old forms of spirituality, set forth on a middle-way path of virtue that avoids both extremes of a situation so as to bring peace. There are similarities but also differences in how such great thinkers as the Buddha, Aristotle or Aquinas arrived at their truths. Let us call the similarities a "transcultural bridge" (based in great part on the four intentional levels of human consciousness: experience, thinking by way of concepts, judging and deciding). Differences stem from culturally-specific factors. We humans can learn to cooperate by sifting through what divides us. In doing so, one can arrive at Aristotle's "middle-path" of virtue (*arete*), a kind of moderation aiming at the mean between extremes. Courage is the mean between fear and overconfidence. With Aquinas, we adopt Aristotle's mean (*Nicomachean Ethics*, 10, 7) that courses between extremes. As has been the case with Christianity, divisions proliferated within Buddhism. The main division is that between the Theravada, way of the ancients (pejoratively called Hinayana, lesser vehicle) and Mahayana, greater vehicle. Thailand, Malaysia and Vietnam and other southern Asian countries were all molded by Theravada Buddhism, while China, Korea and Japan adopted Mahayana Buddhism.

As later occurred in Christianity, so in Buddhism conflicting opinions and doctrines were addressed by Councils. After the Buddhist Second Council of Vaishali, the ancients, opposed to changes in monks' conduct, excommunicated those who held a different view. The latter were in the majority and it is from this group that there eventually arose the Mahayana school. This school's most famous doctrine is that of *Madhyamika*, the Middle Way as taught by Nagarjuna (c. 150–200 A.D). *Madhyamika* means steering a middle path between the extremes of absolutism and nihilism. The Buddhism expounded by the Buddha was not a religion as such but rather an ethical philosophy compatible with Christianity. Nagarjuna's influence within Mahayana is not unlike that of Aquinas in Catholicism. Both strove to steer a *middle course* between extremes. Buddhism's penchant for tolerance has, in the main, led it to play a peaceful role in the history of Asia. Buddhism has had a profound[27] influence in molding the fabric of many Asian nations. Actual conversions to Buddhism and Christianity undergone by persons of all epochs, can still serve as models to help bridge an interfaith dialogue based on the noblest ethical aspects of the human race.

Vatican II's "Decree on the Apostolate of the Laity" notes that lay people should be "sensitive to the movement of the Holy Spirit" (29). It may be that the Holy Spirit is moving Christians, whether they be trained in official Church structures or in informal basic communities, to dialogue with those of other faiths. A basis for such dialogue exists in the middle path of virtue as expressed in Chinese, Greek, Buddhist and Christian philosophies. All of these have developed cognate notions of virtue as a middle way.

To understand the middle ways of Catholicism and of Buddhism, for example, we must advert to the nature of alienation that can mark any person thrown back upon self in the face of evil and that can mark any society as it copes with constant, often unpredictable changes. Existentialists such as Jean Paul Sartre flourished because they realized that modern men and women are often isolated within themselves. Long ago, the Buddha and Jesus also realized this. Both religious founders became itinerant preachers who found solutions in a path of tolerant virtue. Of course, their paths differ in many respects, but they both enlightened their disciples, enabling them to speak "heart-to-heart" even to strangers. For Jesus, a Samaritan—despised by the Jews—becomes a role model of inclusiveness. For the Buddha, all life is sacred; we must respect not only all men and women, but also all of nature—as the ecologists now realize. Jesus taught his disciples to serve. The Catholic tradition, following Aquinas, has deepened its own middle path of virtue wherein the three theological virtues of faith, hope and charity are complemented by practicing justice. We cannot excuse ourselves from this practice by piously giving a few pence to save face and alleviate our consciences. Such a surface remedy betrays Christ's teaching. People become alienated by such self-serving deceptions. Buddhism and Christianity have universal appeal because their founders addressed the deepest human questions. Buddha and Jesus both gathered disciples and taught them to pray and reflect lest they be deceived by the ways of the world. Buddha taught enlightenment; Jesus gave us the golden rule of loving one's neighbor as oneself. Today, innumerable sects within Buddhism and Christianity emphasize this or that aspect of their traditions. Enlightenment and loving one's neighbor as oneself are often viewed as "ideals." With Pope Francis, we insist on trying to realistically live the deeper aspects of discipleship.

INSISTING ON THE DEEPER ASPECTS OF RELIGION TO DEAL WITH ALIENATION

Basic Buddhist and Christian teachings should not be treated as mere ideals. The conversions that Buddha and Jesus taught their disciples are subject to discipline. Discipline and disciple are cognate words. To the extent that Christians practice faith, hope and love they become enlightened; to the extent that Buddhists are enlightened they live with hope and love and an implicit faith. By intelligently responding to and judging about the facts of alienation within self and in society and by taking actions to remedy these, one is living a converted religious life: heart reaching out to heart. By being just and charitable, one educates others and encourages them to learn and practice a virtuous path. The ubiquitous Internet brings people of different cultures and faith traditions into daily contact. Church authorities are called to help the faithful live ethically, spiritually.

Pope Francis knows that Vatican officials ensconced behind their desks can hardly win people's trust. Globalization is not all bad. The Holy Spirit breathes where it wills. If right wing militias in South America have killed many priests and sisters, SCCs inspire people to live ethically lest bogus norms master them. Jesus spoke of the dangers wealth poses to entering the Kingdom. Authentic persons practicing the virtues of faith, hope and charity can make a difference. Melinda Gates exemplifies how a fervent Catholic can do this. She prodded her wealthy, intelligent spouse toward alleviating the sufferings of others. The Gates' concern with education and with medical assistance is a step in the right direction. Pope Francis has been leading the Church into taking the further step of defending the cause of the poor against oppressive forces. To a lesser extent than John Paul II, he, too, was schooled in the world of violence. Both these popes have used their charism in evaluating capitalism. But John Paul II was rather limited by his own Polish ecclesial experience that was a reverse image of Communist unquestioning obedience. He found it difficult to understand American notions of freedom. Francis is not so hampered. Christian trust implies action, but action can depend on one's cultural background. It is necessary to go beyond cultural perceptions by being converted in intellectual, moral, psychic and religious ways. One might say that Christian conversion means serving others. We often use the word "serve" as stressed in the Gospels. Christian service includes a basic attitude of "undoing" wrongs as expressed in St. Francis' prayer, "Where there is hatred, let me sow love. . . . It is in pardoning that we are pardoned."

THE BUDDHIST DOCTRINE OF EMPTINESS IMPLYING THE INTERRELATEDNESS OF ALL THINGS COMPARED WITH CATHOLIC APPROACHES

Our brief Buddhist-Christian discussion is meant to offset some of the limitations of postmodernism.[28] The Buddhist notion of emptiness (nothingness) and the Christian notion of faith can ground a spiritual world bridge. For example, Buddhist *nothingness* is akin to the *nada* or *Nichts* of Christian mystics. Vatican II declared that Buddhism teaches "the radical insufficiency of this shifting world" and that it offers a path in which men and women "can attain supreme enlightenment" (*Declaration on Non-Christians*— no. 2). Such an enlightenment helps one realize the interrelatedness of all things. Buddhist studies do need the expert guidance of specialists to grasp the implications of Buddhist doctrines. Robert Magliola is one such specialist (See Appendix 4). Nagarjuna and Aquinas dialectically addressed their opponents by reconciling conflicting views in deeper syntheses. Pope Francis on his 2019 visit to Asia asked Catholics and Buddhists "to heal the wounds of conflict that through the years have divided people of different cultures, ethnicities and religious convictions." He reminded them that to achieve this unity it is necessary "to surmount all forms of misunderstanding, intolerance, prejudice and hatred."[29] In his November 17, 2019 homily, Francis said:

> Those who speak the language of Jesus are not the ones who say I, but rather the ones who *step out* of themselves. And yet how often, even when we do good, does self's hypocrisy take over? I do good so that I can be considered good; I give in order to receive in turn. . . . That is how the language of the self speaks. The word of God, however, spurs us to a "genuine love" (Rom 12:9), to give to those who cannot repay us (cf. Lk 14:14), to serve others without seeking anything in return (cf. Lk 6:35). So let us ask ourselves: "Do I help someone who has nothing to give me in return? Do I, a Christian, have at least one poor person as a friend?"

These words point to the need of self-emptying so as to be filled with God's love. Recall that Nagarjuna adapted the Buddha's message of emptiness to changed circumstances.[30] Buddhists and Christians have both resorted to popular tales or myths that modern scholars have had to demythologize,[31] but Pope Francis brings us back to love's true meaning as self-emptying. He confronts us with the life-meaning import of religious and philosophical teachings. Language is subject to conventions. Bernard Lonergan's method enables us to view both conventions and language in foundational ways. All humans use the same four basic operations of being attentive, intelligent, rational and responsible; they are interrelated through their common humanity. Humans can become ever more interrelated to the extent that they transcend conventions by adverting to their common cognitive foundations which can lead to self-transcendence. In the measure that we realize this, we can deepen human cooperation among nations. Leo XIII directed that Catholic seminaries and universities were to go back to Aquinas' works and abandon the distorted forms of Scholasticism then in vogue. He also directed that scriptural studies should be taught according to modern scholarship. His foresight was partly responsible for Vatican II's reassessment of the basic teachings of the world religions. Following Leo XIII's directives, Lonergan studied what Aquinas wrote on grace and freedom. This led him to propose eight functional specialties that can link theology with other human studies and to clarify how cognition functions in the minds of all persons, including the ways the scientific method is used to transform the world—not just to deconstruct meaning a la Jacques Derrida (See Appendix 4). Jean-Luc Marion, a staunch Catholic and former student of Derrida, has like Lonergan rehabilitated metaphysics, concerned as he is with today's idolatries.

STRATEGIC CONCLUSION TO CHAPTER 6

We course between extremes to discover truth wherever it is to be found—a traditional Catholic approach! We have identified problem areas in the Church hoping that it will respond to Pope Francis' initiatives meant to plant seeds that would germinate in a future Church Council. We explore ways to foster intimacy so as to avoid the pitfalls of large, faceless organizations. In a world of constant change, Christians must rely on "the Word of God" (91). Church teachings must ever be updated to address intra- and interfaith issues so as to help transform the world ethically[32] and spiritually. We invoke the Middle Ways of Buddhism and Christianity while calling attention to the centrist positions of recent popes. Jesus' parables illustrate how we are to help build God's Kingdom.[33] The revisions of the Code of Canon Law and of the *Church Catechism* stress that the liturgy is an "action" of the whole Christ (*Christus totus*). Those who "celebrate it without signs are already in the heavenly liturgy, where celebration is wholly communion and feast." It is the whole community, the Body of Christ united with its Head, that celebrates" the liturgy—the sacrament of unity (*Catechism*, 1136–40). Our last two chapters examine how communities may contribute to a just peace based on global cooperation. The decline of dogmatic formulations today may actually help the Church play a constructive role. Interfaith and intra-faith dialogues are best achieved in intimate I-Thou communication, not in I-It fashion. We must seek the truth, but ever lurking in the background are the realities of human shortcomings and lacks of communication.

NOTES

1. Cf. John Paul II, Encyclical Letter *Redemptoris Missio*, 56: AAS 83 (1991), 302–04.
2. https://www.nytimes.com/2009/08/09/business/09cerb.html.
3. Cardinal Hamao quoted in "Vatican Official Wants Greater Independence for Local Churches," Catholic World News—cited by Gibson in *The Rule of Benedict*, 35.
4. *Rerum Novarum*, no. 48.
5. John Raymaker, *Empowering Philosophy and Science with the Art of Love* (UPA, 2006) studies how cognitive and spiritual worlds seek to interpret the truth. The Buddhist *Lotus Sutra* makes maximal claims for Buddha. Ancient Hindu, Christian, Buddhist or Taoist texts have to be understood in their original context as well as our own. These contexts have to be bridged so that students of spirituality can communicate in credible ways. In some ways, *Laudato Si*, like Buddhism, reminds us that everything is interrelated. No individual plant or animal, and indeed no species, is an island.
6. C. Otto Scharmer, *Theory U, Leading from the Future as it Emerges* (Sol Press, 2007). Decision makers in industry and education often feel trapped. What is needed is reconciling premodern and postmodern forms of thinking and organizing.
7. John Caputo in *Philosophy and Theology* (Nashville: Abington 2006) reminds us that despite what divides philosophy and theology, the two share a sense of awe, a common gasp of surprise or astonishment. With Job, we can proclaim our innocence in the face of evil; God is the judge,
8. Ian E. Thompson. *Being and Meaning: Paul Tillich's Theory of Meaning, Truth and Logic* (Edinburgh University Press, 1981), 50. Steve Bruce, *God is Dead: Secularization in the West* (Oxford: Blackwell, 2002) supports the Weber-Durkheim thesis on secularism.
9. *Anatman* does not merely replace Hinduism's *atman*, self, nor is it to be confused with a Hindu idea of "not-self"; rather it indicates a "non-self" or an "absence-of-self" notion pointing to one's true nature. In much of Buddhism, what is called the self is only an agglomeration of changing physical and mental constituents.
10. Robert Forman, "What does Mysticism have to Teach us about Consciousness," *Journal of Consciousness Studies* 5 (2):185–201, 1998. He defines mysticism as a set of experiences (conscious events) not to be described "in terms of sensory experience or mental images." One may not be aware of a specific content or thought, but something persists in a PCE contentless consciousness, known in Buddhism (Zen) as *sunyata* (void) or *samadhi* by Hindus. In *Silent Music* (New York: Harper & Row, 1974) William Johnston explores mystical love and silence in the *Gita* and in St. John of the Cross. An apophatic mysticism is devoid of sensory language. If Buddhists see this world as empty, ephemeral ("Only the Buddha world is true") Christians have a sense that a person can potentially foster a true encounter with another person or with another tradition. Buddhist-Christian encounters, for example, may consist in relating Kingdom-of-God justice with Buddhist compassion. This means that members of the two traditions would migrate beyond the intellectual plane to address one another with heart-to-heart warmth.
11. The condemnation ended attempts at an inculturated Christianity in the Far East. Not realizing that the Rites meant respecting (not "worshipping") ancestors, the Vatican action ended the promising start of evangelization in China. In the West, a decadent Scholasticism reinforced the isolation of Catholic thought in Europe.
12. "Some Aspects of Christian Meditation," *L'Osservatore Romano*, January 2, 1990; failing to consult Asians, it ignores Pius XI, *Quadragesimo Anno*, AAS 23, 1931, that "just as it wrong to withdraw from the individual and commit to the community at large what private enterprise and endeavor can accomplish," so it is unjust to turn over to a greater society of higher rank functions that can be performed by lesser bodies on a lower plane. For Asian bishops, Eastern mystic prayer sharpens our awareness of the One "hidden . . . in the heart" (*Asia Focus*, Feb. 10, 1990). The Letter might have avoided problems by giving full amplitude to mystics' response to God's gift; see Raymaker, "The Dilemma Created by the Vatican Letter," *East Asian Pastoral Review*, 27, 1990. In 2010, the Carmelite, Fr. Luigi Borriello, stressed that all are called to mysticism. https:// zenit.org/articles/all-are-called-to-mysticism/. One might compare the approaches to selflessness in Buddhism (as a belief-doctrine) and in Christianity as spiritual ideals.

13. Sakashita Shotaro, *Satori*, tr. by J. Raymaker, *Japan Mission Journal*, Winter 1999, 219–26. Ruben Habito, *Healing Breath: Zen Spirituality for a Wounded Earth* (New York: Orbis, 1993). Arnold J. Toynbee, *A Study of History* (London: Oxford University, 1947), iii, 248, on creative mystics transforming the world through the struggles of history.

14. Thomas Merton, *Zen and the Birds of Appetite* (New York: New Directions, 1975). Paul Knitter, "Thomas Merton's Eastern Remedy for Christianity's 'Anonymous Dualism,'" *Cross Currents*, 31, 3, 1981, 286, sees Merton as overcoming a theological, Platonist "dualism." In parallel fashion, Richard Liddy describes Lonergan's writings as a *Transforming Light* (Collegeville, MN: Liturgical Press, 1993).

15. Heinrich Dumoulin, *Zen Buddhism: A History*, vol 2. (New York: Macmillan, 1990) 233.

16. Paul Leshota, "From dependence to interdependence: Towards a practical theology of disability." *HTS Theological Studies Herv. teol. stud.* vol.71 n.2 Pretoria 2015.

17. Lonergan, (*Method*, 117, 123). See also Hendrik Vroom *Religions and the Truth* (Grand Rapids: Eerdmans, 1989), 378. Vroom suggests how world religions can share transcendence even if they differ in their faith-belief approaches to the apophatic.

18. www.raimon-panikkar.org/english/gloss-ecunemical.html. *Nostra Aetate*, "Declaration on the Relationship of the Church to Non-Christian Religions," 2, *Documents of Vatican II*, W. Abbot (America Press, 1966).

19. Thomas Kochumuttom, *Comparative Theology: Christian Thinking and Spirituality in Indian Perspective* (Bangalore: Dharmaram, 1985) 14

20. Non-Christian Indian theologians long ago developed three basic means (*marga*s) as to how we can attain God, namely *karma-marga* (the way of action), *jnana-marga* (way of knowledge) and *bhakti-marga* (way of devotion). These have parallels in Christianity. Kochumuttom, *Comparative Theology*, 49, stresses *marga* and *karma* action as unselfish and creative. In both Hinduism and Buddhism, *yana* (path) and *marga* refer to a spiritual paths—as does the Chinese *Tao*. Foundational perspectives of Buddhist-Christian thought stress that Buddhist "nothingness" is not mere nihility; it is a relational template virtually interrelating all beings. For Chinese Buddhists "non-self, non-action" relate us to deeper realities—to the void (emptiness= *sunyata*). There is a non-dual relationship (no true separation) between conventional truth and ultimate truth.

21. Kochumuttom, *Comparative Theology*, 25; a guru's authority is a key concept in India's spiritual thinking. One may see Christ as a *Guru-avatara* and "the Church as "the *gurukula*." A Western *gurukula* must respect Asian-African ways of responding to the Spirit. Pope John Paul II's *Faith and Reason*, 72, endorses Asian-African theologians; only natives can inculturate a symbolic system with transcultural categories.

22. The first CELAM Conference in 1968 sought to apply Vatican II to South America.

23. Friends had helped the young Karol Wojtyla escape the fate of prison in Dachau. As Pope, he helped the Polish Solidarity Movement put an end to Communism in Europe.

24. Matthew Lamb, *Solidarity with Victims: Toward a Theology of Social Transformation* (New York: Crossroad, 1982).

25. Thich Nhat Hanh, *Anger: Wisdom for Cooling the Flames* (New York: Riverhead, 2001) helps readers discover the nature of one's anger and obsessions. He explains how the seeds of love and compassion can be strong enough to deal with anger. Anger born of injustice cannot be allowed to take the form of violent attacks upon the presumed "other" (35). Buddhist and Christian perspectives on anger and emotions complement one another. St. Francis de Sales was originally very irascible but he learned to be gentle.

26. In *Jesus: A Revolutionary Biography* (Harper, 1994) John Dominic Crossan calls attention to the "quite deliberate political dramatizations of the priority of one specific leader over another. . . . Those stories are mainly interested in power and authority. They presume rather than create authority" (169). The work of Crossan, a leader of the Jesus seminar, is controversial but his observations on early Church authority are noteworthy.

27. Our efforts to understand the valid claims of Yoga and Zen reject eclecticism. Rather than saying all of Buddhism is compatible with Christianity, we argue that Christian Zen can bridge East-West spiritualities. Because it minimizes words, Zen opens us to apophatic ways of experiencing God. Nagarjuna's Middle Path and the social ethics of Thich Nhat Hanh's are

sound. The Dalai Lama has a personal charism, but left-hand Buddhism and some of the esoteric Buddhism in Tibet call for closer evaluation.

28. Like Eckhart's *Nichts* or Saint John of the Cross' *nada*, the Buddhist "void" (*sunyata, mu*) seeks to "express" an apophatic experience. Gordon Rixon, "Bernard Lonergan and Mysticism," *Theological Studies*, Sep., 2001, 479–97 on Buddhist-Christian apophatics.

29. Pope Francis called on Catholics and Buddhists in Myanmar "to be united" in order "to heal the wounds of conflict that through the years have divided people of different cultures, ethnicities and religious convictions." He reminded them that to achieve this unity it is necessary "to surmount all forms of misunderstanding, intolerance, prejudice and hatred." www.americamagazine.org/faith/2017/11/29/pope-francis-buddhists-and-catholics-must-unite-against-intolerance-prejudice.

30. Edward Conze, *Buddhism: Its Essence and Development* (New York: Harper, 1959), 29, notes that in their desire to adapt themselves to peoples' various mentalities, the Buddhists used mythological explanations for those who thought in mythic terms. The method of wisdom that sees only impersonal forces in enlightenment (*satori*) but seeks to foster interpersonal relations seem contradictory. Stcherbatsky, *Conception of Buddhist Nirvana*, (Leningrad, 1927) 36, notes that the religious revolution moved from an atheistic, soul-denying philosophy teaching the path of personal Final Deliverance and the "extinction" of life, to the establishment of a High Church with a Supreme God a host of Saints and clericalism. Ethically, the revolution was from the ideal of a private "salvation to that of a universal unconditional deliverance of all beings."

31. The biblical scholar Rudolf Bultmann spoke of *existenziell* responses to Jesus' message (*kerygma*). This prompted others to demythologize the Church's dogmas. Modern Buddhist scholars have had an analogous task of explaining basic Buddhist teachings. Lonergan's comments on Bultmann (*Method in Theology*, 158, 169, 196, 318) help us grasp the Bible's message exegetically, historically and existentially.

32. https://earthcharter.org/news-post/fritjof-capra-laudato-si-the-ecological-ethics-and-systemic-thought-of-pope-francis/.

33. Dupuis, *Christian Theology of Religious Pluralism*, follows Pope John Paul II's Kingdom-Spirit paradigms. In *Ecclesia in Asia*, 1999, the Pope stresses Jesus as "gift" proclaimed in dialogue with Asia. His *Dominus Iesus*, 2000, cautions against a pluralism of the type espoused in Roger Haight, *Jesus Symbol of God* (Maryknoll: Orbis, 1999).

Chapter Seven

Historical, Philosophical, and Ecumenical Perspectives on World Problems

Due to the many gaps in our lives caused by secularism, we are in need of concrete structures that would enable us to live the faith intimately. Intimacy with God is an end in itself. The renewed structures Pope Francis is seeking would enable Christians to put their lived experience in the service of a God-centered-intimacy to help establish God's Kingdom on earth. Chapters 1–6 illustrated how religious and mystic experience can help foster dialogue among Buddhists, Christians and Muslims. Jesus demands conversion; he accepts all as brothers and sisters. This chapter first contextualizes issues so as lead into our final chapter on how SCC's could help renew the churches in appropriate ways.

CONTEXTUALIZING HISTORICAL AND ECUMENICAL ISSUES THROUGH INTERDIVIDUALITY AND A METAPHYSICS THAT CAN CLARIFY TODAY'S COMPLEXITIES

Richard Rorty and Gianni Vattimo have written on religion's future.[1] The anticlerical Rorty allows that privatized religion may be a source of consolation for some. In contrast, Vattimo recognizes that it is the advent of Christianity that made possible the progressive "dissolution of metaphysics." He advocates a radical hermeneutics as "the development and maturation of the Christian message" (46–47). He seeks to mediate the transition from Modernism to Postmodernism. He treats nihilism positively—not as something to be overcome. He argues that in developed societies there is a plurality of interpretations due to the media and ever-increasing movements of peoples so that there is no longer any dominant way of seeing the world. Our study of "nothingness" in Buddhism reinforces Vattimo's interpretation of Nietzschean "nihilism." For Vattimo, nihilism does not imply the negation of all values; rather, it removes value and truth from a supposedly ahistorical status. Even the skeptical Rorty recognizes the role of love in life—but he rejects transcendence and metaphysics as illusions. Rather than dissolving metaphysics, Lonergan redefines it as "the department of human knowledge that underlies, penetrates, transforms, and unifies all other departments."[2] Redefining metaphysics on the basis of humans' "pure desire to know" differs from the classical notions of metaphysics rejected by most modern philosophers. Lonergan's *Insight* and his *Method in Theology* develop a method that parallel the views of Rorty and Vattimo but is based on our cognitive operations that leads to his re-grounding metaphysics.[3] His analyses of human understanding led him to develop eight functional specialties that pivot on the criterion of conversion—a solid basis for implementing a cooperative global ethics.

Rene Girard's notion of interdividuality stresses persons' interrelatedness. While people believe that their desires are "authentic," in fact, one creates desires by imitating others. Interdividuality means that we are constituted by parents, authority figures, peers or rivals whom we internalize as models. They become the unconscious basis of our desires. This does not negate the freedom of the will but it does condition it. Humankind, as created in the image of God, is not intended to be identical to the other nor to be subservient to the other. Girard links his notion of interdividuality to mimetic desire, to a scapegoat mechanism and to biblical demystification. Mimetic desire operates as a subconscious imitation of another's desire and the human tendency toward scapegoating. "Our freedom depends on being constituted by the other."[4] Girard's insights can help lay a basis for our own advocacy of intermediate structures that would mediate cross-cultural, interfaith, ethical encounters. While Girard postulates that conflicts are often fought over trivial matters, we seek to integrate interdisciplinary and interfaith insights. Sadly, desires are exploited today; many youths know all about sex, but fail to learn true love—the sad result of shallow secularist thinking. Today, believers are called to re-enlighten the world.

Girard was an atheist until his study of the Bible led him to see things differently. He had expected to find scapegoating dynamics at work in the Bible as he had in other sacred religious texts and myths. Instead he saw the exact opposite: the Bible's stories denounce scapegoating. Many liberals espoused Girard's thought until he expressed his Christian convictions. Faith and conversion do make a difference in how one dialogues! As Girard pleads for atonement to help restore disintegrating cultural values, so we argue for the necessity of a Church Council that would seek to remedy misunderstandings, to find ways to prevent religious and political conflicts. We must learn in "the trenches" as did Teilhard de Chardin, Tillich, Gabriel Marcel who all had their faith strengthened in the midst of violence. Having learned the meaning of atonement, they began to address the complex causes of conflict.

Chapters 1–6 have proposed ways of overcoming secularist illusions that would split people from their very selves and from others. They examined traditionalist and progressive views vying for Catholic allegiance. Traditionalists seek to preserve traditions; progressives argue that this must not hamper our ability to address the future. To mediate between the two views we focus on *conversion* as does Jesus. Interdividuality can help believers overcome individualism. This requires a dialogical process that clarifies how scapegoating and shallow thinking poison human relations.

A VATICAN III COUNCIL THAT WOULD SQUARELY TACKLE CHURCH SHORTCOMINGS

What could a Vatican III council contribute to make people across the world more aware of the dangers of scapegoating? Our panoramic view of history insists on the need of truly listening to others. Practically speaking, both traditionalists and progressives should evaluate the Church's present strong points as well as the way it has survived periods of scandals such as those of the tenth and fifteenth centuries. It was saints and other persons of integrity who rescued the Church. History has much to teach us on this issue. The disintegration of the Carolingian Empire was succeeded by a medieval Christendom. The popes could not prevent the land-hungry European nobility fighting endless civil wars in which the papacy was enmeshed. Consider, for example, Pope John XI (931–935) under whom the papacy reached a nadir. One can hardly say this pope "reigned." As the son of Marozia and her reputed lover, Pope Sergius III, he was his mother's tool until his half-brother confined him in the Lateran until his death. Many popes acted more like politicians than as Christian pastors. During this nadir of the papacy, the Abbey of Cluny launched a reform movement which culminated in Pope Gregory VII's reforms. By deposing the Emperor Henry IV, Gregory translated his personal, mystical convictions into effective action. Papal history, however, points to many other examples of self-serving lacking in Christian principles.

Since Vatican II, many theologians no longer view past dogmatic formulations of the Church as unquestionable. They have re-examined past doctrinal formulations to verify how or in what sense they apply to the present. Indeed, God's ways are mysterious. If the papacy had become the puppet of local Roman politics in the early Middle Ages, the Holy Spirit liberated it. But the rise of the nation-state personified in King Philip the Fair in France managed to make the popes of Avignon a French tool. Pope Boniface VIII resisted Philip's machinations. God intervened again with Catherine of Siena who led Pope Gregory XI back to Rome in 1378. This was soon followed by Urban VI whose stubborn authoritarianism led to the Great Western Schism when three papal claimants threatened the Church's unity. The Council of Constance, which overcame the Schism, declared itself supreme over the whole Church and the "three popes." It condemned the reformer John Hus to be burned at the stake by the civil power after a "trial" that ascribed views to him that he in fact did not hold. Martin V, a scion of the Colonna family whom that Council elected to resolve the Great Schism, initiated another episode of ascendancy of Italian families over the papacy. A theory of Conciliarism emerged which would allow a pope to be judged by the Church from below, but it soon lost influence. The Dominican theologian Cajetan (1469–1534), an opponent of Conciliarism, wanted to unify, defend and reform the institution under clerical control. Meanwhile, Cajetan's Franciscan contemporary, Francesco della Rovere was elected pope, reigning as Sixtus IV (1471–84). Sixtus IV promoted his nephew, the future Julius II, to the cardinalate. Between these two della Rovere popes, reigned Alexander VI who fathered an illegitimate son, Cesare Borgia. Machiavelli modelled *The Prince*—a guidepost for cynical, unscrupulous politicians—upon Cesare Borgia. Such excesses led to Martin Luther's Reformation. Luther needed the help of scheming German princes to carry out his Reform. With Protestantism, it was no longer the sacrament of penance (with an "absolution" allowing the same sins to be repeated *ad nauseam*) that mattered. Rather one was called to constant conversion through a faith that distrusts reason's limitations. The Council of Trent (1545-1563) did its best to reform the Church. Today, we must ask how can a Church which survived scandals re-adapt itself to become an instrument of peace in the twenty-first century? How can Asian and African theological insights help Catholicism move from Western perspectives to global ones?

A POSSIBLE GRAND STRATEGY FOR A POSSIBLE VATICAN III

The impetus of Vatican II reforms was partly undone by John Paul II's naming only conservative bishops. He and Cardinal Ratzinger ignored Vatican Council II texts not pleasing to their mindsets. Vatican II praised the modern world's achievements in human rights, growth of political and religious freedom and development of medical and scientific treatments. But the Church's opposition to the use of contraceptives in family planning have hurt its credibility in the eyes of many. John Paul II's notion of a monolithic Church was patterned on a conservative Polish model,[5] now exemplified in the Kajinski regime. It took Pope Francis to oppose Latin American rightist bishops who had attacked the option for the poor but failed to speak out against militias who killed thousands of those who stood up for justice. In our *Pope Francis, Conscience of the World*, we explore how Francis has addressed both global and local issues (See Appendix 6). His vision may foreshadow themes to be addressed at a Vatican III Council. Historically, Luther's Reformation led to the founding of new religious orders such as the Jesuits. In the post-Tridentine period, popes worked tirelessly to restore papal prestige. The 2019 Synod on the Amazon has made bishops aware that the laity should be more involved in governing the Church. It marked a turning point for the emergence of a truly global Church, one that is still struggling to break free from a clericalism that continues to be an obstacle to the full implementation of Vatican II teachings. The weakness of human nature ever reasserts itself as just noted in our overview of papal history. It was not a divided papacy that resolved the Great Schism but initiatives from the Church from below. Recent abuses in the Church pale when compared with some of the ecclesial failures in past centuries. The question of who can call a Church Council has been disputed. The first Council of the Church in Nicaea was convened by Emperor Constantine. The history of the Councils of Pisa, Constance and Basle during the Great Schism offer other useful lessons. When progressive bishops were pre-empted from exercising a "true-to-the-Gospel" ministry, when liberation theologians were one-sidedly accused of being Marxist (while rightist militias' crimes were tolerated), the Church from below acted. Paul VI who guided Vatican II to its end could not prevent ensuing polarizations. Since John Paul II did not fully understand Western democracies, he let conservatives take over Church leadership in the West—supposedly to maintain Catholic "self-identity." The hierarchy was left free to ignore the pleas of Church reformers. But this has changed dramatically under Pope Francis' watch. Many cultural crossovers are occurring in our globalized societies. How might the Church build on Pope Francis' legacy so as to help the Church fulfill its mission to help save humanity in our crisis-ridden age. Faith here is most important.

The Church is both traditionalist and progressive. In the Apostles' Creed we recite the four marks of the Church: "I believe . . . in One, Holy, Catholic, Apostolic Church." The four marks suggest that the Church fosters a holistic hope in the world while avoiding the fragmented policies of loosely organized sects. Pope Francis stresses that authority must not be used arbitrarily; rather it must be based on persuasive forms of leadership. The four marks presuppose the Church's constant effort to establish the Kingdom preached by Jesus; they are still the identifying traits of a genuine Christianity blessed with loving communities intent on God's justice. Despite the changes in contemporary cultures, the four marks of the Church and its central teaching on love underpin its global ministry. The Christian imperative of love is subject to some conflicting interpretations. We argue that Catholic self-identity is not individualist; through grace, it participates in Trinitarian love. Theologians such as Barth and Rahner[6] sought to balance St. Augustine's view on the Trinity with that of the Cappadocian Fathers. Augustine focused on how God turns our hearts around through grace. He opposed both the Pelagians who failed to address the wounded aspect of human nature and the Donatists who inveighed against corrupt priests. The Cappadocians had a serene theology based on Trinitarian love. Generally speaking, the early Church taught that Jesus and the Holy Spirit jointly mediate the love of the Father in each Christian and in the Church as a whole through grace. Intrafaith Christian debates on the Trinity concern the Church's relations with other religions only inasmuch as these do not accept Church dogmas. Still, in today's pluralist world, the Church must address the concerns of other religions with an open spirit. It can do so by emphasizing social justice. When informed with faith and love, conflicting beliefs can be approached so as to minimize divisions. Only faith can unite believers from different creeds; faith can unite because it transcends beliefs' verbal limitations. The conflicting agendas of orthodox believers in Judaism, Christianity and Islam have led to division and wars. Surely, one should preserve the good in one's tradition—intra-and-interfaith dialogues were both encouraged at Vatican II. That Council led to much interreligious dialogue—as was illustrated in John Paul II's remarkable encounter at Assisi with the world's religious leaders (1986). This was an example of unity-within-diversity. Pope Francis is the first pope who chose to be named after the great saint of Assisi who wanted to rebuild God's Church. Traditionalist and progressive Catholics should address the historical encounters with other religions using the faith-belief distinction. The distinction is consistent with our stress on both a relational theology and on lived experience as crucial to ecumenical and theological encounters. It underpins a possible grand strategy for a Vatican III. It is also key to how the Church can reconcile and integrate such parallel tasks as ecumenism evangelization, and interfaith outreach. These parallel tasks complement another task incumbent upon all religions, that of helping build peace by fostering tolerance.

NEEDED INTERFAITH DIALOGUES WITH ISLAM TO OFFSET TERRORIST VIOLENCE INITIATIVES TAKEN BY POPES JOHN PAUL II, BENEDICT XVI AND FRANCIS

Christianity has played a pivotal role in the West, but a lesser one in other parts of the world. With the rise of Islam, Christianity has declined tremendously in the Near East and North Africa; it has declined in the West due to secularism. The two forms of decline reflect some of the gaps that leave the modern world prone to violence and alienation. Some Islamic extremists violently oppose Western secularism.[7] Many "well-meaning" Islamic terrorists have attacked what they perceive as threats to their values. This has poisoned the atmosphere. In some respects, the birth of globally-concerned societies began in the Middle Ages when Jews, Christians and Muslims created a scientific-technological culture that led to the formation of Western universities in the twelfth and thirteenth centuries. Humbly acknowledging the West's debt to Islam could help blunt the increasingly sectarian nature of Christian-Muslim encounters. Colonization, the result of Western technological prowess has led to migrations from former colonies—provoking more distrust between Muslims and Europeans. If globalization is an irreversible phenomenon with its attendant religious dimensions, we are now faced with the urgent need to learn from history so as to help guide the future. The Church seems particularly well poised to help the West and the wider world understand relevant implications with a view to heal.

In May, 2001, John Paul II became the first pope ever to pray in an Islamic mosque that of the Umayyad Mosque in Damascus, Syria. He had expressed his desire for reconciliation with Muslims in 1985 when he addressed over 50,000 Muslim youths in Casablanca (1984) saying that Christians and Muslims had misunderstood one another:

> We have opposed each other and even exhausted ourselves in polemics and wars. I believe that God is calling us today to change our old habits. We have to respect each other and stimulate each other in good works upon the path indicated by God. In a world that desires unity and peace, but which experiences a thousand tensions and conflicts, believers should foster . . . friendship among (the) single community on earth (*L'Osservatore Romano*, August 1985).

Pope John Paul II had gained Muslims' respect for having opposed the invasion of Iraq. Muslims felt that this showed that the Church was not President Bush's tool as seemed to have been the case with US evangelicals. Still, in recent years, there have been signs of growing discord between the Catholic Church and Islam. Following Pope John Paul' IIs death in 2005, Pope Benedict XVI's announced his opposition to Turkey's entrance into the European Union. This aroused deep suspicion in the Islamic world. A further ambiguity as to Benedict's intentions was fueled by his speech about faith and reason at the University of Regensburg, Germany in September, 2006. In discussing the issue of just or "holy" wars and forced conversions, he quoted a Byzantine Emperor. Without alluding to the difference in treatment accorded those who have the "Book" and the "infidels," the Emperor blurts out: "Show me just what Muhammad brought that was new, and there you will find things only evil and inhuman, such as his command to spread by the sword the faith he preached." The offending quote (tangential to the Pope's intended message) set off many protests.[8] Benedict wanted to stress that it is unreasonable to use force to spread one's faith but his intended meaning got lost in context. Unfortunately, Christians and Muslims find it hard to reconcile their divergent beliefs in Jesus and Muhammad.[9] At Regensburg, Benedict noted the use of the Greek notion of *logos* in the prologue of John's Gospel: "In the beginning was the Word" (*Logos*). For Jews and Christians, reason and the word—both of which were at the heart of Greek thought—are not antithetical to faith. Not intending to offend Muslims, Benedict asked whether a pious Muslim is amenable to reasonable dialogue.[10] Today's reality of religious pluralism has brought such issues into sharp focus. In the face of recent Islamic terrorism, we must not forget that most Muslims are peaceful. Benedict's attempt at Regensburg to clarify the mutuality of the roles of Islamic and Christian believers in a secular world backfired. Failing to consult Islamic experts, he merely quoted the 1996 doctoral thesis of Adel Khoury. Broader consultation with experts would have avoided the worldwide wrath of Muslims. Post factum, Benedict sought to remedy his misstep by meeting with the Islamic ambassadors to the Vatican and acknowledging that dialogue "is in fact, a vital necessity." But he did not back away from his Regensburg remarks, insisting that a condition for interfaith dialogue with Islam is that its leaders try to prevent extremist violence. As to the West, it must reject its "dictatorship of relativism" whose goal is merely to satisfy one's own selfish desires.

Pope Francis has helped bridge some of the cultural gaps between Western democracies and traditional Islamic societies. He has been sharing faith, hope and love so as to help lessen conflicts. For example, in February, 2019, he made the first papal visit to the Arabian peninsula, namely to the United Arab Emirates (UAE), one of the few Muslim majority countries to allow its large Christian minority population to publicly practice its faith. He called for an end to the violence in Yemen which has brought about an ever-worsening humanitarian crisis. Francis' public Mass in the capital city of Abu Dhabi drew about 4,000 Muslims among the 135,000 people present. Many of the attendees were Catholic migrants from places such as the Philippines and South America. In conjunction with the Pope' visit to the UAE, there took place the Global Conference on Human Fraternity in Abu Dhabi. This meeting included 700 representatives from Islam, Judaism, Hinduism, Sikhism, Buddhism and other faiths. In Abu Dhabi the pope said:

> The enemy of fraternity is an individualism which translates into the desire to affirm oneself and one's own group above others. This danger threatens all aspects of life, even the highest innate prerogative of man, that is, the openness to the transcendent and to religious piety. True religious piety consists in loving God with all one's heart and one's neighbor as oneself. Religious behavior . . . needs continually to be purified from the recurrent temptation to judge others as enemies and adversaries. Each belief system is called to overcome the divide between friends and enemies, in order to take up the perspec-

tive of heaven, which embraces persons without . . . discrimination (February 4, 2019).

Our own under-way-strategy is modelled on Pope Francis' original approach to global problems which respects historical realities while opening doors for meaningful dialogue among religious and secularist proponents. This would include Pope Francis' 2019 message on the 19 religious men and women martyred in Algeria between 1994–1996 in which he reminded us that persecutions still occur today fueled by slanders and lies.

RESPECTING RELIGIOUS VIEWS LEST WE BE UNDERMINED BY SECULARISM

During the early Middle Ages, both Christian and Muslim thinkers stressed that God transcends human reason. But the denial of the metaphysical reality of universals by Ockham and the Nominalists in the fourteenth century undermined theology's status in the West. As for Islam, although rationalist philosophers left an indelible mark upon the terminology of later Muslim theology, they gradually became alienated from orthodox elements. After al-Ghazali(1058–1111) refuted them, they exercised little influence upon the main body of Muslim opinion. One of the most important of the Islamic schools was that of the Illuminationists which combined the use of reason and intuition. Along with gnosis, this school has played a vital role in the intellectual life of Islam.[11] Its mystical element combines a "heart-intellect" approach in gaining knowledge. The questions revolving around faith and reason are central to both the Christian and Islamic traditions. It is impossible to reduce either tradition to just one school of thought. A diplomatic blunder, Benedict's Regensburg address threatened to set back Christian/ Islamic relations for years; it illustrates the Church's need to understand the modern world's sensibilities—a point Pope understands very well.

Pope John Paul II was open to non-Catholics, but he marginalized Catholic critics of his policies on e.g., celibacy for priests. He stifled dissenting theologians. He suppressed information about the extent of the pedophilia problem among Catholic priests. He let the Congregation for the Doctrine of the Faith headed by Cardinal Ratzinger enforce his views. Ratzinger had turned from being a liberal theologian at Vatican II to one who called for Vatican II revisions. He was the main author of *Dominus Jesus* that addresses "mistaken" notions of dialogue which fail to "search for objective and absolute truth" with a view to put all religious beliefs on the same plane—this he labelled a "false idea of tolerance."[12] We stress that the Vatican II's "Declaration on the Relation of the Church to non-Christian Religions" notes that the Catholic Church rejects nothing of what is true and holy in other religions. "She has a high regard for the manner of life and conduct, the precepts and teachings, which, although differing in many ways from her own teaching . . . (do) often reflect a ray of that truth which enlightens all men" (no. 2) Still for the Church, Jesus Christ is "The way, the truth, and the life" (Jn 14:6). Interfaith dialogue, part of the Church's evangelizing mission, does not replace its mission to the non-baptized, rather it complements it. Dialogue requires a relationship of mutual knowledge and reciprocal enrichment, in obedience to the truth and with respect for freedom. In 1992, the Vatican declared that being directed toward the "mystery of unity" means "that all men and women who are saved share, though differently, in the same mystery of salvation in Jesus Christ through his Spirit."[13]

More and more young people in the West delay or forego marriage. Has the Church adequately addressed this reality? The best many bishops can do is rail against cultural relativism. Pope Francis has endorsed John Paul II's 1994 policy of not ordaining women to the priesthood expressed in *"Ordinatio Sacerdotalis"* which sought to close further official discussion on the topic; it explored all forms of ministry for women—short of ordination. The Women's Ordination Conference and the Roman Catholic Women Priest movement, however, both seek to make the priesthood more inclusive; they challenge the traditional male dominance in the priesthood. In 2002, women who had been consecrated as bishops in Germany by a Roman Catholic bishop arranged for the ordination of more women to the priesthood. Even though these ordinations may be valid, they will fail to offer women a real opportunity to practice their ministry within a Catholic parishes. The Vatican Holy Office has excommunicated ordained women and their sponsors. A growing number of married Catholic priests and bishops (both men and women) are now serving in alternative forms of Catholic ministry. Many of these meet in homes, retreat centers or universities. The American Church is unique in the world because it functions within a democratic political structure that had been suspect in the Church prior to Vatican II. A Vatican III Council could take the Church into the twenty-first century by giving reform groups a place at the table in dialoguing about the Church's future. With Pope Francis, we seek to lay bridges between Catholic reform and conservative groups that might necessitate new viable Church structures.

THE EMERGENCE OF INDEPENDENT CATHOLIC CONGREGATIONS AND ALTERNATIVE FORMS OF ACTION ON ECCLESIAL AND CIVIL LEVELS

The Protestant Reformation led to the Catholic Counter Reformation in which the lines were hardened between the Catholic Church's clerical-hierarchical system and the newly formed evangelical movements that claimed the Bible as their sole authority. The Catholic religious culture has relied on the centralized authority of the pope who until the modern era often claimed ultimate spiritual and temporal power. Jesus was not a "cleric." Clericalism risks undermining the establishment of God's Kingdom. Our goal is not to polarize. We thankfully acknowledge that the Church has had a vast number of dedicated priests, bishops, sisters, brothers and lay people who have selflessly toiled to bring about Kingdom values. Holiness is not the sole preserve of either clerics or lay people. In reflecting on the history of the Church, on the impact of Vatican II, and in expressing the hope for another Council, we seek to discern how new forms of Christian ministries may help heal and guide our imperfect, rapidly evolving world. Clearly ours is a middle-of-the-way approach. But the Church's clerical cultural has given rise to frequent strife. For example, the Catholic Call to Action group actively supports forms of ministry and community now emerging throughout the world. The 2006 excommunication of Call to Action members in Nebraska indicates that the Church prior to Pope Francis often refused to enter into serious dialogue with its critics. The development of alternative expressions of Catholic identity has led to the emergence of many small Catholic communities in many parts of the USA. Some of these communities have married priests and women priests serving them. Many married priests, however, no longer want to engage in ministry. They prefer other options such as is offered by the Maryknoll Fathers who have encouraged a new alignment between Maryknoll and former members in the "Maryknoll Affiliates." This allows former members to participate in Maryknoll's mission activities without violating Canon Law. The modern world's needs are so great that new Church initiatives are needed to ensure that all can participate in sharing the Good News.

Some question the wisdom of preserving the Church's hierarchical structure. The challenge of modernity in the nineteenth century led to the dogma of papal infallibility as the Church's authority had begun to crumble. The retention of clericalism in the Church did ensure direct papal control over all forms of ecclesial ministry. Vatican II profoundly changed the structures and practices of the church—as intended by Pope John XXIII who wanted to renew the Church. Many of the council's decrees did bring the church into the modern world. The tendency to return to pre-Vatican II ways of doing under Popes John Paul II and Benedict XVI has now given way to Pope Francis' efforts to return to a more collegial type of governance. Francis knows that hierarchism is inadequate in democratic societies that honor the irrevocable rights of conscience to choose one's lifestyle. He stresses that we are now living in a *change of epochs* (or eras) and not just experiencing a period of change. It involves a colossal paradigm shift. Many of the sacred institutions and unique religious symbols that Catholics clung to and defended for centuries are no longer effective in the present change of epochs. The question is what needs to be changed or discarded, what is to be maintained or adapted to present needs? Francis' reintroduction of more collegial-synodal forms in governing the Church is meant to address the present pastoral vacuum on many levels of the institutional Church. The Church's rich tradition has consistently stressed freedom of conscience but not necessarily freedom to act against hierarchical decisions. As to the right of dissenting from unjust civil laws, Martin Luther King, Jr., eloquently said in the 1960's that

> There are two types of laws, just and unjust. I would be the first to advocate obeying just laws. One has not only a legal, but a moral responsibility to obey just laws. Conversely, one has a moral obligation to disobey unjust laws. I would agree with St. Augustine that an unjust law is not law at all. [14]

Church traditionalists insist that the Church did accommodate to previous cultural epochs without loss of its identity or its evangelical mission. Such accommodations must be done with fidelity to the Gospel's core message. Progressives will retort, for example, that no ecumenical council of the Church has declared celibacy to be a doctrinal requirement for the priesthood. The requirement has often been wedded to a Neoplatonic spirituality that separated the earthly and heavenly realms, claiming that marriage and family life were lesser spiritual vocations than that of a celibate life. The epoch in which we live and the emergence of alternative forms of ministry require that the Church seriously consider the alternative forms of thought in the various continents.

SOME ASIAN, AFRICAN, AND LATIN AMERICAN PHILOSOPHICAL AND THEOLOGICAL INSIGHTS AKIN TO INTERDIVIDUALITY THAT A VATICAN III COULD DISCUSS

The blind prejudices within our hearts or one's unacknowledged, uncritical assumptions must be faced. This is why we emphasize Girard's notion of interdividuality and its possible profound implications for Christian life. Unfortunately, interdividuality is subject to aberration. It should transcend the danger of deviated forms of transcendence as happens when religions resort to violence. Sin ever distorts reality. Lest the world's problems remain intractable, we stress the necessity of responsible religious policies that might counter ideologies. How may Buddhism and African or Asian insights be of help here? Buddhists stress four Noble Truths: 1) all in life is suffering; 2) the cause of suffering is desire; 3) suffering ceases by detachment from desire; 4) the eightfold path leads to detachment. Christians find a redemptive role in suffering—not just in a self-driven enlightenment. Both Buddhists and Christians have long recognized the need of community to address the problems of suffering and egoism. Buddha arrived at his ideal construct of *anatman* (non-self) as a way to overcome egoism. A Vatican III Council could further explain how Buddhist-Christian insights into Ultimate reality variously complement one another.[15] Japanese writers have touched on such issues. For the philosopher Nishida Kitaro, "The bottom of my soul has such depth: neither joy nor the waves of sorrow can reach it."[16] Endo Shushaku's *Silence* is a novel on the seeming futility of bringing the Gospel to Japan. It notes some of the ways Japanese distance themselves from Western thought. It stresses the role of culture in evangelizing. For Endo, Japan is a "swamp" that might ingest Christianity unless the latter first learns Asian values. Oe Kenzaburo, the 1994 Nobel Prize laureate for Literature, speaks of a pluriverse universe of harmony and of quixotic windmills symbolizing hope. Lest the Church fall into the realm of the impractical or the quixotic, we ask that it improve its existing intermediate structures by focusing on interrelatedness which is a cornerstone of African and Asian thought. Integrating some of the deeper currents of religion and philosophy is needed to remedy existing confusion between cultures and nations so as to have them adequately interface with one another. Interdividual love in the Church no longer looks for scapegoats. Burning John Hus at the stake was a clear instance of scapegoating to avoid reform. What remains of the Western Church must learn from the vigor of the churches in Africa and Asia—as recent popes have sought to do in the hope of making the Church a truly global one—open to other cultural traditions.

It is helpful to study the trials of those who fought the evils of slavery, or those who now seek to mediate between conflicting views. As the African ability for contrapuntal rhythms[17] guided much innovation in modern musical forms, so a feeling for "rhythmic thought" could help transform conflicting points of view. With Jesus and Pope Francis, we must grasp what are the prevailing forms of oppression today. Culture can meet culture making use of transcultural categories, but only natives can inculturate a symbolic system in a given culture, when, for instance, learning from feminism people begin to transpose their own cultural categories so as to oppose "*dharmas*" that reduce women to inferiority or exploit them. Some Western traditionalists argue that the modern world seems unable to "liberate" us from wrongful desires. Progressives might retort that they have done much to help developing nations meet their overwhelming problems.

It takes groups like Amnesty International or Greenpeace to help people realize that they are part of interrelated communities. Western traditionalists want the Latin Mass back so as to "soothe" their souls; they should learn from the spiritual insights of Africans and Asians. Because the Church realizes that culture can be either a bridge or a barrier to the Gospel, it has nurtured Indian and African theologies to help inculturate Christianity. For example, the 2019 Synod on the Amazon emphasized and praised the roles of indigenous cultures. In a message to that Synod, Pope Francis asked the Church to improve its pastoral ministry in the Amazon region. He warned against building walls and ignoring the traditions of those on the margins of society.[18]

With Pope Francis, we are calling for more healing both in the world and in the Church. Sexual abuse scandals have rocked the Church and called its moral leadership into question. The Church must now do much soul-searching on this issue.[19] A further task for a possible Vatican III Council would be to discern ways to allow more diversity in the Church by, for example, re-incorporating the talents of married priests and ordaining women deacons. New forms of ministry for both men and women would not threaten the Church; they could help make existing types of ministry more inclusive. Celibacy is not a dogma but an ideal mandated by the Church which is now challenged by many. Many reform movements in the history of Christianity remained peripheral for long periods of time before being accepted. As to integrating married priests within the life of the Church, the Church already permits certain married Lutheran and Episcopalian clergy who have converted to Roman Catholicism to function as married priests. Their families may help them be more sensitive than celibates to problems in family life. Pastoral needs should prevail over the custom of priestly celibacy.

The average age of Catholic clergy in some parts of the Western world is well over 60. Vocations lag. As was emphasized in the 2019 Synod of the Amazon, many Catholics now lack the services of experienced clergy. That synod has hopefully opened the doors to more mediation skills that do not close doors to dialogue with prophetic figures. There is, in fact, a need to heal much that is broken in the Church and world.

Celibacy as a discipline within the Church has little if any scriptural foundation; it was never an impediment to the ministry of the Church in the early centuries. For centuries, many of its priests and bishops were married. There is no doctrinal impediment to reinstating the earlier tradition in our day—as Cardinal Hummes had admitted. However, Hummes reversed himself upon his being named prefect of the Congregation for Clergy in 2006. The question is to what extent should the requirement of clerical celibacy be maintained. Some now argue that the Church has lost much of its moral standing due the clergy sexual abuse crisis and its failure to admit its complicity in certain aspects of that scandal. The original objection to the return of married Catholic priests was that it would scandalize the faithful. Some claim that a greater scandal is the failure of the Church to address the pressing pastoral needs of its Catholic faithful. Ironically the conservative approach to teaching young Catholics today can be a "turn off." The Church loses its ability to speak to young people when it polarizes the sexual situation. What it should do is to pray and reflect more on the problems of sexuality in an all too promiscuous world.

CONSOLIDATING SOME GLOBAL THEOLOGICAL INSIGHTS AND INITIATIVES

The Vatican's diplomatic status and its recent tradition of fostering peace and justice in the world should encourage leaders to view issues in their truly global contexts. The history of the Church in Africa and China as well as the events of colonialism and post-colonialism could help the Church reconsider its approach to inculturation on the basis of a global ethic. Only an inculturated global ethic can properly address the many challenges and threats facing Church and world. Consider these two historical examples:

- The Vatican's ban on Chinese rites (1704) led to an ending of Christian missions in China.
- American Jesuits faced the cultural revolution of the 1960's with renewed intellectual commitments.[20]

The Church must realistically face the challenges and threats to religious relevance. Some might argue that the Church's western origins militate against its being a universal religion. Pope Clement XI's condemnation of the Chinese rites ignored the linguistic and anthropological components of non-Western cultures. Overly conservative Western Catholics (who prefer a Church magisterium that quotes only itself) see Vatican II's renewal as endangering the faith. The Church's role in Africa and in Latin America has been ambiguous. Liberation theologies that emerged in South America in the 1970's met resistance in the Vatican. In the 1980's, Vatican officials were allowed to again take matters into their own hands. Their often shortsighted policies—prior to Pope Francis—imposed inadequate policies on the entire Church. We need capable mediators to decolonize theology as pioneered, e.g., in the writings of the African theologian F. Eboussi Boulaga (1934–2018). Boulaga argued that Western missionaries preached a "revelation" that seemed to justify imperialism.[21] One cannot generalize on the Church's role in East and West Africa, where Catholics have had to contend with multifaith heritages and colonialist legacies. The Church's role in Tanzania and Nigeria, for instance, is noteworthy in that the indigenous clergy has been able to build on the sound basis established by missionaries in the nineteenth and early twentieth centuries. In Tanzania, Julius Nyerere's Ujamaa movement influenced the way the Church's 29 dioceses seek to foster justice. Even as Tanzania became somewhat more capitalism-oriented, the Church helped the people assimilate the roots of its Sukuma culture later influenced by Arabians and Westerners. In Nigeria, the legacy of the Biafran War (1967–70) lingers. Nigeria now seeks to balance the many interests of its various Muslim and Christian tribes. More efforts are needed for Nigerians to stabilize their land. As to the complex remnants of colonialism in

Africa, one can single out failure of the Mugabe regime in Zimbabwe. Mugabe, originally a Catholic teacher in a mission school in Southern Rhodesia, went into politics backing Joshua Nkomo. After helping lead the revolution that deposed Jan Smith, he was elected prime minister in 1980. His rule led to tragic consequences due to greed and ineptitude. Relations between him and the Church became strained as its bishops began criticizing his ways of grabbing land in favor of his family and cronies. By 2007, the country's infrastructure had collapsed; electricity was often unavailable. Inflation had reached an annual rate of over 1000 percent and diseases spread due to lack of money for even basic care. Mugabe's successor has not eliminated corrupt practices.

An unjust authoritarianism can have devastating consequences anywhere. On the other hand, consider the legacy of Stephen Bantu Biko, the father of the Black Consciousness Movement in South Africa, who died in 1977 at the age of 30 at the hands of the police during the era of apartheid. His legacy has influenced the African churches. For Biko, black consciousness meant liberating the mind—a psychological revolution seeking to promote African thought and feeling into an amalgam of Black pride and unity."[22] His views greatly influenced Nelson Mandela and the successful transition of South Africa from being an apartheid state to one with a majority-led democracy.

It is not easy to forgive colonialist excesses nor is it easy to govern African nations whose boundaries were arbitrarily settled in the nineteenth century according to the colonial powers' interests—while neglecting tribal realities. As was the case with China and European colonies in South America, African nations have had to defend their cultures against colonialists. The churches on the latter two continents may now have a providential role to play in rescuing a secularized West from materialism. At the 2019 Amazon Synod, Pope Francis insisted that the Church is called to listen so that new ecclesial structures might help us better live the faith. Here, and in our two books, *Steps toward Vatican III* and *Pope Francis, Conscience of the World*, we stress that Christians should establish viable structures to preserve the faith. By addressing local and global problems in relevant fashion, SCC's willing to cooperate with parishes could help the Church as a whole respond to the gospels' global implications. In contrast to some Catholics' uneven approach to Muslim dialogue, let us instance a grassroot way of building peace. In 1974, Muhammad Yunus made his first micro-credit loan to a poor woman living in Bangladesh. His micro-lending initiative grew into the Grameen Bank in 1976.This bank serves hundreds of thousands of poor people; it has disbursed over five billion dollars in funds to over 500,000 borrowers. Almost all of the loan funds come from the deposits of its members. The repayment rate of over 98 percent is almost unheard of in banking history. Grameen Bank has been a model of how poor nations can combat poverty by integrating the poor in community life. The bank even helps the country's beggars—a moral initiative. Yunus was awarded the Nobel Peace Prize in 2006 for having inspired many other developing nations to start similar micro-credit banks.

Judaism, Christianity and Islam share a common prophetic heritage calling believers to find ways to serve the needs of the poor, the destitute. Mother Theresa and her Sisters of Charity exemplify this kind of outreach; Yunus' cooperative bank, involving the poor themselves, embodies another model. Both of these have been motivated by a spiritual core. Implementing the common spiritual heritage of the monotheistic traditions can help bridge some of the divides between the poor in developing nations and the well-to-do.

Gibson Winter pointed the contradictions that can poison Christian love. He argued that suburbanites privatize love and subvert the larger metropolis. Sharing is often limited to acquaintances or small groups. Alienated individuals repress their real selves as the market place co-opts all "values."[23] A Vatican III and the theologians who would prepare for it would have to consider the cultural, historical and ethical implications of the love that should guide Christians.

STRATEGIC CONCLUSION TO CHAPTER 7

The Church must be a living model of what it preaches. The transformation of the Church into a needed collegial model of dialogue and discipleship still lies in the future but many of the elements to achieve such a goal are being developed. A Vatican Council III to reinforce Kingdom priorities would be necessary to confirm what is now happening on the periphery of the institutional Church. Our urging maximum forms of cooperation, our reliance on genuine forms of lived experience and our advocacy of functional specialties to bridge differences are all meant to promote a multicultural-interfaith structured approach to world problems. In a word, we seek theological, interdisciplinary methods to counter both naive eclecticisms and militant secularisms. Since religious experience is not independent of our concepts, beliefs, judgements or actions, we now turn to possible ways of erecting intermediate, fully cooperative structures faithful to the Catholic tradition, yet "semi-independent" of narrow hierarchic control. In many ways, the 2019 Amazon Synod shows that Pope Francis encourages such notions.

NOTES

1. Richard Rorty and Gianni Vattimo (*The Future of Religion*) ed. by Santiago Zabala (New York: Columbia University, 2005).

2. Bernard Lonergan, *Insight: A Study of Human Understanding* (Philosophical Library, 1958), 390. Redefining "being" as the objective of our pure desire to know, he shows how metaphysics proceeds from a correct cognitional theory and epistemology.

3. *In Redirecting Philosophy* (Toronto: University of Toronto,1998), Hugo Meynell argues that Rorty's merit is "to have drawn out the consequences of the principles underlying much contemporary philosophy"(175). If Rorty had drawn those consequences to the bitter end, "he would have revived idealism in an extreme form, since the human mind can become the mirror of nature in "precisely the sense that this is denied by Rorty." By that, Meynell means that by properly using our minds, we can discover what pre-exists our minds. Lonergan's method allows us to "mirror" nature in the sense that we can work out the implications of an independent world. In *The Crisis of Philosophy* (Albany: SUNY, 1990), 213, Michael H. McCarthy notes that Rorty's assessment of our historical situation partially coincides with Lonergan's. But while Rorty denies the possibility of epistemic realism, Lonergan's critical realism integrates human cognition. One of Rorty's less-known works of the late 90's was recently rediscovered. It presciently argues that promoting cultural politics above real politics is to be coupled with a growing awareness that neoliberalism is the working class' enemy This would "combine in many of them abandoning 'the Left' for a nasty populist Right—*realpolitik* in the harshest sense of the term as now incarnated in nationalist ideologies. See www.theguardian.com/us-news/2016/nov/19/donald-trump-us-election-prediction-richard-rorty.

4. Rene Girard, *I See Satan Fall Like Lightning* (Maryknoll, NY: Orbis, 2001), 137. Some use Girard's ideas, but neglect his Christian approach which includes the realities of the Cross. Randall L Rosenberg, *The Givenness of Desire: Concrete Subjectivity and the Natural Desire to See God* (University of Toronto, 2017) on Girard and Lonergan

5. John Paul II had learned from his Polish experience of tolerating no dissent in his effort to foster orthodoxy on Catholic theologians and philosophers in the world's Catholic universities. Canonical visitations were instituted in which each member of these faculties was queried. This also happened in diocesan chanceries. After New York Cardinal O'Connor's interview with John Paul, O'Connor declared an end to any experimentation in his archdiocese. Even films such as that of Elizabeth Kubler-Ross on death and dying became unavailable to New York churches and universities.

6. Neil Ormerod, "Wrestling with Rahner on the Trinity," *Irish Theological Quarterly* 68 (2003) 213–27 argues that Rahner's approach rests on an inadequate distinction between person and nature in his use of quasi-formal causality related to the incarnation.

7. Western secularism has accentuated its differences with traditional cultures (such as Islam). If people in the West no longer want secular affairs to be guided by theologies, what is the alternative? The arbitrary punishments meted out in the Islamic Republic of Iran violate international human rights norms instead of observing norms that support the equality of all citizens before civil law. The moderate President Khatami did respect the rule of law to limit the use of arbitrary theological judgments.

8. (WWW.Vatican.Va—"Regensburg"). Benedict went on to say that "After his forceful expression, the emperor explains why spreading the faith through violence is incompatible with the nature of God or the nature of the soul. For a Byzantine emperor, shaped by Greek philosophy, this would have been self-evident. The Emperor should have known that *sura* 2, 256 reads: "There is no compulsion in religion." Experts say that this *sura* dates from the early period when Muhammad was still under threat and without power. It may be that Pope Benedict had not fully grasped the historical context. The quote he used came from a clearly prejudicial source in the eyes of the Muslim world. The Pope could have used any number of contemporary Islamic scholars to show that the primary meaning of *Jihad* is not a "holy war" but rather a spiritual struggle within the believer to act in accordance with his/her true spiritual nature. In his lecture, Benedict did call for dialogue about the pressing problems in society brought about by the West's secularization. Unfortunately, followers of such traditions may not be able to reconcile the divergent beliefs regarding Jesus and Muhammad. A better forum for such discussion would be one where experts in Christian and Islamic histories could collegially explore needed clarifications. Pope John Paul's Apostolic Constitution, *Ex Corde Ecclesiae*, had pointed out the ideals that must guide a Catholic university's search for truth in our world. Ideals, important in academics' search for truth, should also guide Christians' daily lives.

9. Pope Benedict did not mention Christians' use of force during the Crusades nor how the Inquisition spread the Christian faith in the Middle East, Spain, and Latin America. In 2007, upon his visit to Brazil, he claimed that proclaiming Christ in South America did not alienate the pre-Columbus cultures, "nor impose a foreign culture." Critics retorted that colonizers destroyed Amerindian culture and the missionaries personified European monarchs' authoritarian despotism. See Jan Fisher, *New York Times*, 5/24/07. In contrast, Pope Francis apologized for the Church's grave colonial sins" in a speech (July 9, 2015) at the World Meeting of Popular Movements in Bolivia. www.vatican.va/content/ francesco /en/speeches/ 2015/july/ documents/papa-francesco_20150709_bolivia-movimenti-popolari.htm

10. By focusing on a single Muslim teacher, Ibn Hazm, (994–1064) who stressed God's absolute transcendence, Pope Benedict ignored the diversity in Islamic philosophical traditions. He set up a "straw-man" argument about the nature of Muslim teachings. The noted French Islamist scholar, R. Arnaldez, commented that Ibn Hazm went so far as to state that God is not bound even by his own word, that nothing obliges him to reveal the truth: God is absolutely transcendent—not bound up with our rational categories.

11. Seyyed Hossein Nasr, *Science and Civilization in Islam* (Chicago: ABC, 2001), 294.

12. Cardinal Ratzinger on *Dominus Jesus*, September 5, 2000. To balance Vatican II's teachings with the traditional teachings about the Church's central role in the plan of salvation, *Dominus Jesus* seeks to reconcile two seemingly contradictory positions: affirmation of the truth in the major religious traditions and the Church's role in uniting all humanity. Reaffirming Christianity's centrality among the world's religions, it insists that the Church is a unique bulwark against secular relativism and atheism.

13. Pontifical Council for Interreligious Dialogue and the Congregation for the Evangelization of Peoples, *Instruction, Dialogue and Proclamation*, 9, 29: ASS 84 (1992), 417–24. (cf. Vatican II's *Gaudium et Spes*, 22).

14. https://slate.com/human-interest/2014/10/mlk-s-letter-from-a-birmingham-jail-and-other-great-open-letters.html

15. Amos Yong, "On Doing Theology and Buddhology: A Spectrum of Christian Proposals." https://www.jstor.org/stable/41416537?seq=1

16. Nishida Kitaro, *Intelligibility and the Philosophy of Nothingness* (Honolulu: East-West Center) 1958.

17. Contrapuntal refers to the ability to incorporate counterpoint (material added above or below an existing melody—as occurs in Bach's music. Jazz and African music in general develop harmonizing rhythms. The African genius is manifested in the Afro-American verbal rituals that develop communal experience.

18. https://cruxnow.com/vatican/2019/10/27/pope-closes-amazon-synod-warning-of-walls-neglect-of-traditions/. See also Stephen P. Judd, "The Indigenous Theology Movement in Latin America," in *Resurgent Voices in Latin America*, edited by Edward L. Cleary and Timothy J. Steigenga. (Rutgers Univ. Press, 2004), 210–30.

19. On bishop accountability as to this issue: www.bishop-accountability.org/

20. www.britannica.com/event/Chinese-Rites-Controversy. Raymond Schroth, *NCR*, February 23, 2007, 3.

21. Fabien Eboussi Boulaga, *Christianity without Fetish: An African Critique and Recapture of Christianity* (ISBN10: 3825850773, 1984). Samuel Rayan, "Decolonization of Theology," *Sedos Bulletin*, Nov. 1998, 297–306. Brian Cronin, *Foundations of Philosophy*, (Nairobi: Consolata Institute, 1999) describes his futile search for a transcultural method for teaching philosophy in an East African seminary that would respect the cultural givens of his students. He found in *Insight* a way of addressing self-appropriation within the contexts of contemporary problems and of African culture.

22. Steve Biko, *Black Consciousness in South Africa* (New York: Random House, 1979), xiv.

23. Gibson Winter, *The Suburban Captivity of the Churches* (New York: Doubleday, 1961). In his Ph D dissertation, John Raymaker coordinated Winter's social ethic and pointed out shortcomings in G.H. Mead's symbolic interactionism and in Max Weber. Winter, *Elements for a Social Ethics* (New York: Macmillan, 1968) uses intentionality to correct behaviorist notions. Alfred Schutz *Collected Papers* (The Hague: Nijhof, 1964) analyzed Weber's views on the

foundations of the social sciences, concluding that Weber failed to distinguish between an action in progress and the completed act, between the meaning of the producer of a cultural object, my own actions, and the meaning of another's action. Weber did not identify the unique relation existing between a self and other selves. Clarifying that relation is essential to understanding "lived relations." Acts of reflection that turn us inward allow us to reach a meaning as a clear, distinct entity.

Chapter Eight

Solutions Based on Small Christian Communities Striving for Social Justice

Some of the Ironies in the Fall and Rise of SCCs in Christian History

We are endeavoring to situate Christian debates within the larger problematics of the Church engaged in a secularized, pluralist world. Having analyzed some of the problems besetting our world, this final chapter asks how SCCs may help Christians better realize that the Kingdom is within us and that it is to be shared ever anew.

History is full of ironies. With the legitimization of Christianity in the Roman Empire, the important role of home churches was eroded. If both the symbol of *ichthus* (standing for "Jesus Christ, Son of God, Savior") and SCCs were eroded subsequent history,[1] we seek to develop a Church model that integrates a pursuit of social justice and dialogue with all manners of people. Our focus on SCCs means that we value forms of Christian intimacy amidst alienation as well as the conscientization of SCC members as to social problems in the light of the Gospel. A Vatican III Council would have both an evaluative and architectural function in devising sound policies for faithful SCCs—but this may first need a priming from SCCs (as these represent the church from below).

The 2019 Amazon Synod shed light on such possibilities. It suggested that many of the laws about the nature of ministry in the Church have little or nothing to do with Catholic doctrine and could be changed to meet the needs of the present century. It also suggested that the Church's canon law could be amended to allow for the ordination of married men (*Viri Probati*), first in Brazil, and of women deacons in other areas. Such changes could help Christians live their faith more authentically. Opponents of Pope Francis, such as Cardinal Robert Sarah, attempted to draw Pope Benedict in opposing the ordaining of married men in the book *From the Depth of Our Hearts*. Although written primarily by Cardinal Sarah, Pope Emeritus Benedict was listed as a co-author. Benedict, however, asked that his name be removed. That Pope Francis in *Querida Amazonia* (Feb. 12, 2020), felt constrained to yield to conservatives in postponing a decision on the ordination of married men and/or women deacons, is another indication of the need of a Vatican III Council to more fully explore controversial issues in the Church. Besides the fact that many are deprived of the Eucharist due to a shortage of priests, an additional factor is that this is also an inculturation-bridge-building issue inasmuch as it touches on one of central tasks Pope Francis has taken on. Let us approach this from mystic-world-religions perspectives.

CHURCH AND WORLD IN THE LIGHT OF PHILOSOPHY AND THE WORLD RELIGIONS

The Council of Trent decreed that the three sources of revelation are the Scriptures, Tradition and the Magisterium. Evangelicals argue that Catholicism gives priority to Tradition and to the Magisterium but discounts a personal appropriation of Scripture. To help clarify these diverging views, let us consider three levels on which Catholics appropriate their faith and engage in various form of dialogue with others.

First, on a personal level, Catholics engaged in the mystical life as were the European mystics of the Rhenish School, the Spanish Carmelites or St. Therese of Lisieux do not need a "Christian Zen." But many young Catholics who have drifted from their faith because they found it "irrelevant," would benefit from reading the popular works of Thomas Merton, William Johnston or Ruben Habito which give Westerners insights into the possibilities and reality of a Christian Zen (see note 125).

Second, on a historical level, the relations between Judaism, Christianity and Islam have been marked by conquest, the Crusades, terrorism, as well as by such positive encounters that occurred in the complementary reflections of Avicenna, Maimonides and Aquinas.

Third, on an intercultural faith level, the Church must adequately communicate Christ's message in cultural categories relevant to each culture, be it in Hindu India, in Buddhist nations such as Thailand, Korea or Japan, in Africa, or in the now secularized West.

Pope John Paul II approached such realities by giving conservative groups such as Opus Dei a privileged position. We appeal to the open-mindedness so evident in the lives of popes John XXIII and Francis. The excesses of both left and right are a problem. Arguing that intermediate Church structures are needed, we suggest areas of human endeavor that could benefit from how some Catholic thinkers have reflected on such matters. First and foremost, we look for solutions in the lives of Jesus and of the early Christians. Today's marginalized Christians must forge new ways to help individual Catholics combine intimacy and effective methods of promoting the Church's Kingdom-oriented mission. There has been persistent forms of dualism in Western thought stretching from Plato, St. Augustine's notion of "Two Cities" (one of God and one of man) through Cartesian and Kantian philosophies. Gilbert Ryle called it the "ghost" in the Western mind.[2] Westerners tend to bracket out the spiritual part of reality in our lives. We tackle Ryle's ghost by appealing to non-Western thinkers' *non-bracketing* views. Such views reinforce our own theological strategy of seeking new mediating structures based on a relational theology. We seek to draw lessons from a *kairos*-inspired, relational theology by focusing on SCCs that combine intimacy and social concerns with a dynamic faithfulness to Christ. We stress "dynamic." Those who fear the dynamic realities unleashed by Vatican II tend to interpret Thomism in static ways. They have not adequately fathomed how Karl Rahner, Yves Congar and Bernard Lonergan have helped us discover the dynamic implications of a *living* Thomism engaged with the modern world. We shall now focus on how SCCs have pioneered new forms of Kingdom-oriented ministries.

NEW FORMS OF COMMUNITY MINISTRIES AS "LIVING BRIDGES" THAT IMPLEMENT THE PRINCIPLE OF SUBSIDIARITY

The *sentido de comunidad* of Basic Christian Communities (BCCs) refers to their being interactive transformative communities in which members are joined in continual, integrative, evolutionary types of growth that strengthen over the years. In the early Christian communities, those who presided over the celebration of the word and the Eucharist were chosen do so because of their moral authority and because they belonged to the community. These two conditions no longer hold today when pastors mostly come from the outside; all too often they not relate well to their parishioners and have little moral authority. Such outsiders can become stumbling blocks to those seeking a genuine Christian spirituality. Despite such drawbacks, the Church is still in a unique position to help unify mankind and its many traditions amidst a rampant globalization. Pope Francis has helped reshape Church authority in ways that can more effectively promote new ministries required to engage the Church with the contemporary world.

In Brazil alone, there are 80,000 BCCs.[3] Prior to the 2019 Amazon Synod, thousands of married priests had organized themselves into a number of associations in Brazil. There are indications that the Synod laid a path to reactivate some of these married priests to foster the growth of BCCs. Such communities are a leaven for social justice in the developing world torn by the enormous divides between the rich and the poor. Yet, they receive only marginal support from the official Church. They have formed Bible Circles that meet regularly to discuss Scripture from liberation-theology viewpoints. This replicates how early Church communities were led by those with moral authority. In effect, we are here invoking the Catholic principle of subsidiarity that what individuals can accomplish on their own should be respected by higher authorities. Lower levels of Church organization such as SCCs and BCCs can help bishops bring about needed ecclesial transformations including laying the groundwork for a Vatican III. In the hope of stimulating dialogue on mobilizing the Church's spiritually creative role in the world, we invoke both intra-faith and interfaith "dynamics" in a world subject to constant change. The Church must explore how believers can help transform partial views into holistic ones. In accord with our twin on-the-way strategy, we evaluate theologies that can unite rather than divide the world. If guerilla warfare has prompted governments to use more "sophisticated" weaponry, a relational theology "revolutionizes" the heart by appealing to Jesus' new-wine-and-salt-of-the-earth teachings. With Pope Francis, we advert to Christian principles, seeking a viable bridging theology that can help develop new ecclesial paradigms in teaching, sanctifying and governing the Church across the planet. The hearts of the truly engaged faithful ever burn upon reflecting on Christ's words. With the disciples of Emmaus, we wounded healers should hasten to hear the Lord's words so as to engage in the many tasks facing the Church.

SINFUL STRUCTURES IN NEED OF REFORMING AND MORE PROFOUND TYPES OF INTIMACY

Pope Francis has sought to reform the Church's administrative structure so as to make it responsive to local churches' needs. The question is to what extent should the Church be decentralized? In this chapter, we explore how SCCs foster personal reflection on how to implement Jesus' Kingdom vision. Our relational theology seeks to integrate and harmonize the spiritual and secular aspects of people's lives. One must realize that there are many barriers impeding Jesus' vision. We have seen that the path of Western spirituality went through many stepping stones such as that of the spirituality of the hermit, the monk and the mendicant orders. Such spiritualities arose due to crises occurring in the societies in which religious founders lived. As individual persons, St. Anthony, St. Francis of Assisi, St. Ignatius of Loyola, Mother Seton, Dorothy Day or Mother Teresa, each responded in creative, often heroic ways. Today, Western societies are challenging the Church. They often rely on views bereft of the divine. An incarnational spirituality and a relational theology both call for various forms of personal conversion. The Church gathers its members to help the-not-yet, or only-partly converted. We advocate SCCs as ways to deepen people better realize what conversion implies. Vatican II left us a creative agenda—one that was in some ways usurped when John Paul II began to appoint "orthodox" bishops. A "too conservative" episcopate is unwilling to pursue the true Catholic genius which calls for adequate ways to meet societal needs.

Bernard Lonergan can help people come to grips with deeper insights into meaning and value that molded the past but are also relevant to our present situation. He offers us a complex way of studying how various forms of psychic, affective and moral conversions are necessary for Christian ministry if it is to be done in the name and in the spirit of Jesus. Ministry requires the personal faithfulness of the minister, an awareness of one's limitations and the study of history which helps one overcome one's limitations. Such study can help us understand, for example, how ministers of former times dealt with such problems as scrupulosity when forms of rigorism or Jansenism flourished in the Church. It is not helpful when clerics, intent on preserving cherished prerogatives, keep lay people from sharing in new forms of ministry that might enrich their lives.

Many balanced mediating positions have been proposed to help guide the Church toward a Vatican III Council so as to help unite the churches of Asia, Africa, Europe and the Americas cooperate in Kingdom-of-God solutions. Among such positions are those that seek to find the proper balance between the need for intimacy and public responsibility. There are many kinds of human intimacy. We think first of the intimate relations between husband and wife, parents and children. Such intimacy can be shattered by infidelity. Old Testament prophets used this notion of infidelity to describe how Israel had broken its Covenant with God by turning to false gods (Is 1:21; 57:7–13; Ez 16 and 23; Je 2:20; Ho 1–3). In the Lord's Prayer, Jesus calls us to a new kind of profound intimacy with God. Here, too, problems can arise when such an intimacy is lost due to unfaithfulness, or misunderstandings. We have noted that some priests find it difficult to be intimate in fulfilling their task. Our vision for alternative forms of ministry is conscious of intimacy-infidelity-immaturity problems and of viable forms of SCCs that might foster personal, communal, and spiritual intimacy.[4] Present forms of Church ministries must be reconsidered so as to fill the gap between present needs and a dearth of ministers duly authorized to minister to the needs of the faithful and to announce the Gospel. What is needed are an incarnational spirituality and relational theologies able to promote SCCs that can respond to people's needs in our secularized world. SCCs embody models of Christian life in that they practice spiritual intimacy so as to better share the Good News.

SOME UNPLEASANT AND REALITIES TO BE ADDRESSED SPIRITUALLY

Despite the high ideals and profound hopes that have inspired the Church, some serious realities must now be faced. Let us touch on three such realities relating to 1) Church teachings, 2) the dwindling[5] number of men now willing to commit themselves to the celibate priesthood and 3) ways to promote spiritual intimacy in ministry today.

1) Many of the Church's positions on moral questions (divorce and remarriage, birth control homosexuality, and abortion) have alienated millions of people in the West.

2) Most of the Church's pastoral needs in twenty-first century America will probably be met by lay persons serving in specialized ministries. Gerald Grudzen recently visited Detroit 's Sacred Heart Seminary where he had studied over 40 years earlier. The seminary, located in an inner city neighborhood, had guards posted at the entrance and in the main building. It had once housed several hundred local seminarians. Only 95 seminarians were now attending. Some of the students came from as far away as China. A seminary classmate (now a married priest serving as parish administrator of an inner-city parish) indicated that the celibate pastor of his parish was also responsible for three other inner-city parishes. He was not sure whether his parish would survive further budget cuts. Under present circumstances, the Church's future outreach in inner-city areas will have to rely on lay ministers or on former clerics. Those willing to participate in these challenging ministries would be well-served if supported by growing networks of SCCs. Without some new mediating structures, the Church will lack the ability to touch the larger human family with its message of forgiveness and redemptive love.

3) Conversion often occurs within the context of community. For this reason we argue that SCCs could be one of the most effective agents to live the Gospel in the twenty-first century. The breakdown of intimacy in Western societies is part of the fast-paced, individualist culture pervading life. The Church's mission should foster spiritual intimacy which is a real challenge.[6] Jesus' standard of intimacy requires forgiveness when necessary. Married people are challenged to be intimate with self, spouse and others amidst conflicts. From a religious viewpoint, one must add God-intimacy, believer-intimacy even intimacy with atheists. Although atheists reject Christianity's notion of a forgiving Father, they, too, must beware that they not fall into the ways of Chinese or North Korean totalitarianism. This may present problems

to those who forget that we need symbols to live as rational animals. Studies of symbols are of strategic help in overcoming one-dimensional man and in establishing various forms of interreligious dialogue. In Paul Ricoeur's theology of love, the father image is recovered as a symbol grounding God's love. His theology progresses from mere resignation to fate to a poetic life of love.[7] Biblical history, the psalms and the prophets testify to the power of love and poetry to reanimate suffering people on the margins. The unpleasant realities of a dearth of priests and of a lack of intimacy must be evaluated within the context of society at large. For some 200 years in the West, alienated people have been relegated to the margins of a faceless, industrialized society—as dramatized in the theater of the absurd. SCCs are a way for Christians to transcend their marginalized status so as experience intimacy anew. We stress that the Church is One, Holy, Catholic, Apostolic. Apostolicity denotes a criterion of what SCCs are all about. SCCs should help unify the Church rather than divide it. Conscious of their status on the margins, they open new ways of living the faith and of interacting in holy, apostolic ways. Striving for holiness (living holistic lives) helps them bridge personal and communal forms of alienation. Taking seriously the catholic nature of bridge-building across the centuries, SCC ministries are or seek to be in communion with Church authorities and people of good will. Some questions do arise: how long is it tenable that (as St. Benedict in Detroit shows and as replicated in much of the Catholic world) parish priests serve as "circuit riders" celebrating Mass while other ministries are performed by others? If the Church is determined to preserve the celibate priesthood (mostly because it does not want married priests promoted to the episcopacy) what alternative is possible between circuit-rider priests and the gathering of people in SCCs without a priest? As partial answers to these questions, we shall examine A) the source and nature of community; B) various types of SCCs functioning both outside of and within Church structures and the need for more.

THE SOURCE AND NATURE OF CHRISTIAN COMMUNITIES

At no time in history have so many people lived communally. There are now more ways of living in communities than previously, such as in kibbutz, intentional communities, virtual communities (Internet based), housing cooperatives or "eco-villages." Such communities restore forms of intimacy and sharing amidst a depersonalized, secular world. Surveys have shown that between 30 and 40 percent of Americans now belong to small communities. The Church has a rich tradition of community life as embodied in its many types of religious orders and congregations of men and women. We have touched on some of these such as the Benedictines, Franciscans and Jesuits. Our intent, however, is to focus on the needs today's Church now faced with a lack of religious vocations, on the one hand, and an ever increasing need for viable forms of community life in secular societies. Too often, government programs fail due to poor management, greed and graft. Individual volunteers are often not adequately supported. Many NGO's exist to fill a vacuum between government inefficiency and personal limitations. The blind prejudices within one's heart and consumerism must not be ignored. In this section, we study the problems SCCs face and the promises they offer in helping individual Christians and the Church as a whole engage in "intimate" yet communal forms of joint apostolates.

Some authors on SCCs have noted problems and crises that can occur in renewing Church structures. We have stress the importance of a viable intimacy whereby humans can feel at home within a responsive, responsible community. This section examines what may be viable alternatives. We argue that the source and nature of Christian communities is embodied, for example, in SCCs and the hope they offer in ameliorating Church structures. SCCs are loci of lived Christian experience. But as happens in any new development, mistakes can be made. Reflection is needed. Let us reflect further on Latin America's BCCs, on SCCs in the USA that function within existing Church structures and on "marginalized" communities that could eventually prove pivotal to the Catholic Church's future.

SOME ROLES OF LIBERATION-THEOLOGY-DERIVED BCCS AND OF SCCS

So as to foster deeper forms of dialogue, we argue that BCCs and SCCs are ecclesial organisms that engage believers in the work of implementing a "morally coherent world view." This requires more than defensive mechanisms—as may be illustrated with an appeal to and interpretation of Pope John Paul II's view on interreligious dialogue as expressed in his *Redemptoris Missio*: "Dialogue does not originate from tactical concerns or self-interest. It is demanded by deep respect for everything that has been brought about in human beings by the Spirit who blows where he will." For John Paul, dialogue is based on hope and love. "Those engaged in it must be consistent with their own religious traditions" (no. 56). John Paul's words are directed to those engaged in interreligious dialogue but they also apply, we argue, in intra-faith dialogue. There we get into the grey areas of hierarchic privilege as when this same Pope regularly edited and put his own finishing touches on the debates of the bishops assembled triennially in Rome in the Synod of Bishops. If interfaith dialogue needs "inner purification and conversion" (Ibid), so does intra-faith dialogue. "Dialogue" in itself has the somewhat abstract goal of seeking to arrive at the truth; it has the more proximate goal of fostering a recognition of shared humanity. Our suggestions for fostering SCCs so as to help renew Church structures *do try* to balance Catholicism's hierarchic setup with the duty to educate the young in their faith and to help evangelize the non-churched in a changing Church. It is a hopeful sign that the highest strata of Church leadership has had to tolerate Paulo Freire's conscientization method. Freire conscientized the poor through small community activities. His conscientization method preceded liberation theology; the two then jointly helped give birth to BCCs and to clarify the divisive issues separating the Church's conservative and progressive voices. While the latter see Latin America's BCCs as a blessing, the former dismiss them as being unable to viably remedy capitalist distortions. With Freire, we insist that the word of God must be reflected on so as to help transform the world. Conscientization should not be accompanied by violence; it is meant to sharpen people's perception as to how viably oppose injustices. We have been suggesting ways to bridge traditional and present interpretations of Church structures. We have traced the history of BCCs in Latin America and touched on the important role Christian ashrams have played in laying a groundwork for peace and understanding among the world religions. We now turn to examine other types of SCCs in the Christian world. Some SCCs work within traditional Church structures such as the parish. Other SCCs, made up of disaffected Catholics and other Christians, stand on the margin of Church structures or outside them.

Among the latter are progressive SCCs engaged in multi-faith communities. We shall address in turn SCCs that work within traditional Church structures in the USA and those that for one reason or another tend to work independently of Church structures. Just as religious orders have traditionally played a role auxiliary to the Church's hierarchy, so we envision SCCs as also playing such an auxiliary role but on a different canonical basis. John Paul II made Opus Dei an entity responsible only to the Pope. We would add that SCCs can be auxiliaries with various modes of "flexible" types of accountability to Church authorities. For us, community renewal in the Church differs from structural or institutional renewal. Our relational theology perspective does not confuse official Church structures with the need authentic Christians have of participating in meaningful communities. It is a matter of priorities. If their faith is to flourish, Christians need communities where they can discuss issues with a hope of being heard. Due to secularism, the collective Christian conscience has been diminished; promoting the faith stands in need of a "personal touch." Constrictive structures snuff out faith initiatives. To the extent it is in touch with people's needs, the Church's leadership can help the grain of faith grow in people's lives. Perceptively integrating SCCs within the institutional, Church would help the institution as a whole and localized SCCs better promote Christian faith and love. This is so because people who have truly experienced the grace of God feel empowered to share that grace with others. Having a listening heart can help bishops guide the faithful in fulfilling the Church's mission. The Church's goal is not to have structures, but to help establish God's Kingdom on earth by living the Christian life—a point made by many who have written on SCCs. Most BCCs and SCCs seek to work within, not against the Church.

HOW SCCS CAN ENLIVEN TRADITIONAL CHURCH STRUCTURES—IF NOT MARGINALIZED

We now briefly review four books on SCCs operating within the American Catholic Church. Stephen Clark argues that "the Church should be restructured"[8] through SCCs. Structure of itself can snuff out faith and the initiatives of faith. Church leadership, in touch with peoples' needs, should subordinate structures to ways of supporting communities in which the grain of faith can grow and charity live.

Arthur Baranowski seeks to restructure parishes so that people might help one another more effectively. He recognizes the powerful role of the counterculture that now keeps parishes from being the center of Christians' lives. New ways of being Church as practiced in such programs as RENEW and Marriage Encounter means that such groups do not remain mere small groups but rather "become church at a new, more basic level."[9] Building SCCs involves a three-phase process, that of beginning, praying (alone and together) and "being Church for the Long Haul" (25). "Crisis can and will strike" (38) within SCCs. To deal with crises, able pastoral facilitators must be found who lead in consistent ways. Thomas Kleissler and alii expand on Baranowski's strategy, stressing that from 30 to 40 percent of Americans have belonged to small faith communities.[10] At the dawn of the twenty-first century, we live in the "rarest of moments" one that calls for a new evaluation of the quality of community (7). Spirituality, centering forms of prayer and other practices are SCCs cornerstones.

Bernard Lee supports his research on SCCs with theological and sociological reflection. He discusses Karl Rahner's 1974 admonition that "the Church of the future will be one built from below by basic communities as a result of free initiative.[11] While SCCs "are not, in any simple way, the future of the Catholic Church, there is probably no future that will not find itself shaped by their worldwide emergence" (3). Perceptive forms of criticism are needed based on one's "conscience and "personal experience" (65). Soundly organized SCCs can best deal with conflicts that may arise. Lee uses the metaphor of "margins" to help us understand the present Church. He asks us to think of the Church's present institutional self-understanding "as the written text on the page." In this thought experiment, the "post-conciliar, postmodern church is coming into existence." It is a not-yet written text. The margins, then are the spaces where the unwritten text begins to interrogate the written text." All of us have seen borrowed books with scribblings in the margins. Such scribblings impinge upon the text for the scribbler felt that "something else needs to be said that the text does not say (119). As with the scribbler, SCCs are both insider and outsider. Many have been warmly supported by bishops and pastors, but there is official ambivalence about marginal activity. Still, SCCs have no official canonical status. The Church informally admits that SCCs may be important for the future—but it has not yet fully integrated them into its life—they remain on the margins. The problem of marginalization in society and in the Church can be addressed with Jesus' parables of the Good Samaritan which concludes that everyone is one's neighbor (Lk 10:25–37). Other parables in Luke stress that he came to save the "lost." "Getting lost" in today's societies reflects the reality that we need language to communicate. Migrants must either learn a new language—or create new ghettos. Tourists are accommodated with the quasi-*lingua franca* that English has become, but when it comes to renewing the Church through community only the language of Christian love that reaches to those on the margins will do. At issue here is also the need to inculturate the Gospel message today.

Experts agree that North American SCCs are pastoral in nature. Still, many clerics get defensive about SCCs as a way of being Church—even though the shortage of priests and religious makes SCCs an almost indispensable means to educate the faithful and to foster spiritual life. SCCs in the USA have for the most part avoided the confrontation that greeted Latin America's BCCs but they still await more official Church recognition—another reason for a Vatican III Council. Theologians and sociologists have been re-examining the Church's original structures. A Vatican III Council could evaluate how the Church's original structures developed through the centuries. It could adapt present structures so that the Gospel may be made known, its Good News lived. We live in an age of unprecedented changes and crises. Europe is very much secularized. Few still go to Sunday Mass; among those who do, Mass attendance does not significantly affect their daily lives. In the USA, attending the Sunday liturgy tends to reinforce already held views of what life is all about. Only those who do not rush home from the Church parking lot so as to reflect and share in deeper ways grow as Christians. How many bishops are willing and able to renew parish life? Vatican II's renewal of the Liturgy has helped motivate many but alienated others. Other Vatican II reforms opened new perspectives for Christian participation in the world. If the Vatican and traditionalist bishops seek to micro-manage the laity, they risk stunting growth and snuffing out Vatican II's the spirit of renewal. Large parishes that allow only the voices of the Pope, the bishop or parish priest defeat the aim of assembling Christians to pray and build community. A lack of priests and other circumstances call for renewed Church structures that can foster genuine SCCs. Westerners are conditioned to think in terms of organization and task-oriented groups, rather than in environmental and/or communal terms. SCC advocates speak of "restructuring" the Church so as to better foster the faithful's spiritual lives based on a sense of community. Our explorations of incarnational-relational theologies and spiritualities are steps in that direction. One might speak of two revolutions that of love and of the internet. SCCs working in tandem with parochial and diocesan structures can help Christians "transvalue" values in our age. A delicate task in life is to discern and share one another's hidden truths that prompt persons to live a life of love. Deep in our hearts of hearts, we are called to love. Love is to be shared personally and communally. Love prompts one to work for the greater good—not for profit. Psychologically, one is tempted to protect one's turf or interests. Christian love transcends this drive by letting the profit motive dominate life. Hopefully, the Church of the future will more adequately recognize and respond to people's needs for intimacy and for personally reading and sharing the meaning of Scripture. Such a recognition and a deeper cooperation between clerics and laity, experienced in fields unknown to most clerics, would foster rather than stifle community. This in itself would open up new forms of ministries able to reach out to a secularized culture and to believers in other religions. Establishing God's Kingdom on earth necessitates putting Church structures at the service of communal life so as to better honor Kingdom imperatives.

FCM AND MARGINALIZED SCCS OPERATING OUTSIDE OF OFFICIAL CHURCH STRUCTURES

The Federation of Christian Ministries (FCM) was founded in 1973 in New York. It opened a way for new Christian ministries adapted to today's realities—this was some 450 years after St. Ignatius wrote his *Spiritual Exercises*. FCM has developed new forms of ministry and fostered community life. It models the way the early Christians gathered together to pray; it implores the Holy Spirit to guide us in our uncertain age. One may ask how do the admonitions of Jesus and St. Paul that married persons are less free to serve God apply today? With the Church, one must uphold the traditional ideal of selfless service that foregoes marriage for the good of others—but it is an ideal that fewer young Catholics are willing to embrace. Many vocations to the priesthood now occur much later in life than in previous generations. To make up for the lack of priests today, we ask whether and how a possible Vatican III might reinstate a married priesthood. FCM has pioneered ways in which a married priesthood might function. Today, married priests can only work on the Church's fringe. FCM promotes SCCs which it sees as an appropriate means to live and share the Gospel today. Under present circumstances, FCM members mostly exercise their ministry outside of official Church structures. While many bishops under Paul VI were willing to experiment with new forms of ministries, many conservative bishops today have stopped most new forms of ministry dead in their tracks. FCM members are left to engage in a vision of the church as an inherently cooperative community of faith. They cooperate in tackling today's challenges. The inspiration for renewal groups such as FCM originated in Vatican II's documents that encourage a new understanding of the Church as the People of God and of its mission to the contemporary world. In FCM, one joins like-minded persons faithful to the Gospel. In the midst of our ever-so-busy world, FCM members seek to lovingly share the truth. They meet to reflect on Christian life and support one another. Some of its members participate in parish activities; some restrict their activities to SCC ways of doing in the hope that a Vatican III will authorize a married clergy. They feel that the Church is shooting itself in the foot, as it were, when despite a lack of clergy, trained married priests are suspended from ministering. The Church's should be more concerned with having the Gospel preached to all than with preserving the ideal of a celibate clergy. Limited forms of lay ministry often depend on the whims of local bishops. To address current needs, FCM sets up informal ministerial structures and avoids conflicts with hierarchic Church. While some married priests abandon all forms of ministry despite ecclesial training, FCM members, both women and men, are encouraged to live the Gospel in theologically informed ways.

FCM communities help its members love God and one another by "transvaluing" values in ways Nietzsche had not dreamed of. FCM reaches out to people of all faiths or to those without faith. From the beginning, it has helped married priests and their wives, while developing ever broadening forms of ecumenical and interfaith ministries. Let us cite some examples of how FCM members have been reaching out to others.

A first example touches on the need to integrate personal and community experience within realistic socio-cultural situations. Several FCM members, including Anthony Soto, a married Franciscan priest-sociologist, founded the Center for Employment Training (CET), based in San Jose, CA as a way to meet the needs of migrant workers. Grudzen worked with Soto in CET's early stages. Both men found this to be a logical way to implement FCM's social justice advocacy. CET now exists in several U.S. cities. It has trained more than 100,000 migrant workers for skilled employment. Several members of *Communidad*, a SCC founded by Soto and his wife, still meet to discuss active ways of participating in the larger community.

A second example is that of FCM members who exercise a legally recognized ministry without provoking conflicts with the hierarchy. FCM provides legal ministerial credentials many married priests and nuns still wishing to exercise a public ministry.

A third example is how some FCM members visit and minister to prisoners in local jails. Jesus blessed those who visit "him" in prison. Our prisons hold truly spiritually needy persons often due to the shortcomings of criminal justice systems.

A fourth example of FCM's vision is in the founding and staffing of the Global Ministries University (GMU)—an online theology training program for those preparing to assume ministerial roles. GMU is faithful to Catholic tradition. It serves several independent Catholic communions such as the Ecumenical Catholic Communion. It teaches its students to understand their own faith and share it from the heart lest parochial beliefs impede dialogue with secular-minded persons, with those of other religious affiliations.

The said examples of FCM's outreach is in line with the Church's mission to the world of sharing Gospel values as best one can amidst globalization. We believe that a Vatican Council III would confirm many of the reforms that Catholic renewal groups have advocated over the past six decades. An important reform would be to redefine the roles of SCCs which recall the roles of small Christian assemblies in the early centuries of Christianity. Lay Christians could assume some of the roles now reserved to clerics. SCCs enable Christians to build deep reflective communal relationships allowing them to relate on more than the superficial levels as is often the case in large parishes. Could the day have come for new types of non-hierarchical religious organizations? FCM is one model of such a paradigm. Other organizations similar to FCM such as CORPUS have also developed new forms of community that could serve as models for the future. Social-justice-oriented communities have also emerged such as the Maryknoll Affiliates. The Affiliates offer ways for lay Christians to participate more fully in the Church's Peace and Justice Mission while promoting international forms of Christian fellowship. A Maryknoll Affiliate group based in California's Bay Area, for example, has supported several projects in the Middle East featuring Palestinian cultural and artistic groups. It has raised thousands of dollars to fund scholarships to allow students to finish their education

Another example of how SCCs conduct projects to help heal a broken world is that of the St. Patrick's Church in downtown Chicago. By 1983, this inner-city parish had only four registered parishioners. A small group of lay persons and clergy devised a plan to renew this historic Church. Today the church has been completely remodeled. It has a dynamic social justice ministry with over 3,500 households participating. It often supports victims of natural catastrophes and conducts job-search and adult education seminars. It is known for its artistic exhibits based upon Irish-Celtic traditions.

FURTHER THOUGHTS ON OUR NEED FOR RENEWED SCCS: DEEPENING OUR SENSE OF CHRISTIAN LIFE IN AN AGE OF SPECIALIZATION

SCCs can empower people in the midst of contemporary forms of marginalization. People are empowered by the dynamics of community acceptance. SCCs help marginalized Christians develop new forms of Christian ministries. Faithful SCC members find lasting friendships and engage in forms of service that complement existing ecclesial forms of diocesan and parochial ministries. In view of the decreasing number of candidates to a celibate priesthood which leads to a circuit-rider type of ministry and to a lack of intimacy in ministry amidst creeping forms of marginalization, the Church could adapt a dual-track priesthood. It would ordain men who would be allowed to either forego marriage or forego their chances of becoming bishops. Obviously, this would remedy our acute priest shortage. Those who forego episcopal promotion could, for instance, animate SCCs. This must be put within a much larger perspective. The Church must develop ethical policies in a world in which humans starve due to conflicts. Ideally, SCCs are aware of the Church's four marks: One, Holy, Catholic, Apostolic. SCCs can help unify the Church rather than divide it. Despite their status on the margins, SCC members have opened new ways of living the faith. Striving for holiness helps them bridge personal or communal forms of alienation. Taking seriously the Catholic nature of bridge-building, they minister in communion with Church authorities while collaborating with people of good will. A Vatican III Council could decide whether present Church structures are adequate or must be modified. Vatican II's "Decree on the Bishops' Pastoral Office in the Church" states that the welfare of the "flock" is the first priority of any diocese. In practice, that welfare has been subjected to the whims of bishops or of the Vatican. Some SCCs do work within parish and diocesan structures, but neither the laity nor priests will feel empowered if they can be arbitrarily silenced when they venture into controverted areas. The present model of married deacons might serve as reference point for a dual-track priesthood. Married deacons function well within present structures; a dual-track priesthood could solve the scarcity of priests problem.[12] Gary Wills claims that the papacy has fostered structures of deceit. If Vatican II was a brief respite from the Vatican's bent on working in secrecy, restoring transparency depends on whether the Church can make its structures more responsive to the faithful. Wills quotes the eminent Catholic moral theologian, Bernard Haring: "Since the role of the priest is primarily that of a credible witness, it is of the utmost importance that all Church structures, all basic relationships within the Church, and the whole of moral formation promote and encourage absolute sincerity and transparency" (Wills, *Papal Sin*, 231). Such sincere transparency may remain an ideal in our too imperfect world. For our part, we seek a middle ground that might enable people to live ethically in spite of human imperfections. If the powers that be tend to marginalize others, we argue that SCCs, which take people as they are, can be fitting model to foster a Christian, ethical renewal that can address world problems. On the models of the apostolic Church and of the Church in pre- and post-Constantinian times, cooperation between married and unmarried priests would serve as a model of a Church in which Christians are a sign of selfless love in an alienated world.[13]

Catholic life means more than a Sunday Mass experience. But how best deepen genuine modes of intimacy in ways that foster the Church's mission? Ira Progoff proposes being creative based on self-knowledge and deepening relationships with others. His Intensive Journal method can help persons cope or even thrive amidst today's vertiginous changes; it is used by retreat directors to help people live an incarnational spirituality. We have reflected on how the Church could motivate people strive for Kingdom values—as Jesus prompts us to do. The Church has suggested new ways of living holistic lives in our secular world, but due to the dysfunctions affecting the world and the Church, these suggestions are all too often put on a back burner. Since Vatican II, many wars have occurred and the phenomenon of the Internet has changed ways humans communicate. Climate crises now complicate matters. New technologies have made the waging of war even more terrible. Increasing forms of specialization means that no one can now be a universal genius as were Da Vinci or Benjamin Franklin. Even geniuses have to restrict the scope of their interests. This means that interdisciplinary bridges and a method that can ensure deep communication among specialists are now needed. Lonergan's method can be of great help here for it bridges faith and reason, science and religion. We cannot here go into the details of his method. Suffice it to say, that the functional specialties he pioneered in his *Method in Theology* can help humans cooperate. Progoff helps people get in touch with self. Lonergan can help them communicate and cooperate in depth.

The two men help us integrate the complexities of our lives. Our focus on ongoing transformations anticipate how a Vatican III Council may face such issues. Generally speaking, in chapters 1–6 we argued that the faith is endangered in much of Western Europe, but that in the USA the intervention of Church leaders such as Cardinal Gibbons on behalf of workers and immigrants still energizes people's faith. Chapter 7 has been outlining some of the ecclesial developments in the developing world. Missionaries were farsighted enough to prepare the way for native bishops to inculturate Christ's message in native theological categories. We turn to consider further challenges and possibilities.

A CALL FOR CHURCH-FROM-BELOW CONVOCATIONS FOCUSED ON SPIRITUALITY AND ETHICS AND SOME ORGANIZATIONAL ASPECTS OF CHURCH RESPONSIVENESS

A Vatican III Council could help heal our broken world. Pope Francis has taken some of the first steps to let the Church from below get more involved in Church leadership. Our own analysis of deficiencies in Church leadership has prodded us to stress two traditional functions within the Church, the *sensus fidelium* and *sentire cum ecclesia* (to think and feel with the Church). While a recentralized post-Vatican II Church has tended to make *sentire cum ecclesia* a view in which laypeople merely "pray, pay and obey," we have appealed to the spirit of Vatican II that advocated structures to enable the faithful to help guide Church teaching. Some are asking whether Pope Francis' reforms are modest or radical. He has said from the start of his pontificate that he dreams of a Church for the poor. Being a Vatican outsider who had never studied or worked in Rome, his modest reforms have upset those who cling to static structures and ways of doing (or not doing) things. Traditionalists realize that once things begin to move forward, there is no going back. In the April 2, 2018 edition of *The National Catholic Reporter*, Sr. Joan Chittister wrote that after five years of Francis' papacy, the momentum seems to have stalled. No doubt Francis has dramatically changed the style of church governance, but many had hoped for more. "His humble, pastoral approach demands greater compassion, and care for the poor and the migrant." Yet, many resist even Francis' most Gospel-oriented actions such as his fulfilling Jesus' command "to wash the feet of one another. Some have made it clear that certain people's feet were not to be washed. We wait for divorced and remarried "Catholics to be allowed to share in the sacramental life of the church, but the church remains stingy with its largesse. Are female deacons on the horizon?" Many doubt this. Critics allege Francis has been uncertain in addressing women's issues in the church.

> He lacks a complete understanding of what needs to be done to ensure equality for women, and why that is so important for women and the church. His efforts at addressing sexual abuse issues have faltered. He sometimes seems strong, and at other times his moves are confusing. Francis himself seems to have tired of the struggle. It's almost as if he feels he has gone as far as he can and is discouraged from continuing to push for change. The resistance is winning. The conservative hierarchy is unwilling to relinquish power and seems to have the wherewithal to maintain it. Why is Francis' council of eight cardinals who were to govern the church not doing more? We have to change but 'it's the average layperson living out the faith in the temper of the times who shapes the future.' Only a visionary can move the church from one age to another (Ibid).

Even though the world is in dire need of an effective global ethics, most people do not have time to be "bothered," being too busy coping. We have argued that the Church's social doctrine is one of its best kept secrets. The Church needs more people of integrity including bishops, priests and laity able to work in dialogical relationships in both intra-and extra-Church activities. For such reasons, we conclude our book with a call for a first Church-from-Below Convocation to focus primarily on spiritual and ethical questions but also on Church responsiveness. Christians "on the way" in the Third Millennium need deeper forms of conscientization. We have spoken of liberation theologians and SCCs. But if communication barriers impede an effective "feeling with the Church", deeper forms of conscientization are needed. We cannot let the dysfunctions affecting the world and the churches hinder efforts to realize Christianity's basic mission. There is a need to motivate the hierarchy to dialogue with the Church from below—a step that Pope Francis has been fostering. The Pope realizes that without ongoing dialogue, the Church will fail to adequately preach the Gospel. In view of this, the Church from below must help establish structures that foster further conscientization. The time is ripe, we argue, for the first "Church-from-Below Convocation" to be held at a time and place most convenient to concerned parties. In the light of some of the themes we have addressed, it could focus on the dynamics of developing resilient Church structures through

- Examining the state of the Church in the light of Vatican II and discussing the merits of having the pope convoke a possible Vatican III.
- Exploring new forms of ordained ministries that could complement present forms.
- Focusing on reconciling Church factions while exploring new approaches to Evangelization and renewed Church structures focused on moral conversions.
- Cooperating with those who foster understanding among the worlds' religions.

Such a Convocation would gather Catholics of good will and experts on ecumenical and interfaith issues. Our middle-of-the-way strategy that seeks to mediate between conservatives and progressives would not let the first Church-from-below Convocation be under the official sponsorship of Call to Action due to its problematic relations with the Vatican. But in the spirit of what we have written, we would welcome its unofficial backing. Canon Law reserves the right to call an Ecumenical Council to the Pope, but a convocation of the Church from below would debate how the Church leadership is doing on such themes as spirituality, ethics and Church responsiveness. It could give helpful input for the larger theme we have discussed, namely advising the present pope or a successor in identifying issues to be addressed at a future Vatican III Council.

STRATEGIC CONCLUSION TO CHAPTER 8

A Vatican III, if and when such a Council is called, could benefit from the thinking and activities of informed Catholics and from those engaged in interfaith initiatives. It would be up to the hierarchy to respond to proposals from the Church-from-below. If the lessons based on official Church's pronouncements on liberation of theology and from the activities of SCCs have been learned by both sides, a proposed first convocation would be a means to discuss issues more in depth—not to provoke tensions. It would assess the two forms of Catholic self-understanding that have divided the Church since Vatican II. Not being divisive in intent, such convocations would seek to overcome the excesses of egoism through an ethics of Kingdom justice. We have explored ways to root such initiatives in a relational theology and in a deepened sense of interfaith spiritualities. This is needed to promote the ideal conditions for Church and world renewal. Our proposed convocations would involve those who can legitimately call themselves Catholics and are willing to cooperate in exploring themes a Vatican III would have to address. Our moderate middle-way approach concludes with a biblical symbol, that of the Slain Lamb. Washing in the blood of the Lamb is said to make one "whiter than snow" (Rev. 7:14). Such a washing is a symbol of reconciliation with God and humanity. Jesus still reconciles us as symbolized in baptism. Christian life is to be ever renewed through forgiveness and through helping overcome the injustices faced by so many humans.

NOTES

1. The symbol of the fish *(ichthus)*, a secret way of expressing belief in Jesus as Savior, is much less prominent in Christian iconography. The symbol was adopted by Darwinists as a rallying point against fundamentalists who denied evolution. We accept Church teachings on evolution but argue that the ancient Christian home churches anticipated the roles of today's SCCs which help Christians nurture their faith by clarifying the nature of the conflicting notions of worldly and Christian "success."

2. Gilbert Ryle, in *The Concept of Mind* (London: Great Library, 1949) and later works sought to dispel the Cartesian Myth that distinguishes between the inner and outer world.

3. Brazil has long advocated a married priesthood: its development of BCCs is consistent with the Church's teaching on subsidiarity.

4. Throughout history, the Church has given birth to many types of movements which it integrates as best it can. While some movements are beyond the pale if they lead to rupture, we study SCCs from our middle-way, bridge-building perspective.

5. *The National Catholic Reporter* (April 6, 2007) on how the dwindling number of priests and sisters who formerly staffed US Catholic schools has led to a two-tiered model of governance, ministry juridic persons (MJP's), that could transform the Church for they are founded for the sake of ministry In school MJP's, a predominantly lay board oversees a school's daily

operations while the sponsoring community retains some say. Such a model has led to fruitful cooperation between religious and laity. MJP's are the official link between a particular ministry (e. g. a health system or a university) and the church—just as religious communities were in the past. MJP's do not primarily promote a way of life in search for holiness. Juridic persons are not new. Every church entity that has official canonical status—diocese, religious order, parish—is a juridic person. In *Commonweal,* Nov. 12, 2019, "Making Ministry Whole," Charles Bouchard, O. P. reflects on the 2019 Amazon Synod. He notes that new MJP's are a way to renew the Church and maintain the identity of Catholic institutions. MJP's are not merely advisory: their authority comes directly from the Holy See—giving them a canonical status.

6. Steven Solomon and Lorie Teagno, *Intimacy after Infidelity* (New Harbinger, 2006).

7. Alasdair MacIntyre and Paul Ricoeur, *The Religious Significance of Atheism* (New York: Columbia, 1969). Daisaku Ikeda, *Embracing the Future* (Tokyo: *The Japan Times,* 2008) writes that "The eyes of a poet discover in each person a unique humanity. While arrogant intellect seeks to manipulate the world, the poetic spirit bows with reverence before its mysteries."

8. Stephen B. Clark, *Building Christian Communities: Strategy for Renewing the Church* (Ave Maria Press, 1992) is a highly recommended book.

9. Arthur Baranowski, *Creating Small Church Communities* (St. Anthony, 1996) 13.

10. Thomas Kleissler, Marge LeBert, Mary McGuinness, *Small Church Communities* (New York: Paulist, 1997), ix.

11. Bernard Lee, *The Catholic Experience of Small Christian Communities* (New York: Paulist, 2000), 3.

12. A. W. Richard Sipe, *A Secret World: Sexuality and the Search for Celibacy* (Routledge: 1990) claimed that half of Catholic priests in the US had at any given time been involved in some form of sexual activity. In *The Church with a Human Face* (Crossroad: 2005), Edward Schillebeeckx asserts that clerical celibacy originated partly in pagan notions of sexual purity. The Council of Nicaea (325) and the Council of Trullo (692) both rejected proposals requiring celibacy for all priests.

13. Garry Wills, *Papal Sin: Structures of Deceit,* 98. Lonergan's method for integrating experience, ideas, reason and actions in spiritual, ethical ways on the basis of conversion can help us toward Christian transparency. His method has also been used in ways that are culturally insensitive and therefore wrong.

Appendix 1

Tyrrell's Argument that Church Authorities had Usurped the Laity's Role

One must situate Tyrrell in historical perspective. Early on, he had espoused Newman's views on the development of doctrine, but later abandoned Newman's nuanced restraints so that he ran into the opposition of both his Jesuit superiors and the Vatican. His theology—one in which an immanent deity communicates with the human spirit through one's conscience—stands in contrast to theologies of transcendence in which the deity speaks to mankind primarily through hierarchically appointed Church officials. For Tyrrell, the authority of the Church rests primarily in the body of believers who gather together in the name of Christ.

> It is surely in accordance with this notion of authority as immanent in, and emanating from the highest in man that Christ says: 'Where two or three are gathered together in My Name, there am I in the midst of them' To say that all spiritual and moral power is inherent in the people and derives from the people, in no wise constricts the truth that it derives from God and is divine. It is only to insist that, for us, God's highest and fullest manifestation is given, not in the clouds, not in the stars, but in the spirit of man, and therefore most completely in that completest expression of man's spirit which is obtained in the widest available consensus, and is the fruit of the widest collective experience, of the deepest collective reflection (*Tradition*, 98).

Tyrrell went on to claim that hierarchical Church authority usurped the power of the laity by its abandonment of consultation with the laity about matters of Church doctrine and governance. The imperial power of the Roman Empire had been transferred from the civil sphere into the centralized institution of the Church. The democratic nature of the Church expressed in the early period of the Christian movement was largely lost or subordinated to its hierarchical structure. For Tyrrell, under the influence of an imperial conception of authority and its historical policy of assimilation, the democratic nature of the Christian priesthood had been gradually "forgotten" (*Tradition*, 101). Tyrrell presciently noted that Church structures did not fit well with the liberal political culture that was emerging in the West. The concept of popular sovereignty was foreign to Church officials who still claimed a direct line of divine authority given to the Apostles and passed down to the hierarchy over the centuries. Such an ecclesiastical culture also limited the participation of women. It took such movements as the enfranchisement of women and feminists' deliberations to force the Church to "adapt" to more Tyrrellian-like perspectives.

Appendix 2

The Hindu Notion of Bliss Consciousness, Saccidananda. Brahma, Brahman, Mantra — and a Contemporary Ideology

The Indian Catholic philosopher and theologian, Thomas Kochumuttom argues that Indian notions of consciousness and mantras can help the West better understand what life in God may mean and to deepen its traditional views of spirituality and ethics. "*Saccidananda*" developed by Hindu thinkers seeks to explain how we may share in God's life through consciousness and bliss. Since, for Christians, the Father is the sole possessor of existence (*sat*) and since the Son (for Christians) is God's own wisdom (*cit*) and the Holy Spirit is born of the mutual devotion and love of the Father (*ananda*, bliss personified) and the Son, we may appreciate East-West theologians' efforts to help us get some insights into what life in God may mean. *Brahma* is not be confused with *Brahman,* who is the supreme God force present within all things. Etymologically, both are related to the Greek root *morphe* (form); later, it came to mean the revealed Word of the Vedas symbolized in OM, the greatest of mantras that "embodies" the essence of the universe manifesting itself to humans as sound (*sabda*). Hindu grammarians made use of the theological understanding of *sabda*, tracing the multiplicity of words and beings to an unmanifest *sabda*—Brahma in his absolute nature is inaccessible to humans but manifests himself as sound (*sabda*). A mantra, in Hinduism, is a sacred utterance (syllable, word, verse, OM) that is considered to possess mystical or spiritual efficacy. Various mantras are either spoken aloud or merely sounded internally in one's thoughts. They are either repeated continuously for some time or just sounded once. *Samadhi* (concentration) is likened to a sleepless sleep, a sense of pure isolation without an "I."

A contemporary ideology has resurfaced in India since 2014 due to Prime Minister Modi, a member of the Party responsible for the assassination of Gandhi in 1948. Modi's Bharatiya Janata Party wants to rehabilitate Godse, Gandhi's assassin, portraying him as a Hindu patriot. It has requested Modi to install a bust of Godse—so far to no avail. The deep insights of *Saccidananda* can all too easily be ignored due to political expediency.

Appendix 3

How the Church May Help Us from Falling Victim to the Hyperreality of Images

The philosopher Baudrillard (1929–2007) confused the distinction between systems of signification and those of communication; he let the real "implode" into the hyperreality of images. Christian and Buddhist sages teach that the image should not be mistaken for the real. If Baudrillard substituted a relational immanence for the complete "disappearance" of the transcendent, a Christian philosopher should be "hypersensitive" to God's "*uncoded logic*" that affects our hearts. This would correct Baudrillard's "hyperrealist" fantasies that mistook codes for rules. Rules underly and guide coded systems. A bridge of the type we seek would help the Centers and Peripheries of world entities re-center in a new viable world order. We need not sweep Tradition away, but must remain God-centered in an evolving world. We should avoid both postmodernist-hyperrealist projections as well as outdated forms of Christian ministries. Church leaders such as the late Archbishop Quinn of San Francisco and bishop McElroy of San Diego have striven to better include the laity in ecclesial matters. Pope Francis' ecclesial and evangelizing mission and his emphasis on synodality means that he is sensitive to what affects human hearts so as to spare us from hyperreal images. This theme, too, could benefit from prudential discernments made by the bishops at a Vatican III Council.

Appendix 4

Fathoming how Mystics, Philosophers, and Theologians Address the Unfathomable: Pioneer Christian Thinkers Rephrasing Ancient-Medieval Thought in Modern Terms

HOW MYSTICS WOULD RELATE US TO THE INTERRELATED WHOLE

John Arblaster and Paul Verdeyen, in "The Reciprocity of Spiritual Love in William of Saint-Thierry and Hadewijch" (*International Journal of Philosophy and Theology*, Vol. 78, 2017) show that relationality is the hidden side of the apophatic. They examine the mystical anthropology of the two medieval mystics, William of Saint-Thierry and Hadewijch who have recently attracted the attention of scholars. Arblaster and Verdeyen explore the Trinitarian theology of the two mystics, arguing that it provides a foundation for a mystical anthropology. William radically argued that the human soul is structured according to the pattern of the Trinitarian life. He advocated a reciprocal, mutual encounter between the soul and God in which each touch and pass over into one another, becoming one Spirit. In the thirteenth century, Hadewijch drew on William's fundamental insights, integrating them into her own mystical-theology. Unlike her contemporaries, Hadewijch maintained that the soul has the natural potential to be united with God without a created intermediary, and that in mystical union, the soul becomes God in love.

Richard Kearney in his *Anatheism: Returning to God After God* (Columbia Univ., 2009) argues for a third anatheist way: a "sacramental return to the holiness of the everyday." It invokes a "yes" in the wake of no," which marks the potential return to God after 'God.' *Ana-theos*, a creative unknowing, requires us to break with former sureties; it invites us to forge new meanings from ancient wisdoms such as "re-speaking" of God. Having 'traversed' the dark night of the soul, one emerges on the other side, into a 'second faith, an ethical imperative of loving even in the face of injustice. One encounters religious wonder anew. Situated at the split between theism and atheism, one responds in deeper, freer ways to what we cannot fathom or prove. Anatheism is an inaugural event lying at the heart of every great religion—a wager between hospitality and hostility to the stranger. Kearney shows how a return to God is possible for seekers leading to a birth of a more liberating faith. For Kearney, "Epiphany manifests a paradoxical structure of time that Paul called 'eschatological,' exemplified in the ancient Palestinian formula for "remembering the one who is still to come"—a phenomenon that Jewish philosophers such as Levinas, Benjamin and Derrida have called "messianic" times. It envisages a singular form of "anticipatory memory" that recalls the past into the future through the present: a temporal anomaly. Levinas calls this the paradox of posterior anteriority." Gerard Manley Hopkins called it "aftering" or "over-and-overing," an ana-esthetic process that enables us to bear witness to the being dwelling within one (*Anatheism*, 2). "Creative unknowing" is significant—as Robert Magnolia has shown.

The Greeks were quite perplexed as to how relate human nature to divine reality. In the *Symposium* (202d13-e1), Plato stresses metaxy that emphasizes an "*in-between*" or a "middle ground. He defines Eros as "a great *daimon*": the "whole of the daimonic is between (metaxy) god and mortal. Metaxy Eros acquires a mysterious reality that Socrates regarded as the most important force animating our lives. We emulate both Simone Weil who saw the Greeks as building bridges between the temporal and the eternal, and Pope Francis' efforts to find spiritual, ethical foundations for our lives.

HOW ZEN'S NOTION OF *PRAJNA* CAN HELP CHRISTIAN ENLIGHTENMENT

Zen arose in Chinese monasteries that had used the Indian mental concentration of *dhyana* that cuts short one's reasoning process by excluding extraneous thoughts so as to heighten one's consciousness. It is as if one focuses on the subject of meditation so as to attain enlightenment with pure thought. Hui-Neng (d. 713) opposed this view. He recast *dhyana* into *ch'an* (Zen in Japanese) by stressing *prajna*'s noetic principle whereby a synthetic apprehension "of the whole becomes possible." Zen awakens *prajna* from the depths of consciousness to find that ultimate reality is at once pure being, pure awareness. *Prajna*, at work in our conscious mind lets us grasp, be grasped by ultimate reality. It makes one truly aware of this Reality (God for a Christian). Consciousness realizes itself as illuminated by an unconscious in such a way that there is no longer any division between the two. "It is not that the empirical mind is absorbed in *prajna,* but simply that *prajna* is. . . . Nothing else has any relevance except as its manifestation." *Prajna* breaks through our empirical consciousness, floods our whole being and all that is around us, transforming us in its light." We "become that light." Zen neither denies nor affirms subjects or objects; it refuses to translate experience into words. It focuses on private spheres rather than on public domains; one can sublate it with Christian values as needed.

HOW ROBERT MAGLIOLA RELATES US TO THE INTERRELATED WHOLE IN BUDDHISM

Scholars often labor in obscurity but they show their grit when they are able to connect ancient wisdom with modern needs and problems. Robert Magliola is one such scholar. He proposes a "Buddhist-deconstructionist logic" that not only anticipates but helps solve some of the riddles of existence that have puzzled postmodernist philosophers and such an astute "deconstructionist" commentator on language as Derrida. According to Magliola, Derrida was concerned about the entrapment of language. In his *Derrida on the Mend* (Lafayette: Purdue, 1984) and his *On Deconstructing Life-Worlds: Buddhism, Christianity, Culture* (Atlanta: Scholars 1996), Magliola argues that for Nagarjuna, Buddhist "wholeness" (the interrelatedness of all persons with one another) was expressed in the paradoxical phrase that all things are "empty" (being "nothing" in themselves, they must be grasped as part of an interrelated whole). The entrapment of language comes in when we lose sight of the Buddha's or Jesus' holistic insights. The whole is "beyond knowing"; still, we can arrive at some form of enlightenment free from the limitations of language. Magliola speaks of an "and/or" relation that seeks to capture the Buddhist view of an interrelated whole. When we declare that a thing is "devoid" of existence we mean that it is "empty"; yet, this does not apply in relation to ultimate reality. By "negating the reality of a thing, a Buddhist declares it to be devoid of existence in itself. With Buddhists, we, too, can assert that all realities are interlinked. In other words, unlike modern "deconstructionists" who focus on the separateness of lived experience, Buddha taught that all things are "empty," devoid of individual essence or absolute permanence but they *are vitally linked—holistic.* The Buddhist *Heart Sutra* asserts that "Form does not differ from Emptiness; Emptiness does not differ from form." Nagarjuna rejected both absolutist and nihilist interpretations of this teaching. He rejected the absolutists' contention that because the ultimate nature of reality transcends rationality, any meaningful discourse is impossible. He also rejected the nihilist claim that nothing really exists. His solution is to reject the assumption that reality can only be characterized through the categories of realist metaphysics. His is a type of relational philosophy: like Buddha, he teaches that all things are interrelated and depend on one another. The "emptiness" of things is not that of utter ineffability nor utter non-existence. "The emptiness of all phenomena is just their conventional reality, which is itself likewise thoroughly empty."

The main forms of Buddhism known in the West are "logocentric" in Derrida's sense; that is, we think of identity or causality and label them "ideas." Buddhist enlightenment helps one realize the interrelatedness of all things ("nothingness") furnishing a context that can bridge words and realities. Such a task needs the expert guidance of specialists. We merely point out with Magliola that with one and the same stroke, a holistic world view allows us to have it both ways in non-paradoxical, ever altering ways that reconcile the validity of words and values with the deeper mystery of faith. This may spare us from alienation and help people from various cultures speak with one another. See Jean-L. Marion, *God Without Being*, tr. Thomas Carlson (U. of Chicago, 1991) on God's distance and the implications of mysticism and the iconic that confront Derridean logocentric fears. In *Orality and Literacy: The Technologizing of the Word* (London: Methuen, 1982) 166, Walter Ong faults Derrida for neglecting "historical continuities."

GOD'S MERCY IN THE WRITINGS OF ISLAMIC MYSTICS

Many Muslim-Sufi mystics have lived their religious ideals faithful to their own tradition of God's mercy. Such ideals are helpful in establishing love-faith bridges of mercy. William C. Chittick, "The Anthropology of Compassion," The Muhyiddin Ibn 'Arabi Society' 48 (2010) 1–17, argues that "mercy pertains to the very stuff of reality. God cannot give priority to wrath over mercy ... because that would be to give priority to unreality over reality (...) to others rather than to himself. It would contradict the (...) truth upon which the universe is built, the fact that there is no reality but God, there is no true existence but God's existence." Sufi scholars define *Tasawwuf* (تصوف) as "a science whose objective is the reparation of the heart and turning it away from all else but God. It refers to the inner or esoteric dimension of Islam ... (to be) complemented by outward practices." It is a practice of the heart—a possible relevant dialogue partner with mystics of other religions. Al-Ghazali (1058–1111) was dissatisfied with the philosophy of his day rooted in observable phenomena. For him, the Divine reality transcends all such phenomena. As did Kant later, Al-Ghazali realized that the methods of science and philosophy could not help a believer find certitude in his/her belief. He went through a period of clinical depression that eventually led him to experience a mystical Dark Night of the Soul. Having affiliated himself with a Sufi community, he travelled throughout the Middle East. During this period, he wrote his masterwork, *The Revitalization of the Religious Disciplines* explores *ilm* (secular knowledge) and *ma'rifa* (mystical knowledge). In his *The Niche of Lights,* Al-Ghazali explains the Sufi experience of *fana* and *fana al fana* (self-annihilation and the annihilation of self-annihilation). *Fana* means losing oneself completely—being one with Divine Truth; *fana al fana* expresses a further experience of annihilating the "self" in the experience of identity with the One Divine Truth. As with the Buddhist Oxherd, a mystic eventually returns to ordinary life to help others be enlightened. In his book, *Hizmet Means Service: Perspectives on an Alternative Path within Islam*, Martin E. Marty explores how the *Hizmet* movement founded by Fethullah Gülen inspires acts of service without alienating other faiths.

HOW LONERGAN HELPS US DEEPEN INTERFAITH DIALOGUE

Lonergan's acumen in dialectics has to be complemented by his openness to a foundational eye of love, evident, for example, in the teachings of great mystics. For Lonergan, our ability to question in unrestricted ways underlies our capacity for self-transcendence; being in love in an unrestricted fashion is the proper fulfilment of that capacity. That fulfillment stems neither from our knowledge nor our choice. No! Love dismantles and abolishes the horizon "in which our knowing and choosing went on and it sets up a new horizon in which the love of God will transvalue our values and the eyes of that love will transform our knowing" (*Method in Theology*, 106). One is transported into a new conscious dynamic state of love, joy, and peace. Lonergan transvalues Nietzsche's transvaluations—thus supplying an important missing link in atheist discourse. While Nietzsche sought to undermine Christian notions of values and morality, Lonergan helps us on our quest for the common good. He reinterprets Christian faith so that it may better address today's realities. As did the Buddha, Jesus, and Muhammad in their own day, Lonergan radicalizes the tradition he inherited; he identifies missing foundational links in modern thought. In negative theology, an "experience of the Divine" cannot be expressed in words. Humans cannot define the infinite-yet-unified complexity of the divine. Any attempted description of the Divine is mistaken. Lonergan avoids this dilemma by emphasizing interiority and reintegrating the spiritual and communal dimensions of life. Prayer transforms us. Whether one meditates silently as do Zen practitioners, or whether one dances communally as in Africa, or whether one bows in prayer as do Muslims, believers pray in their various traditions. This also applies to their patterns of thinking. The greater the thinker, the more apt he/she is at identifying missing links that can help reintegrate personal and communal experience within the societal.

Appendix 5

How Philosophers and Historians Have Developed Notions of Lived Experience which can Buttress Integrating Bridges Based on a Global Mysticism

"Lived experience" sounds tautological in English since all experience is lived. It took historians and philosophers centuries to discover the deeper implications of "lived experience" (*Erfahrung*) of which Kant wrote. Hegel assigned it a technical meaning. For Wilhem Dilthey (1833–1911), lived experience acquired evaluative connotations of what a person selects from the vast manifold of everyday life as having a personally "lived" (*erlebt*) significance. "*Erlebnis*" is derived from the verb, *erleben* (live to see). On the face of it, this neologism connotes what one personally experiences. Dilthey provided an alternative to nihilism with his detailed considerations of lived experience. While scientists study electrons and viruses etc., Lonergan, like Brentano and Husserl, studied human intentionality. Husserl set the tone for modern philosophy when he wrote of immanence as the flux of a lived subjectivity. But his attempts to unite science and philosophy failed to solve the philosophical crisis as he had hoped; they did give rise to phenomenology which studies lived experience as a mix of empiricism and the transcendental. Lonergan builds on Dilthey (*Method in Theology*, 206, 210–12, 264, 318).

The modern world that began in the seventeenth century has led to a pluralist world dominated by science and capitalism. Theologians were called to find a surer foundation. Lonergan found this foundation in intellectual, moral and religious conversions. Humans share common basic cognitional operations. There are as many versions of such common basic cognitional operations as there are persons. Lonergan has shown that science is not omnicompetent—even scientists need to be intellectually converted. Scientists using the scientific method have accomplished much; but, in fact, the foundation of science does not consist in any of its principles or conclusions. Both of these are subject to revision. Both science and theology depend on a foundation that can generate ways to revise as needed accepted laws and principles. Whatever scientists or theologians do is grounded in the method they use. Lonergan emphasizes this by carefully studying how all persons personally experience, understand and use his/her four native operations when judging and acting. They all use common sense in everyday life whether engaged in mathematics, science or theology. Philosophers of science such as Karl Popper and Thomas Kuhn have shown that science is open and evolutionary in nature. Science, according to Popper, seeks not a fixed certitude but rather the best explanation for questions and problems that humankind may be asking at a particular point in time. Science, like theology, need not be dogmatic in nature. In his *The Structures of Scientific Revolutions*, Kuhn shows how science has revolved around different paradigms that may be incommensurable with each other. This may occur because science, like theology, seeks answers to specific questions that may differ from age to age. Lonergan explores how scientists and theologians reason. The latter explore the mysteries of God, the former appeal to causality, but they all use their four basic human operations that make model-based reasoning possible; these operations include lived experience. Lived experience is the starting point for all areas of human life. Each one's lived experience depends on one' personal background. These may be so different that little communication is possible unless each one understands the basic operations they share in common. Lonergan's method is meant to build bridges among all areas of human life and knowledge. It helps theologians reapply dogmas in ways that do not contradict the past.

The basic recurrent operations common to all humans are bases for pursuing intra-faith, interfaith and secular dialogue, erecting viable theologies based on conversion and practicing justice. Lonergan's method can help humans of various background cooperate in our constantly changing, fast-moving world. One may be morally and religiously converted as demanded by Jesus. One may be intellectually "converted," but unless the various conversions are processed through the psychic makeup of individual persons and the communities they live in, we shall not arrive at the type of relational theologies that lie at the core of the biblical message. Historically speaking,

> In the mid-nineteenth century, after the Romantic movement had shifted the emphasis in much religious thinking from theology to individual experience, a growing interest in ecumenism led to the invention of the term mysticism and its extension to comparable phenomena in non-Christian religions. The com-

petition between the perspectives of theology and science resulted in a compromise in which most varieties of what had traditionally been called mysticism were dismissed as merely psychological phenomena and only one variety, which aimed at union with . . . God—and thereby the perception of its essential unity or oneness—was claimed to be genuinely mystical. / www.britannica.com/topic/mysticism

John Raymaker, in his *Empowering the Lonely Crowd*, explores how Lonergan studied humans' cognitional-volitional-spiritual faculties and how mystics can help illuminate humanity's role on earth. God's Kingdom is a reality-in-the-making. Humans are potentially endowed with an "inbuilt bridge" that can clarify, link, reconcile controversial issues. *Empowering* was published ten years before Pope Francis' papacy; in retrospect, Francis has displayed the qualities just described. His life has been one of reconciling while trying to bring the Church "kicking and screaming" into the twenty-first century.

Appendix 6

Pope Francis' "Glocal" World View

Conservatives and progressives must be open to one another's diverging views. They must listen to one another. The first of Alcoholic Anonymous' 12 steps is to admit the existence of one's drinking problem. Catholicity implies diversity within unity, which means that Catholic thinkers must allow a diversity of emphases. Since traditionalists and progressives see problems from different perspectives, one must mediate between the claims of traditionalists and of those who want to critically adapt the Church to the modern world. Pope Francis has displayed to an amazing degree the ability to interrelate the local and global implications of the many issues facing the Church. In our *Pope Francis, Conscience of the World*, we stress that *glocal* combines the implications of both global and local; we point to the simultaneous universalizing and particularizing tendencies in contemporary life. In the business world, companies are advised to think and act globally while servicing customers locally. Globalization should benefit not only large enterprises from developed countries but also developing countries' interests. In fact, the latter are often exploited. Glocalization, on the other hand, would promote dynamic relationships between these two realms so as to insure the well-being of all. Seehttps://fabrikbrands.com/glocal-warming-and-glocalisation/Pope Francis has insisted that the only sustainable future for a glocal world is one in which people practice solidarity. There are close links between local climate, for example, and the occurrence of diseases in other parts of the world. This is why a glocal-ethical theology is needed. "A Glocal Theology in the Pope Francis Era,"www.kings.uwo.ca/kings/assets/File/academics/centres/carct/Glocal-Theology.pdf features glocal theologies developed in Canada. Many now write about possible repercussions of the actions of individuals and organizations worldwide. This reinforces our stress on interdividuality, on sharing in our all-too-divided world. Pope Francis has reached deeply into our psyches, even our souls through his contagious charisma: the world needs more such charismatic, down-to-earth leaders.

Glossary

As does our entire text, the glossary focuses on searches for the spiritual in world religions. This would include the charisms and dreams of great religious leaders.

Aggiornamento: Renewal. Our text explores the need, possibilities of Church renewal.
Anatheism: an inaugural event lying at the heart of every great religion— a wager on the possibility that seekers after the truth can return to God through a liberating faith. It implies a sacramental return to the holiness of the everyday.
Anatman: Buddhist "non-self" or the "not self" of a person's true nature: it offsets Hinduism's atman (self as eternal core of one's personality).
Apophatic transcends subject/object dichotomies. It refers to what cannot be put into words as opposed to the kataphatic which can be verbalized. One instance of the apophatic is the "dark night of the soul" experienced by mystics.
Dharma: Buddha's universal truth applying to all beings and common to all Buddhist sects; the void of self-nature as affirmed in Buddhist metaphysics.
Dhyana: Mental concentration that cuts short one's reasoning process. Zen Buddhists recast such mental concentration by stressing prajna's noetic principle whereby a synthetic apprehension "of the whole becomes possible." Zen awakens prajna from the depths of consciousness to find that ultimate reality is at once pure being, pure awareness.
Hermeneutic: Interpretation of literary texts.
Inculturation-Enculturation: Enculturation is the process by which people learn the dynamics of their culture and acquire values and

norms appropriate to that culture and worldviews. Inculturation is used by missiologists to refer to the adaptation of the way Church presents its teachings to non-Christian cultures. We emphasize inculturation, but implicit in our text is the fact that people have to learn the dynamics of their own culture.

Kairos: The God-appointed time for realizing salvation in this world.

Ki, Chi, prana: Spirit, mind, soul in Far Eastern thought. They indicate one's aesthetic feelings or the vital elements that motivate persons within one's culture.

Logos: "Word" used in St John's writings to refer to Jesus as manifesting the godhead.

Marga: A "path" in Indian religions that leads to salvation.

Mysticism: seeking union with God or even the "absorption" into absolute. It is a form of spiritual apprehension inaccessible to the intellect but sought after in contemplation.

Prajna: A noetic principle whereby an apprehension of the whole becomes possible.

Prana: See Ki.

Saccidananda: Hindu mystical notion of bliss consciousness—a sharing in God's life

Samadhi: Meditative absorption, attained by the practice of *dhyāna*. See Sunyata.

Sangha: Association, especially of spiritual practitioners. The term is used in many traditions such as yoga and Buddhism to denote communities devoted to the spiritual.

Spiration: The Holy Spirit is called the Spirit of the Father (Mt 10:20) and the Spirit of the Son (Gal 4:6). It points to the mutual love of the Three Persons within the Trinity.

Sufism: A mystical form of Islam, a school of practice that emphasizes the inward search for God and shuns materialism. It has produced some of the world's most beloved literature such as the love poems of the thirteenth century Iranian jurist Rumi.

Sunyata: The Buddhist equivalent of Hinduism' samadhi; the void of Zen Buddhism understood not as negation but as undifferentiation or dynamic self-determination.

Selected Bibliography

Andraos, Michel. *The Church and Indigenous Peoples in the Americas: In Between Reconciliation and Decolonization* (Eugene OR: Cascade Books, 2019).
Arendt, Hannah. *The Human Condition* (Chicago Univ., 1958).
———. *The Origins of Totalitarianism*. Orlando, FL: Harcourt, 1968.
Baranowski, Arthur. *Creating Small Church Communities* (Cincinnati: St. Anthony, 1996).
Barbour, Ian G, *Religion and Science: Historical and Contemporary Issues* (Harper, 1997).
Bouchard, Charles. "Making Ministry Whole: How MJPs Could Transform the Church" www.commonwealmagazine.org/Nov. 12, 2019.
Boulaga, Fabien Eboussi, *Christianity without Fetish: An African Critique and Recapture of Christianity* (New York: Orbis, 1984).
Bulliet, Richard W. *The Case for Islamo-Christian Civilization*. New York: Columbia, University Press, 2004.
Clark, Stephen, *Building Christian Communities: Strategy for Renewing the Church* (Ave Maria Press, 1972, revised in 1992.
Conze, Edward, *Buddhism: Its Essence and Development* (New York: Harper, 1959).
Crowe, Frederick E. *Appropriating the Lonergan Idea*, ed. by Michael Vertin (Catholic University, 1989).
De Lubac, Henri Cardinal. *The Religion of Teilhard de Chardin*. New York: Image Books, 1967.
Dumoulin, Heinrich. *Zen Buddhism: A History*, vol 2 (New York: Macmillan, 1990).
Fenn, Richard. *The Secularization of Sin* (Louisville: Westminster-Knox, 1991).
Francis, Pope. *The Joy of the Gospel*, Vatican City, 2013. *Laudato Si*. Vatican City. May, 2005.
———. "Message for the 105th World Day of Migrants and Refugees," 27 May 2019. *Praedicate Evangelium*.https://www.ncronline.org/news/opinion/francis-draft-curial-reform-fundamentally-reimagines-vaticans-role.
Freire, Paulo. *Pedagogy of the Oppressed* (New York: Seabury, 1970).
Griffiths, Bede. *A New Vision of Reality: Western Science, Eastern Mysticism and Christian Faith* (Springfield, IL: Templegate, 1989).
Grudzen, Gerald and Rahman, *Reason, Revelation and Science: Friends or Foes?* (Bloomington, IL: Authorhouse, 2014).
Grudzen, Gerald and John Raymaker. *Steps Toward Vatican III* (Lanham: University Press of America, 2008).
Girard, Rene. *I See Satan Fall Like Lightning* (Maryknoll, NY: Orbis, 2001).
Lee, Bernard, *The Catholic Experience of Small Christian* Communities (New York: Paulist Press, 2000).
Leo, XIII, Pope. *Rerum Novarum*. Encyclical, 1878.

Lonergan, Bernard, *Insight, A Study of Human Understanding* (New York: Philosophical Library, 1958).
———. *Method in Theology* (New York: Herder, 1972).
———. Theology in its New Context," in *A Second Collection* (Philadelphia: Westminster, 1974).
MacIntyre, Alasdair and Paul Ricoeur, *The Religious Signiificance of Atheism* (New York, Columbia University, 1969).
Merton, Thomas. *Zen and the Birds of Appetite* (New York: New Directions, 1975).
Nasr, Seyyed Hossein, *Science and Civilization in Islam* (Chicago: ABC International Group, 2001).
Nishida, Kitaro, *Intelligibility and the Philosophy of Nothingness* (Honolulu: East-West Center) 1958.
Noonan, John. *The Development of Catholic Moral Teaching* (Notre Dame University, 2005).
Peacocke, Arthur. *Paths From Science Towards God* (Oxford: One World, 2002),
Raguin, Yves. *La Profondeur de Dieu* (Desclee de Brouwer, 1973).
Raymaker, John. *Empowering Philosophy and Science with the Art of Love: Lonergan and Deleuze in the Light of Buddhist-Christian Ethics* (Lanham MD: University Press of America, 2006). Ricoeur, Paul. *The Symbolism of Evil* (Boston: Beacon, 1967).
Rosenberg, Randall L. *The Givenness of Desire: Concrete Subjectivity and the Natural Desire to See God* (University of Toronto, 2017).
Taylor, Charles. *The Ethics of Authenticity* (Cambridge: Harvard, 1991).
Teilhard de Chardin, Pierre, *Building the Earth* (Discus Books, 1969).
———. *Divine Milieu: An Essay on the Interior Life* (Harper, 1960).
Tracy, David and Hans Küng's *Toward Vatican III* (New York: Seabury, 1978).
Vroom, Hendrik, *Religions and the Truth* (Grand Rapids: Eerdmans, 1989).
Wills, Garry, *Papal Sin: Structures of Deceit* (New York, Doubleday, 2000).

Index

Al-Ghazali, 163
Aquinas, Thomas St., 61, 62, 71, 95, 146, 148, 150
Arab Spring, 30
Ashrams, 75
Atheism, 27
Augustine, St., 14, 58, 65, 97

Benedict, St., 14, 99
Boff, Leonardo, 120–121, 124n6, 130
Boulaga, Fabien Eboussi, 169
Buber, Martin, 8
Buddhism, 16, 31, 133, 136, 147
Building Cultural-Religious Bridges, 14, 57, 59
Bulliet, Richard, 25

Catherine of Siena, St., 157
CELAM, 142
China, 31, 33, 40–41, 169, 180
Christian-Buddhist Relations, 34, 81n34, 141, 148, 149, 150, 158
Christian-Islamic Dialogue, 23, 43, 45, 155, 162
Conrad, Joseph, 58
Constantine, Emperor, 14, 117
Council of Trent, 157

Dalai Lama, 1
Day Dorothy, 102, 178
Descartes, Rene, 53

Dilthey, Wilhelm, 68
Dupuis, Jacques, 68, 73

Ethics, its Essential Roles, 39, 127
Ezekiel, Prophet, 116

FCM (Federation of Christian Ministries), 186–187, 188
Focolare, 15
Francis of Assisi, St., 64, 89

Galileo, 97, 132
Gandhi, Mahatma, 101
Girard, Rene, 156, 172n4
Globalization, 24, 34, 35, 39
Gospels, 113, 115, 118, 119
Griffiths, Bede, 1, 75
Grudzen, Gerald, 81n33, 180
Gutierrez, Gustavo, 121, 142

Hinduism, 133
Human Rights, 40, 95

Interdividuality, 157
Islam, 28, 31, 40, 45, 155, 162

Johnston, William, 11, 79n4

King, Martin Luther Jr., 5, 75, 77, 101, 146
Kingdom of God, 12, 17, 67, 70, 107, 139, 140

Knitter, Paul, 75
Kyoto Declaration on the Environment, 35
Kochumuttom, Thomas, 141
Koran, 28
Küng, Hans, 15, 99

Latin America, 120, 128
Laudato Si , Encyclical, 31, 42, 114
Lazarus, Emma, 33
Liberation Theologies, 120, 169
Lived Experience, 68, 73
Lonergan, Bernard,, 1, 59, 70, 90, 105, 155
Luther, Martin, 157

Marcel, Gabriel, 12, 75, 88, 125
Marx, Karl, 1, 85, 120, 129
Merton, Thomas, 71, 77, 102
Middle-East, 28
Migrant Workers, 38, 95, 130
Modernism, Post-Modernism, 85, 90, 101, 102, 108n10, 155
Moltmann, Jürgen, 13
Mother Teresa, St., 104, 178
Muhammad, Prophet, 71
Mysticism, 23, 27, 73, 101, 134, 136

Nagarjuna, 147
Newman, John Henry Cardinal, 14, 88
Nietzche, Friedrich, 68, 73, 75, 85, 88, 102
Noonan,John, 98, 108n8
Nouwen, Henri, 18

Palestinians, 29
Philippines, 33
Pope Benedict XVI, 59, 62, 99, 104, 165
Pope Francis, 6, 17, 36, 57, 72, 106, 132, 149, 150
Pope Gregory IX, 157

Pope St. John XXIII, 14, 55, 64, 78, 89, 106, 144
Pope St. John Paul II, 6, 8, 11, 15, 59, 97, 104, 106, 137, 146, 182
Pope Leo XIII, 88, 89, 102, 108n5, 128
Pope Paul VI, 86, 104
Pope Sixtus IV, 157
Prayer, 103, 136
Process Theology, 60

Rahner, Karl, 1
Raymaker, John, 136, 152n5
Romero, Oscar St.,

Said, Edward, 29
Saint Paul, 14, 62
Secularization, Secularism, 61, 62, 101
Small Christian Communities (SCC's), 17, 70, 103, 125, 178, 180, 182
Symbols and Spirituality, 74
Synod of Bishops, 1, 65, 67

Tagle, Luis Cardinal, 21
Technology in People's Lives, 63, 104
Teilhard de Chardin, Pierre, 74, 97, 125, 133
Teresa of Avila, St., 92
Thich Nhat Hanh, 50n18, 153n25
Tillich, Paul, 62, 67, 125, 132, 137, 156
Tyrrell, George, 87, 88

Vatican II Council, 13, 15, 24, 36, 65, 102, 120
Vatican III Council, Possibility of, 13, 39, 65, 72, 157, 188, 191, 193

Zen Buddhism, 136

About the Authors

John Raymaker earned his doctorate in social ethics at Marquette University based on the work of Bernard Lonergan (1977). He is the author of such books as *Empowering Climate-Change Strategies with Bernard Lonergan's Method* and *Steps toward Vatican III* co-authored with Gerald Grudzen.

Gerald Grudzen is the founder and president of Global Ministries University. He has worked on educational and development projects in Bangladesh, Turkey, Egypt and now in Kenya for the past eight years in addition to his teaching at several colleges and universities in the United States. Grudzen is also the author of *Burying the Sword: Confronting Jihadism with Interfaith Education* (2017)

www.ingramcontent.com/pod-product-compliance
Lightning Source LLC
Chambersburg PA
CBHW032042300426
44117CB00009B/1158